Don Troiani's Civil War

Corporal, 5th New York Volunteer Infantry, "Duryée's Zouaves"

Don Troiani's
CIVIL WAR

Art by Don Troiani
Text by Brian C. Pohanka

STACKPOLE
BOOKS

Copyright © 1995 by Stackpole Books
Images © 1995 by Don Troiani

Published by
STACKPOLE BOOKS
5067 Ritter Road
Mechanicsburg, PA 17055

All rights reserved, including the right to reproduce this book or portions thereof in any form or by any means, electronic or mechanical, including photocopying, recording, or by any information storage and retrieval system, without permission in writing from the publisher. All inquiries should be addressed to Stackpole Books, 5067 Ritter Road, Mechanicsburg, Pennsylvania 17055.

Images in this book may not be removed and sold, framed or unframed, for any commercial purpose. All images copyright Don Troiani, all rights reserved. Any form of reproduction, alteration, or mutilation is a violation of copyright. No images may be reproduced in any form or by any means without written permission of the artist.

Printed in China

First Edition

10   9   8   7   6

Library of Congress Cataloging-in-Publication Data

Troiani, Don.
    Don Troiani's Civil War / art by Don Troiani; text by Brian C. Pohanka.—1st ed.
       p.   cm.
    ISBN 0-8117-0341-X (Hardcover)
    ISBN 0-8117-2715-7 (Paperback)
    1. United States—History—Civil War, 1861–1865—Pictorial works.
2. United States—History—Civil War, 1862–1865—Art and the war.
3. United States—History—Civil War, 1861–1865.   I. Pohanka, Brian C., 1955–   . II. Title.
E468.7.T76 1995
973.7'022'2—dc20   95-3678
                                                                           CIP

*To the American soldiers, North and South,
whose legacy is an inspiration
and whose courage shall not go unrecorded;*

*To my understanding wife, Donna,
who lives with my obsessions on a daily basis;*

*To my parents, who got me interested
in all of this as a child;*

and

*To the memory of Jean-Baptiste Edouard Detaille,
the greatest soldier painter of them all.*

CONTENTS

Foreword — xi

Acknowledgments — xiii

Introduction — xv

1861

8th Company, 7th New York State Militia — 2
1st Regiment, South Carolina Rifles — 3
"Up Alabamians" — 4
1st Rhode Island Volunteer Infantry — 7
First at Manassas — 8
Company K, 69th New York State Militia — 11
2nd U.S. Cavalry — 12
1st North Carolina Cavalry — 13

1862

United States Marines — 16
The Stars and Bars — 17
Men of Arkansas — 18
19th Tennessee Infantry — 21
Washington Artillery of New Orleans — 22
8th Texas Cavalry — 23
The Red Devils — 24
Southern Cross — 28
"Old Jack" — 32
Federal Infantryman — 34
Corporal, 2nd Missouri Volunteer Cavalry — 35
The Diehards — 36
2nd Wisconsin Volunteer Infantry — 39
Colonel of the Confederacy — 40
Lone Star — 42

CONTENTS

Until Sundown	45
9th New York Volunteer Infantry	48
Confederate Drummer	50
Corporal, 2nd Regiment United States Sharpshooters	51
J. E. B. Stuart	52
Bronze Guns and Iron Men	54
Clear the Way *(Faugh-a-Ballagh)*	57
Federal Cavalry Picket in Winter	60
The Advance Picket	61
Emblems of Valor	62

1863

General Robert E. Lee	66
165th New York Volunteer Infantry	68
1st South Carolina Infantry, U.S.	69
Before the Storm	70
"Charge"	73
Eagle of the 8th	76
Pioneer, Army of the Cumberland	79
Confederate Infantry Corporal	80
The Gray Comanches	81
The Fight for the Colors	83
76th Pennsylvania Volunteer Infantry	86
The Boy Colonel	87
45th New York Volunteer Infantry	89
Battle in the Streets	90
Cemetery Hill	91
Decision at Dawn	95
"The Men Must See Us Today"	98
The Texas Brigade	101
20th Georgia Infantry	102
"Don't Give an Inch"	103
Lions of the Round Top	106
Bayonet!	109
53rd Georgia Infantry	110
Saving the Flag	111
Barksdale's Charge	114
114th Pennsylvania Volunteer Infantry	117
Retreat by Recoil	118
1st Minnesota Volunteer Infantry	122
Band of Brothers	124
1st and 2nd Maryland Infantry, C.S.A.	127
The High Water Mark	128
"Give Them Cold Steel, Boys"	132
Private, 72nd Pennsylvania Volunteer Infantry	133
First Sergeant, 13th Pennsylvania Reserves	134
A Confederate Officer with His Men	135
10th New York Volunteer Infantry	136
Union Drummer	137
Rebel Yell	138
Trooper, 7th Virginia Cavalry	140
Union Standard Bearer	141

1864

Confederate Standard Bearer	144
Excelsior	145
146th New York Volunteer Infantry	148
155th Pennsylvania Volunteer Infantry	149
Lee's Texans	150
The Bonnie Blue Flag	153
The Forlorn Hope	156
One of Forrest's Men	159
Southern Steel	160
Federal Infantry Officer	163
Thunder on Little Kennesaw	164
29th Alabama Infantry	167
33rd New Jersey Volunteer Infantry	168
Waiting for Dispatches	169
12th Virginia Cavalry	170
3rd New Jersey Volunteer Cavalry	171
Ranger Mosby	172
Forward the Colors	175
Opdycke's Tigers	176
Pat Cleburne's Men	180

1865

The Last Rounds	182
Confederate Pickets in the Snow	183
The Gray Wall	184
Crutchfield's Virginia Heavy Artillery Battalion	186
The Last Salute	187
From American to American	191

FOREWORD

It was a visual war from the outset. In the North—the old Union—three major "illustrated" newspapers, *Harpers, Frank Leslie's,* and the *New York Illustrated News,* brought weekly issues filled with crude yet graphic woodcuts of the armies and their battles, based upon on-the-spot sketches made by staff "delineators." In the South—the new Confederacy—the *Southern Illustrated News* attempted to do the same before scarcity of just about everything but battles put it out of business. Behind all those battlefield artists came the photographers—no one knows how many, but they numbered in the hundreds. Behind them they would leave a visual record of more than a million images, ensuring that *this* war would be remembered as no other.

Considering this, it should hardly be a surprise that the nation's fine artists have been drawn to the Civil War as a subject too, from the moment the guns started to bark right on down to the present. Indeed, in our own time a score and more of talented painters have been turning out their own recreations of the "look" of the Civil War for nearly a generation.

Among this small legion, Don Troiani stands alone. None can match the drama of his battle scenes. No one equals his attention to detail and accuracy in every fine point of uniform and equipment. Few if any can capture the face of war and warriors as he does in dozens of studies, from grand battle panoramas to insightful character studies of a single soldier.

Here is the charge of Barksdale's Mississippians at Gettysburg as it must have looked, the splendid color and terrible beauty of the scene almost masking the dreadful work they were about. Here is the resplendent zouave in the gaily colored uniform that make him so striking on the battlefield, and such a great target. Here are the men of Blue and Gray in camp and field, living the true life of the soldier—talking, eating, and waiting.

Seeing these wonderful paintings, it is no wonder that Troiani's work hangs in galleries and government buildings all across the country, nor that the United States Mint has commissioned him to illustrate commemorative coinage with Civil War scenes. He knows the *look* of that conflict and its people and retells it with his brush better than any other.

Yet adding further illumination—if more is needed—to his art is this text by distinguished historian of the common soldier Brian C. Pohanka, himself widely acknowledged for his attention to detail and accuracy. He provides the historical context for each of the works here presented, and his words combined with Troiani's art offer a feast both for the eye and the mind. *Don Troiani's Civil War* is, in fact, a window on *everyone's* Civil War, an experience that belongs to all Americans—indeed, all the world—and now made more vivid and real. Every page is a journey to yesterday.

William C. Davis
Mechanicsburg, Pennsylvania

ACKNOWLEDGMENTS

Special thanks go to Brian Pohanka, my good friend and historian *par excellence*. Also thanks to Earl J. Coates, Les Jensen, James Kochan, and Howard M. Madaus, true historical experts and good friends, always willing to share their wealth of knowledge.

My deep appreciation to all the other authorities, dedicated researchers and students of history, always ready to share, and whom I am fortunate to count as friends: Bill Adams, Harris Andrews, Tom Arkis, Cricket Bauer, Bruce S. Bazelon, Edwin C. Bearss, Brian Bennett, Herman Benninghoff, Robert Braun, William L. Brown III, Chris Calkins, Duncan Campbell, René Chartrand, Charles Childs, Ed Christopher, Jo-Val Codling, Dr. Charles Cureton, William C. Davis, Thomas Desjardin, Kirk Denkler, John Duillo, Fred Edmunds, Mark Elrod, Bill Erquitt, Dr. David Evans, Pat Eymard, James Frasca, William A. Frassanito, Dennis Frye, Joe Fulginiti, Fred Gaede, Dr. Gary Gallagher, Al Gambone, William Gladstone, Michael Gnatek, Eric Goldstein, George Green, A. Wilson Greene, Randy Hackenberg, Holly Hageman, Clark B. Hall, Peter Harrington, Kathy Georg Harrison, Dr. Joseph Harsh, Scott Hartwig, Dan Hartzler, Ralph Heinz, John Hennessy, Greg Heppe, Steven Hill, Kim B. Holien, Bob Huntoon, James Hutchins, Larry Jones, C. Peter Jorgensen, George Juno, David Jurgella, Ross Kelbaugh, Ross Kimmel, Don Kloster, Frank Kravic, Robert K. Krick, Robert E. L. Krick, John Henry Kurtz, Juanita Leisch, Paul Loane, Collin MacDonald, Roy Marcot, Bill Marvel, Greg Mast, Michael J. McAfee, Tom McDonald, Stephen McKinney, Dan Miller, William J. Miller, Jim Muir, Dr. John M. Murphy, Craig Nannos, Donna Neary, Deane Nelson, Nick Nichols, John Ockerbloom, Julia Oehmig, Seward Osborne, Steve Osmun, Ron Palm, Bob Parker, Herb Peck, Rick Poucher, Dr. Walter Powell, Kenneth Powers, Russ A. Pritchard, Dr. Walter Rodgers, Dr. Richard A. Sauers, Stephen Sears, Paul Smith, Charles Smithgall, Mark Snell, James Stamatelos, Larry Strayer, William Style, Wiley Sword, Stephen W. Sylvia, Dean S. Thomas, Richard Tibbals, Alice Trulock, James Trulock, Ron Tunison, Bill Turner, Dr. Gregory Urwin, Ed Vebell, Joseph Whitehorne, Michael J. Winey, Steven Wright, Robert J. Younger.

I hope to be forgiven for those I may have unintentionally omitted who have also provided their generous assistance.

Don Troiani
Southbury, Connecticut

INTRODUCTION

"I TRY TO PAINT IT HOW IT WAS." THUS DON TROIANI, THE DEAN OF American military painters, expresses his artistic credo. Through his unique combination of historical research and great skills as a painter, Troiani has crafted an unprecedented pictorial record that captures all the valor and tragedy of America's bloodiest war.

Born in New York City on June 16, 1949, Don Troiani was not drawn to the subject of the Civil War through any direct ancestral connection. His grandfather, a native of Lacquila in the Abruzzi region of Italy, came to America in the 1890s as a tourist and decided to stay. Troiani's mother's family, of Polish and Rumanian origin, arrived about the same time; his maternal grandfather helped to design the Central Park Zoo. Since Don Troiani's father was a commercial artist and his mother an antique dealer, art and history were early parts of his life.

When Troiani was two years old his family moved to Pound Ridge in Westchester County, New York. He attended elementary school there and graduated from Fox Lane High School in 1967. "My first efforts at military art began as soon as I had crayons," Troiani recalls. "I drew stick figure battles and Davy Crockett at the Alamo, and was very interested in anything to do with the Roman Empire. I always wanted to draw soldiers and would not be swayed from it."

When Troiani was in sixth grade, a family vacation to Paris provided a significant stimulus to his artistic and historical aspirations. Excited by the vast collection of military uniforms and memorabilia in the *Musée de l'Armée*—the Army Museum at *Les Invalides*—he convinced his mother to leave him there for an entire day. "The place was full of sleeping guards, and a bit like a mausoleum," he remembers, "but I had a great time." As the twelve-year-old roamed the vast hallways, with their displays of colorfully uniformed mannequins and regimental banners so evocative of past glories, Troiani was particularly taken with the paintings of Napoleonic battle scenes, many of them by an artist named Edouard Detaille. "I didn't know what they were," Troiani says, "but I was awed by them."

Troiani's parents were supportive of his decision to pursue an artistic career, and in 1967 he entered the Pennsylvania Academy of Art in Philadelphia. He augmented his four years at the academy with summer courses at the Art Students League in New York City; and while Troiani is quick to point out his training was not of the same caliber as that of his late–nineteenth-century precursors, it was the best available at the time.

Unfortunately, the then-prevalent emphasis on abstraction proved a frustrating obstacle to Troiani's realist approach. "You could go in there

Don Troiani. PENCIL DRAWING BY JOHN DUILLO

and paint circles and squares the first day and still be painting them the day you got out," he recalls. Representational art was frowned upon, and the instruction not only deemphasized classical training but often seemed to denigrate the very idea of realism. "Criticism was considered destructive of creativity," he says. "Everybody wanted to paint like a child, and the only reason children paint badly is because they can't paint well." One teacher gave Troiani a failing grade because he refused to paint in an abstract manner.

Although the few remaining instructors from the old school took him under their wing, Troiani profited more from studying nineteenth-century art in the academy's museum, and even illustrations in books, than he did in the classroom. "Eventually I started hanging around with old-time illustrators like Ed Vebell and John Duillo, both of whom took pains to explain to me how to look at art, when a technique worked, and when it didn't," he says. In the end, he asserts, "I essentially wound up teaching myself."

Over the decade following his graduation in 1971, his work focussed primarily on episodes of the American Revolution—an era that remains a strong interest of his, and one that tied in nicely with the nation's bicentennial. Troiani did over one hundred watercolors for the National Park Service and created a series of spirited, if somewhat unsophisticated, Revolutionary War battle scenes for *American Heritage* magazine. He also executed a number of paintings dealing with the history of the American frontier, including several cavalry subjects set in the Civil War period. From age eleven an active collector of military memorabilia, Troiani began to concentrate on Civil War uniforms, weapons, and accoutrements, which were far more plentiful than Revolutionary War items.

His first venture into the field of limited-edition prints came in 1980, with the issue of "Come On You Wolverines!"—a scene of General Custer at Gettysburg. Two years later, with the successful release of "Confederate Standard Bearer," the artist became firmly established in the lucrative vocation that in 1984 led him to establish his own company, Historical Art Prints. Freed from the restrictions and demands of commercial publishers and galleries, Troiani was now able to choose his own subject matter, ensure historical accuracy, and maintain quality control of the finished product. His success fueled a popularity of Civil War art prints that continues unabated. Today at least a dozen artists work in that highly competitive field, while nearly twice as many more have tried their hand at Civil War themes.

From the moment the first shots echoed over Charleston Harbor in April 1861, America's greatest conflict spawned an outpouring of sketches, engravings, lithographs, and paintings. Although the Civil War was the first war to be widely covered by the relatively new medium of photography, the long exposure time of mid-nineteenth century cameras was unable to record movement. Artists like Alfred Waud, Edwin Forbes, Winslow Homer, Frank Vizitelly, and James E. Taylor accompanied the Union and Confederate armies in the field, braving bullets and shellfire to capture the action in spirited pencil sketches. These rough, sometimes impressionistic renditions became the basis for woodcut engravings, from which illustrations were printed in popular journals like *Harper's Weekly* and *Frank Leslie's Illustrated*.

The appeal the war held for American artists did not end with Appomattox. The 1880s and '90s found painters Julian Scott, William L. Sheppard, Gilbert Gaul, William T. Trego, and Thur de Thulstrup, to name a few, concentrating their work on Civil War subjects. Teams of artists turned out huge circular panoramas of the battles of Gettysburg, Atlanta, Shiloh, Missionary Ridge, and the fight between the *Monitor* and the *Merrimac*. Traveling from city to city and displayed in round exhibit halls, these "cycloramas," as they were commonly known, were for a time a lucrative precursor to the cinema. Well into the third decade of the twentieth century artist-illustrators Howard Pyle and N. C. Wyeth often executed Civil War scenes for novels and magazine articles.

Despite the vast legacy of American Civil War art, in his style and his approach to rendering military themes on canvas Don Troiani draws his strongest artistic inspiration from European rather than American precursors. He speaks the names Meissonier, Detaille, de Neuville, Rochling, and Menzel with a respect that borders on reverence—artists whose paintings exemplified the drama, realism, and above all a dedication to historical authenticity that he strives for in his own work—and figures he believes deserving of greater recognition today. "I can't say anything bad about them," Troiani states. "Any one of them would be better than any five contemporary American military artists put together. They are practically invincible."

Jean-Louis-Ernest Meissonier (1815–91) was a fervent French nationalist who saw his military art as a "patriotic mission," through which he sought to evoke the glories of the First Empire and Napoleon Bonaparte. A favorite artist of the great emperor's nephew, Napoleon III, Meissonier accompanied the French General Staff during the 1859 war with Austria and won wide acclaim for his realistic portrayal of the battle of Solferino. But it was for his series of stirring depictions of earlier campaigns that Meissonier was best known, particularly the thundering charge of steel-breastplated cuirassiers past their emperor at Friedland, which he titled "1807."

"I did not intend to merely paint a battle," Meissonier said. "I wanted to paint Napoleon at the zenith of his glory; I wanted to paint the love, the adoration of the soldiers for the commander they believed in, and for whom they were ready to die." Meissonier worked on his large canvas for fifteen years, displaying an almost obsessive attention to detail, even in the distant background figures. One critic noted, "Each soldier is unique in his appearance, in what I would call his biography." "It is probably the greatest military painting ever done," Don Troiani says of Meissonier's masterpiece, now a part of the collection of the Metropolitan Museum of Art in New York. "It is absolute perfection—as good as military art can possibly be."

Fond as Troiani is of Meissonier's work, he reserves his greatest admiration for another French military artist, Jean-Baptiste Edouard

xviii INTRODUCTION

Detaille (1848–1912). At age seventeen Detaille commenced his prolific artistic career under the tutelage of Meissonier. From his childhood a collector of military artifacts, the teenager heeded his master's dictum: "Do like I do; naturalism, always naturalism!" He soon began to surpass even Meissonier in his earnest fixation on detail. By 1869 Detaille was a respected painter in his own right, and his military service in the defense of Paris during the Franco-Prussian War gave him firsthand knowledge of the sights and sounds and actions of men in battle.

In crafting his art Detaille drew upon his own wartime experiences, and he frequently attended military parades and maneuvers to gain inspiration. Like Meissonier a militant nationalist, Detaille was welcome in army circles. But above all it was by posing and photographing models who had been uniformed and equipped from his huge personal collection of militaria—much of it from the Napoleonic era—that he succeeded in accurately capturing the period authenticity he craved.

"I am, and I want to remain a painter of History," Detaille said. "I want to show the reality of a battlefield, without conventional poses, without an outlandish composition, and without any of the childish improbabilities that the public welcomes with great good faith. Each figure has his role, without worrying himself about the viewer. . . . I want to create an accurate record, but at the same time a moving tableau in which I seek to give an impression of grandeur."

Don Troiani's fascination with the work of Edouard Detaille began with his 1961 visit to the Army Museum in Paris—where Detaille's uniform collection became the foundation of an immense collection of original uniforms, weapons, and artwork—and continues unabated to this day. "He is my mentor," Troiani says, "I would love it if someday someone referred to me as 'the American Detaille.' It would be the

Edouard Detaille's 1893 painting of a patrol of the 4th Hussars circa 1800, now in Troiani's collection, is a treasured reminder of the great French military artist Troiani calls his "mentor." PHOTO COURTESY DON TROIANI COLLECTION

highest possible compliment." He notes that Detaille combined the technique of an accomplished academician with an unparalleled sense for the dramatic moment. But most importantly, the intimate knowledge Detaille gained from documentary research and the collecting of original uniforms, weapons, and accoutrements is the same hands-on approach that Troiani takes in his own work.

"The way he worked is the only way you can do it," Troiani says of Detaille. "You have to have fully uniformed and equipped models with all the correct gear right in front of you to get it right. An artist can never make up something better than the real thing." He points out that Detaille's paintings are so accurate they can be used as literal references to period detail, something that cannot be said for much of the Civil War art being produced today.

Although his style of painting was a bit more impressionistic than Detaille's, Alphonse de Neuville (1835–85) was another veteran of the Franco-Prussian War whose paintings of that bitter but heroic French defeat were rendered with dramatic and historical realism. He collaborated with Detaille on two battle cycloramas, "Champigny" and "Rezonville." When one art critic asked de Neuville, "Why constantly evoke memories of a tragic past?" the artist replied, "Because we should remember precisely what we would prefer to forget." Troiani remarks that the same question has been put to modern-day painters of Civil War subjects. While he prefers Detaille's ultrarealism and concentration on the period of the First Empire to de Neuville's broader brush strokes and focus on Franco-Prussian War scenes, Troiani still considers de Neuville a "superb" exponent of the genre.

Though most influenced by the French school of military art, Don Troiani also cites the work of several German artists. Adolf Menzel (1815–1905) was a master draftsman whose pen-studies gained him much recognition. Fascinated by the life of Frederick the Great, Menzel executed numerous drawings and paintings of *Der Grosse König* and his army in a manner that emphasized the candid and realistic attitudes of his subjects. Richard Knötel (1857–1914) was another German painter of military themes whose uniform plates remain an accurate reference on the armies of the Seven Years War and Napoleonic era. Troiani calls Karl Rochling (1855–1920) "a master of the panoramic battle scene, a little more rigid than the French, but every bit the expert." Designated the official military painter for the Prussian kaiser, Rochling typically included hundreds, and even thousands of figures in his action-packed compositions. In that aspect, Troiani admits, Rochling was superior even to Detaille.

Karl Rochling's depiction of the charge of Prussia's Grenadier Guard at the battle of Hohenfriedeberg reveals the German artist's talent for rendering large-scale battle scenes. PHOTO COURTESY ANNE S. K. BROWN MILITARY COLLECTION, BROWN UNIVERSITY LIBRARY

In Troiani's view no artist of the American school quite rose to the level of the European military painters. The sketches by Waud, Forbes, and Taylor are invaluable for their immediacy; and perhaps the best painter was Winslow Homer, who parlayed his brief 1862 visit to the front lines into a series of genre studies focussing primarily on camp life in the Union Army. While Julian Scott and William L. Sheppard were both veterans of the conflict, and generally accurate in their rendition of period details, Troiani finds their work sometimes primitive, lacking in emotion and in providing a sense of the chaos and ferocity of combat.

Of the next generation of Civil War artists, Troiani considers Gilbert Gaul to have been the best painter but notes he did not take as much care as his precursors to get the details right. Some of Gaul's figures, for instance, appear to be sporting uniforms and accoutrements of the 1880s rather than the 1860s. Pennsylvanian William T. Trego, whose hands and legs were crippled following a childhood bout with polio, "was superb in light of his physical disabilities," but also, like Gilbert Gaul, was occasionally guilty of period anachronisms. The same can be said of the cyclorama artists. "Being mostly Europeans they were absolute masters of their craft, and the artwork is wonderful," Troiani asserts, "but there are usually major problems with historical accuracy and uniform details."

When it comes to the early-twentieth-century painter Howard Pyle and his famous protégé N. C. Wyeth, Troiani is less charitable. "Pyle and Wyeth were excellent illustrators but terrible historical artists," he says. "Pyle's painting of the battle of Bunker Hill looks magnificent, but from a historical perspective it's garbage. The British are wearing Napoleonic coatees and carrying Civil War–period knapsacks." As illustrators both men were habitually working to a deadline, Troiani notes, and were in no sense students of the subjects they portrayed.

In selecting a subject for one of his larger paintings, Don Troiani usually looks for an incident that contains what he calls "the good dramatic moment." He does not concern himself with the politics of the war, who was right or wrong: "There were brave Americans on both sides," he states. Troiani often chooses to highlight the valorous exploits of a particular Union or Confederate regiment as its men follow their commanders and their flag into the jaws of death.

The process usually begins when Troiani reads an account in a regi-

Don Troiani at work on his painting "Give Them Cold Steel" in 1987.
PHOTO COURTESY RON TUNISON

mental history, soldier memoir, or diary and thinks, "God, this will make a great painting!" As he visualizes the event he begins the historical research that either reinforces his image or shatters the illusion. About half of the concepts pass this first test. Then Troiani continues to gather as many contemporary accounts of the incident as he can locate,

The initial pencil drawing of "Retreat by Recoil," Troiani's painting of Captain John Bigelow's 9th Massachusetts Battery at Gettysburg. PHOTO COURTESY DON TROIANI COLLECTION

and whenever possible he photographs the location where the event occurred at the same time of day as the battle and often on its anniversary. Without a sense of the terrain, the type of crops and fences, the color of a particular house or barn, and the weather conditions and lighting, it would be impossible to capture the moment with the accuracy he desires.

For these and other aspects he profits immeasurably from the expertise of a wide network of historical specialists who regularly serve as consultants for his artwork. "I have been fortunate to develop a tremendous resource among museum personnel, archivists, collectors, and historians," he says. "Some of them have spent years studying a single regiment, and their assistance is invaluable." Troiani also scans his own three thousand-volume library and research files—the latter consisting of hundreds of folders containing specific details on regimental uniforms, armament, and flags, as well as photographs of unit personnel. If he cannot find enough information on an event, he will not attempt a painting of it, though it may be possible to put the research to good use in a smaller painting depicting a typical soldier of a given regiment.

On average, each of Troiani's major canvasses requires two years' or more worth of research, and he tries to paint no more than four such works a year. "If I did more than that the quality would deteriorate," he claims. "I never paint toward a deadline. I want my pictures to stand the test of time." When all obtainable information has been gathered, Troiani marks the file "ready to be painted."

As Don Troiani begins work on a painting, the first step is to pose and photograph models, clad in period attire, who enact the frenzied grapplings of Civil War combat in the backyard of the artist's Connecticut home or in nearby woods and fields. From hundreds of images, often made over a period of several weeks, he selects specific figures for the scene, penciling them on his canvas, and he begins to rough out the painting when the arrangement is complete.

"Posing is a problem," Troiani admits. "Some people can never get the right expression, while some are naturals and get it right away." If a model is too stiff, Troiani will have him jog up and down his driveway a few times, wearing a wool uniform and toting a knapsack and musket. "That gets him breathless and sweaty, and gives his face the pained, exhausted look I'm after," he says. "If he is a chronic smiler, a cupful of vinegar will sour his puss right up."

Over the years Troiani has assembled a pool of nearly two-hundred models. While he prefers some Civil War reenactors, many of his models are people he meets on the street who have the period look he is after. "I don't want handsome fashion plates," he remarks, "I like gaunt, hardened faces. I don't want them too tall or too short, and they can't be overweight or a body-builder. They have to be physically fit and very thin to be true to the period. Civil War soldiers were lean from marching. They would look like a jogger does today." Troiani rarely uses a model with a waist larger than thirty-two inches. Hairstyles, posture, and attitude are all factors in the selection of models. "Some people just have a nineteenth-century look and some don't," he says.

Troiani is highly critical of other artists who base their figures on photographs taken at large Civil War reenactments. "Many reenactors do not wear well-researched and correctly reconstructed uniforms, and many are far too heavy. It seems like one in three wears glasses; but even if the lenses are in period frames, the fact is very, very few Civil War sol-

Halfway to completion, "Retreat by Recoil" would later be revised so that in the finished work the central figure wears a red shirt rather than an artillery jacket, giving the painting more contrast and a visual center of interest. PHOTO COURTESY DON TROIANI COLLECTION

diers ever wore spectacles in the field." Reenactor officers will often carry their swords hooked to their belts "sticking out like a rooster's tail, with their hand on the hilt; it just was not done that way in the mid-nineteenth century. The sword was hooked to the belt with the hilt to the rear, so that it hung parallel to the left leg." Other reenactors fail to shorten the straps of their haversacks and canteens by knotting them as their historical precursors did, or they shape the brims of their forage caps like modern baseball caps rather than flipping them up, as many Civil War soldiers preferred.

"Paying attention to these details can make all the difference in the world," Troiani believes, "between painting something that looks like a Civil War battle, or painting something that looks like a Civil War reenactment."

He cites the example of an artist who photographed a reenactor artillery crew, then flopped the negative so that in the finished painting the cannon would be pointing in the direction he desired for his composition. "The only problem," Troiani smiles, "was that the regulation positions of the gun crew were now reversed, and they were all left-handed!"

Troiani is able to supply his models from a veritable arsenal of one hundred original weapons—including three full-scale artillery pieces—along with drums, bugles, band instruments, and a collection of hundreds of reproduction uniforms, flags, knapsacks, saddles, and horse equipment. Most of the clothing has been carefully reconstructed in correct nineteenth-century materials, based on research on original items in museums as well the artist's extensive collection of period uniforms and headgear.

In what would be the envy of many museums, Troiani's is one of the most comprehensive private collections of militaria in the United States. It includes original horse equipment, saddles and tack, knapsacks, mess gear, shoes and boots, and rare uniforms like the colorful hussar jacket and talma of the 3rd New Jersey Cavalry, Zouave outfits from the 5th New York and 76th Pennsylvania, and one of only two known examples of the green frock coat worn by Berdan's Sharpshooters. These garments provide invaluable insight into the peculiarities of nineteenth-century tailoring, so different from the clothing of our own time.

Terming his collection "a crucial aspect" of his work, Troiani declares, "You have a really good idea of what the soldier was like when you know what his equipment was like. A historical artist must have an in-depth knowledge of the equipment, its scale, how it was worn, how it works. You can't work from pictures out of reference books. It can only

On June 4, 1863, the men of Company K, 1st Pennsylvania Reserves, posed for the camera at Fairfax Court House, Virginia. For Troiani, capturing the physical appearance and bearing of the Civil War soldiers is as important as ensuring the scrupulous accuracy of their uniforms, weapons, and accoutrements.

PHOTO COURTESY RICHARD K. TIBBALS

be learned by doing, touching, feeling." Pointing out that his idol, Edouard Detaille, shared the same philosophy, Troiani thinks anything less than this hands-on approach "would be like trying to learn about sex out of a book, without doing it."

It is likewise important, he feels, to study period tactical manuals in order to ensure the accuracy of the military formations and the way a soldier carried his weapon under a given circumstance. While formations might become disordered in the confusion of battle, Civil War officers strove to preserve the linear choreography of company and battalion drill, in which every soldier knew his proper place and maintaining "the touch of elbow" was a constant refrain. Troiani decries artists who depict Civil War combat "like a Spartacus-type gladiatorial epic, with everybody evenly sprinkled over the battlefield fighting hand to hand. The only thing missing is someone picking up an opponent and tossing him onto two others."

Troiani finds the current popularity of Civil War art a decidedly mixed blessing. While the fascination the war holds for the American public has fueled demand for his own work, it has also attracted the attention of artists he refers to as "Historical Philistines." "Anyone who can pick up a brush can try to exploit it," he says. "Some of them are certainly prolific; they pride themselves on their speed. But you simply can't do the research in so short a period of time. This is serious work here, we owe it to history—and to the Civil War soldiers—to get the details right."

Differentiating between "artists who paint historical subjects" and "the true historical artist," Troiani defines the latter as "an expert on his subject, who can answer detailed historical questions about his product." Rejecting "artistic license" out of hand, he finds statements like "I was going for a mood" to be a painter's thinly disguised excuse for not doing his homework. "You can certainly endow a painting with mood and drama and still have it be as accurate as research can make it. Everyone makes mistakes, but there is a difference between an educated mistake and a pattern of stupid mistakes."

Although he considers applying his well-honed and rewarding merger of history and art to other eighteenth- and nineteenth-century American conflicts, the mix of pageantry and horror, romanticism and suffering that was the Civil War remains Don Troiani's spiritual passion and artistic mission. When asked if he thinks he will ever run out of ideas he replies, "There is no end in sight. I could just paint Gettysburg and nothing else, and never run out of ideas. I'll be dead before I run out of ideas."

Don Troiani's artwork was recently selected as the design for a series of commemorative coins issued by the U.S. Mint. Proceeds from the sale of these coins will be used to preserve threatened Civil War battlefield sites, a cause the artist strongly supports by donating numerous prints to preservation organizations.

1861

8th Company, 7th New York State Militia

Perhaps America's finest prewar militia unit, the 7th New York was said to be to the National Guard what West Point was to the Regular Army. Many a young New Yorker preferred to serve as a private in the 7th Militia rather than as an officer in a less elite organization. With a membership composed in large part of the blue-blooded sons of Manhattan's oldest families, the well-tailored gray uniform—a color worn by many militia units, both North and South—was a frequent sight at parades and celebrations. And, when called upon, the well-drilled 7th New York was also used to quell the occasional civil disturbance.

On April 19, 1861, the 7th New York marched down Broadway, nearly one thousand strong, bound for Washington and the war. "Was there ever such an ovation?" one soldier wrote. "The marble walls of Broadway were never before rent with such cheers as greeted us when we passed." One of the first units to reach the national capital, the 7th was personally greeted by President Lincoln, and the regiment was widely acclaimed as the saviors of the largely undefended city.

Although the 7th New York would soon return to Manhattan and would not fight in any major battles of the war, many of its soldiers went on to promotion, fame, and glory—proud veterans of the "Dandy Seventh."

PRIVATE COLLECTION

1st Regiment, South Carolina Rifles

On July 20, 1861, the 1st South Carolina Rifles became the first unit from their state to be mustered into Confederate service for the duration of the war. The regiment was popularly known as "Orr's Rifles" in honor of its commanding officer, Colonel James Lawrence Orr, a rotund middle-aged politician who would be elected to the Confederate Senate in December 1861.

Orr's Rifles was unusually large by Civil War standards, with more than fifteen hundred men serving in its ranks during the initial training and organization on Sullivan's Island, near Charleston. Fort Moultrie, the former Federal bastion that came under Confederate control prior to the siege of Fort Sumter, was garrisoned by the Rifles and was a popular destination for Southern civilians. They were certain to receive a cordial welcome from the troops, whose distinctive green-trimmed frock coats and trousers denoted their status as riflemen. Those who envied Orr's Rifles their privileged status soon dubbed the 1st "The Pound Cake Regiment." But the South Carolinians would soon have to prove their merit on the battlefields of Virginia.

Beginning with the bloody battles of the Seven Days, Orr's Rifles served with honor and distinction and paid a heavy price for their valor. At Gaines's Mill, Second Manassas, Fredericksburg, and Gettysburg, they fought bravely and well. By the time the unit surrendered with Lee at Appomattox, only 157 men remained of the proud 1,500 who had answered the call of the Confederacy.

PRIVATE COLLECTION

"Up Alabamians"

The 4th Alabama at First Bull Run, July 21

Confident that one great battle would settle the fate of their divided nation, fledgling soldiers of the Union and Confederacy clashed on a hot Sunday afternoon along the banks of a stream called Bull Run. In an engagement marked by blunders on both sides, Southern forces led by Generals P. G. T. Beauregard and Joseph E. Johnston ultimately triumphed, forcing Federal General Irvin McDowell's army to retreat to the defenses of Washington.

The battle was difficult. Several times during that bloody day the Confederate forces seemed on the brink of defeat. But the gallantry of the officers and the pluck of their soldiers enabled the Southern troops to prevail.

Particularly dedicated to the cause of the South was Confederate Brigadier General Barnard E. Bee. A South Carolinian and member of the West Point Class of 1845, Bee was a tall, striking figure, who had performed heroically in the Mexican War and entered the Confederate service still clad in the blue frock coat of the U.S. Army.

The men of Barnard Bee's brigade shared their commander's determination, if not his military experience. Three days before the first battle, one of Bee's men, Private James G. Hudson of the 4th Alabama, noted, "The boys are all in a high state of glee and excitement under the impression that they are to be led out to attack the Northern vandals." Still innocently unaware of war's grim realities, the Alabama unit comprised a polyglot of militia companies and wore a variety of uniforms including both gray and blue frock coats. Their arms included .69 caliber Model 1842 U.S. muskets and .54 caliber Mississippi rifles, while many accoutrements dated to the pre-war militia era. Largely indifferent to the complexities of battalion maneuver, the volunteers would rely on patriotism rather than tactical proficiency to vanquish the hated Yankees.

By late morning of July 21, as the firing along Bull Run grew in intensity, General Bee's troops, along with Colonel Francis Bartow's Georgia brigade, arrived on a hilltop near Judith Henry's farmhouse. To their north, the brigade of Colonel Nathan Evans was bearing the brunt of the Federal onslaught, fighting valiantly against a numerically superior foe. Holding Bartow's Georgians and his two Mississippi regiments in reserve, Bee led the 4th Alabama downslope, across Young's Branch and the Warrenton turnpike, and up the flank of Matthew's Hill, where Evans's forces had launched a desperate counterattack against the oncoming Union brigades.

As the seven hundred Alabamians waited along the fence-lined edge of a cornfield, panting in the sweltering heat, Bee rode forward to assess the situation. Moments later, the general came galloping back, flourishing his cap and ordering the soldiers to their feet with the cry, "Up Alabamians!" Over the fence and forward through the corn they went, relieving Evans's decimated formations and opening fire on the advancing Yankees of Colonel Ambrose Burnside's brigade one hundred yards to their front.

The commander of the 4th Alabama, Colonel Egbert Jones, rode along his embattled line until his horse was shot beneath him. As the colonel struggled to his feet, another bullet ripped through his thighs, inflicting a mortal wound. The lieutenant colonel and major also fell wounded, and though the arrival of Bee's remaining units and Colonel Bartow's Georgians bolstered the Southern line, the enemy pressure proved too great to resist. After an hour and a half of furious combat, the Confederate troops began to stumble

COLLECTION OF U.S. ARMY NATIONAL GUARD BUREAU

back down Matthew's Hill in disorganized retreat. As the Alabamians scrambled past their dying colonel, Jones implored them, "Men, don't run."

The shattered remnants of the brigades of Bee, Bartow, and Evans managed to rally on Henry House Hill, where Brigadier General Thomas J. Jackson's Virginians were offering determined resistance. Exhorting his troops to hold the line, Barnard Bee shouted, "There stands Jackson like a stone wall!" and what was left of the brigade paused and prepared to reenter the battle.

As the Confederacy began to dominate the fighting, General Bee galloped up to the surviving Alabamians with the query, "What regiment is this?" An officer responded, "Sir, don't you know your own men? This is what is left of the 4th Alabama." The general led his troops back into battle but soon reeled in the saddle with a fatal wound. One of Bee's staff officers, the aristocratic and aptly named Colonel States Rights Gist, took charge of the Alabamians and led them through the chaotic struggle until victory was assured.

By day's end the men of the 4th Alabama had learned the terrible cost of war. More than two hundred of their number had been killed or wounded, the greatest regimental loss of the battle. But their bravery, and that of their fellow Southerners, had won glory on the fields of Manassas.

1st Rhode Island Volunteer Infantry

Among the war's first volunteers were the men of the 1st Rhode Island Infantry, a unit enlisted for a term of three months and led by the future commander of the Army of the Potomac, Ambrose E. Burnside. Colonel Burnside's soldiers were clad in a distinctive overshirt, or smock, peculiar to Rhode Island troops, and wore gray trousers. They were also distinguished by their red blankets, and like other early volunteers, many of the Rhode Islanders sported a linen havelock worn over-top their kepis.

By the time of First Bull Run, Colonel Burnside had been elevated to brigade command, and the 1st Rhode Island went into battle led by Major Joseph Balch. Exhausted by a strenuous march in the sweltering heat and humidity, the Rhode Islanders spearheaded the initial Federal assault and performed well in the fight for Matthew's Hill. But when the North began to lose the battle, the bloodied New Englanders joined in the general withdrawal, which soon gave way to panic and collapse.

This canteen, from the Troiani collection, belonged to a soldier of Company E, 2nd Rhode Island Infantry, the companion unit to the 1st Rhode Island in Burnside's brigade. According to regulations, every soldier was issued a regimental number that was marked on his arms and accoutrements—hence the "No. 86" on the canteen.

PHOTO COURTESY DON TROIANI COLLECTION

PRIVATE COLLECTION

First at Manassas

Battle of Bull Run, July 21

Manassas—as the first major land engagement of the Civil War was known in the South—would be remembered as the first great Confederate victory; and for the North, the defeat suffered by Brigadier General Irvin McDowell's troops would haunt the Federal high command—and the Lincoln administration—for months to come.

No Yankee unit marched into battle on July 21, 1861, with more confidence and promise of military glory than the 11th New York Fire Zouaves. Recruited from the stalwart and largely Irish ranks of Manhattan's volunteer firemen, the 11th New York embodied the physical strength and devil-may-care spirit that characterized nineteenth-century firefighters. During a visit to New York City, English author Charles Dickens concluded, "It is evidently the manner with them to affect recklessness, so as not to appear to be drilled and drummed about."

The 11th New York had been recruited by twenty-four-year-old Colonel Elmer Ephraim Ellsworth, who a year earlier had toured the Midwest and Northeast with his fifty-man U.S. Zouave Cadets of Chicago. An ambitious military enthusiast and close personal friend of Abraham Lincoln, young Ellsworth had fueled a "Zouave craze" that swept the ranks of the prewar militia and inspired dozens of units to march to war clad in exotic garb modeled on the uniform of the famed French Zouaves. On May 24, 1861, Colonel Ellsworth's death at the hands of a Virginia innkeeper made him the first Northern martyr and incited his soldiers to vengeance. Some Zouaves had "Revenge Ellsworth's death" inscribed on their tasseled red or blue fezzes.

The colorful Fire Zouaves made good press, and their red shirts and fierce demeanor gave them a brigandlike air that seemed to portend great deeds on the battlefield. In truth they were as new to war as any volunteer unit, and Ellsworth's successor, Colonel Noah Farnham, had been frustrated in his efforts to instill the firemen with a sense of military discipline and deportment. Like so many soldiers at Bull Run, the 11th New York was little better than an armed mob, and their fighting ability had been further weakened by a hot and tedious march from the defenses of Washington to the field of battle at Manassas.

With McDowell's army on the offensive, and the engagement going in favor of the North, the Fire Zouaves found themselves called upon to support two batteries of Federal artillery occupying a strategic crest known as Henry Hill. As the sweating New Yorkers jogged into line of battle at the double-quick and began to advance toward a tree line, their formation was raked by Confederate volleys. The Virginia brigade of General Thomas J. Jackson was not about to yield Henry Hill without a fight.

Heedless of their officer's entreaties, some Zouaves returned fire, while others dropped to the ground or stumbled back down the slope in confusion. The rearmost companies were still attempting to deploy when out of the woods on their right flank thundered 150 Rebel horsemen, flourishing sabers and firing pistols and carbines. Colonel J. E. B. Stuart of the 1st Virginia Cavalry launched his troopers at the disorganized mass of men in red "like an arrow from a bow."

Still clad in his prewar U.S. Army uniform, the brawny auburn-bearded commander led the charge into the Zouave formation. A ragged volley brought down several horses and their riders, but Stuart's Virginians slashed their way through the New Yorkers, causing

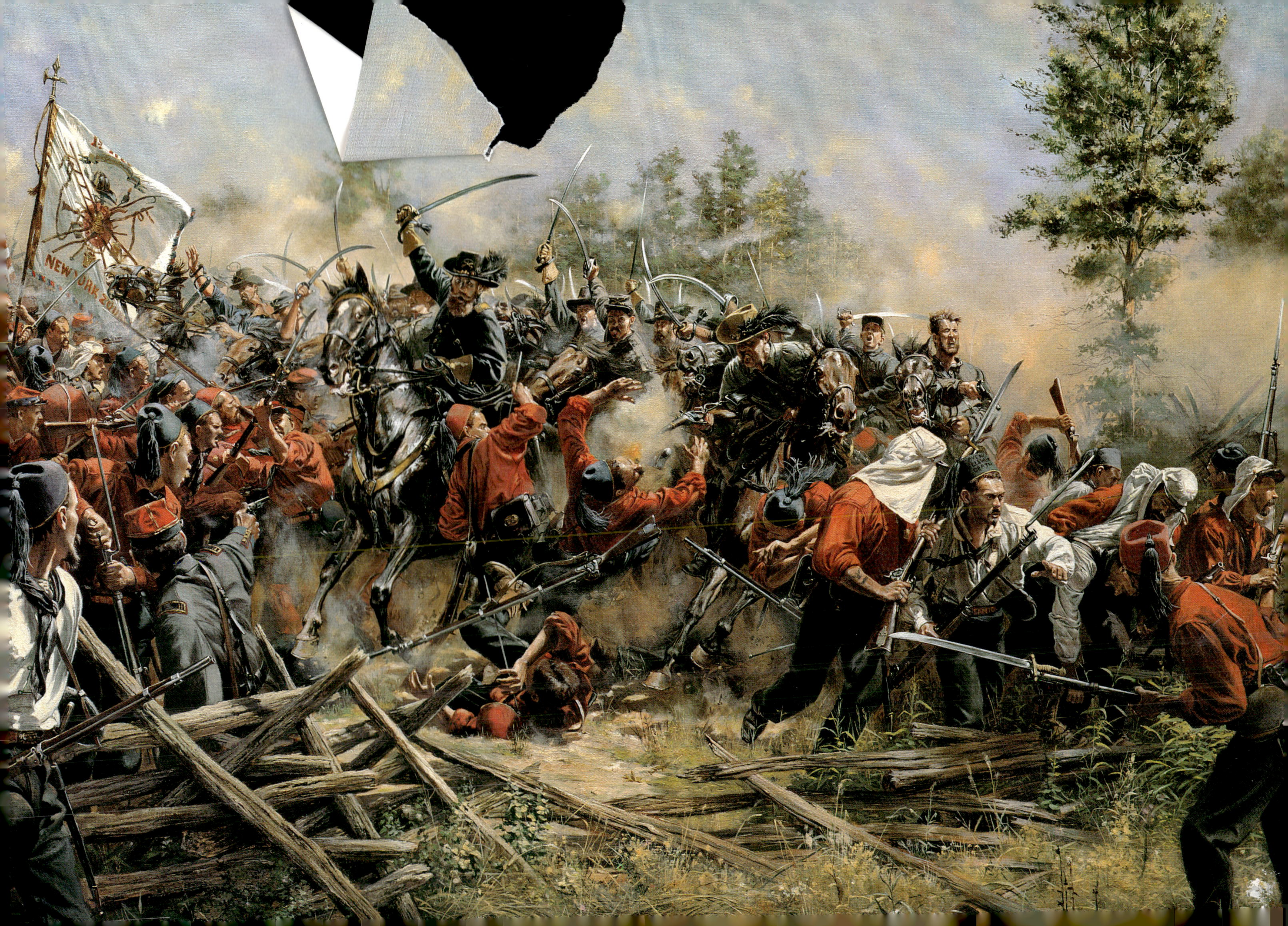
NEW YORK

chaos. Lieutenant William Blackford felled one Zouave with a point-blank blast from his carbine, and others were cut down and trampled underhoof.

Though a relative handful of men were killed or seriously wounded in the clash, by the time Stuart's charge was over, the 11th New York was not able to defend the batteries entrusted to its care. Colonel Farnham had been wounded and his companies were hopelessly intermingled, and when the Confederate infantry attacked, the Fire Zouaves were caught in a deadly cross fire and put to flight. Though the disputed batteries would change hands several times during the battle, Jeb Stuart's daring charge on the Fire Zouaves had helped ensure Confederate victory at Manassas.

Recalling the 1st Virginia's charge on the Fire Zouaves, Lieutenant William W. Blackford wrote, "The tremendous impetus of horses at full speed broke through and scattered their line like chaff before the wind." As Blackford's horse, Comet, bowled over one Zouave, the lieutenant—who carried a Sharps carbine in addition to his saber and revolver—jammed the weapon into the New Yorker and "blew a hole as big as my arm clear through him." PHOTO COURTESY BILL TURNER AND LARRY JONES

2ND U.S. CAVALRY

WITH THE VETERAN SOLDIERS OF the Regular U.S. Army preparing for their part in putting down the rebellion, there was no prouder unit in the "Old Army" than the men who wore the orange-trimmed uniforms of the 2nd United States Dragoons.

Organized at Jefferson Barracks, Missouri, in the summer of 1836, the 2nd Dragoons had slogged through the swamps of the Florida Everglades in pursuit of the wily Seminoles and had stormed the defenses of Mexico City. They fought a grim and deadly war of ambush and retaliation against the hostile Indians of the northern and southern plains, and intervened in the bloody sectional strife of pro- and antislavery factions in Kansas Territory.

Four years before the outbreak of the Civil War, the tough horsemen had spent a frigid winter in the foothills of the Rocky Mountains, policing the defiant Mormon settlers who refused to recognize the authority of the U.S. government.

With the opening shots at Fort Sumter, their twelve companies were gathered from their scattered stations and hurried to the theater of war. Company K was on hand in time to participate in First Bull Run. Less than a month later, on August 10, 1861, all U.S. mounted troops were redesignated as cavalry—and much against their wishes, the 2nd Dragoons became the 2nd U.S. Cavalry.

Though yellow was the official cavalry trim, the Dragoons were permitted to maintain their distinctive orange stripes and taping until the clothing wore out—and so jealous of their heritage were these hard-bitten troopers that it would be two years before they were fully amalgamated into the cavalry arm.

COLLECTION OF U.S. CAVALRY MUSEUM, FORT RILEY, KANSAS

Company K, 69th New York State Militia

Irish Zouaves

BATTLE OF BULL RUN, JULY 21

"Gentle when stroked, fierce when provoked." So reads the regimental motto of the 69th New York, emblazoned on its crest beneath the noble figure of an Irish wolfhound. At the outbreak of the Civil War, the 69th New York was by far the most distinguished Irish-American militia unit in the United States. The regiment's commanding officer, Colonel Michael Corcoran, was a leading figure in Irish nationalist circles, and in 1860 had gained considerable notoriety for refusing to parade his troops before the visiting prince of Wales.

Another who cherished hopes of a free and united Ireland was the fiery orator Thomas Francis Meagher, who had escaped imprisonment by the British and emigrated to America, and who, like Corcoran, became a prominent member of the Fenian Brotherhood. When the 69th New York answered President Lincoln's call for volunteers, Meagher organized a contingent of Zouaves, which was designated Company K of Corcoran's unit. Their modified version of the Zouave uniform—made famous by Elmer Ellsworth's prewar tour—reflected Meagher's previous association with the Phoenix Zouaves, a quasimilitary adjunct of the Fenian Brotherhood.

At Bull Run the fighting 69th New York played a gallant, though ineffective, part in the Union assault on Henry House Hill. Colonel Corcoran was captured during the Federal retreat, while Captain Meagher's bravery would soon earn him the rank of general and command of the famed Irish Brigade.

COLLECTION OF WILLIAM RODEN

1st North Carolina Cavalry

Organized in Warren County a month after Bull Run, the 1st North Carolina Cavalry arrived at the seat of war in Virginia in October 1861. Initially commanded by Colonel Robert Ransom, a West Point–educated veteran of the 1st U.S. Cavalry noted for his harsh discipline, the Tarheels became a distinguished unit of J. E. B. Stuart's famed mounted force.

Clad in the regulation North Carolina sack coat, trimmed in yellow to denote their status as cavalry, the Carolinians initially received a varied mix of weaponry and accoutrements. One company was issued the artillery version of the Colt revolving carbine, while many troopers carried Model 1836 pistols, converted from flintlock to percussion. The Model 1840 heavy cavalry saber was much in evidence, slung from white buff belts of the pattern issued to U.S. Dragoons in the Mexican War. Horse equipments included one hundred Texas Ranger saddles and bridles.

By the spring of 1862 most of the early uniforms and accoutrements had been discarded, and the Tarheels' distinctive attire gave way to more generic garb that rendered them indistinguishable from the other mounted units that followed Stuart's plume.

COLLECTION OF M. FLANAGAN

1862

UNITED STATES MARINES

North Carolina Coast

THE UNITED STATES MARINE Corps saw limited action in the epic land battles of the Civil War—First Manassas and the January 1865 assault on Fort Fisher being exceptions—but Marines did fight aboard ship and participate in countless raids and forays on the Southern coast. These amphibious operations were the offensive arm of the Union blockade that slowly but surely tightened its stranglehold on the Confederacy.

Marine landing parties were outfitted as infantry, according to the 1859 uniform regulations. Their undress (everyday) frock coats were worn over white linen trousers, eminently suited to the warm and humid weather of the Carolina coast. Sporting a French chasseur-style kepi with a hunting horn insignia reminiscent of that worn by Federal infantry, they carried the Model 1855 rifled musket, one of many long arms in the Marine arsenal. Among the more distinctive aspects of the Civil War Marine were the white buff accoutrement belts and the yellow silk chevrons—worn points-up rather than points-down as was the custom in other branches of the service. Officers were likewise set apart from their army counterparts by their double-breasted frock coats and "Russian knots" rather than shoulder straps to indicate rank.

Though they were often stationed in less glamorous theaters of war and denied the press attention lavished on the great armies of the interior, the United States Marine Corps did its part to achieve victory for its country.

PRIVATE COLLECTION

The Stars and Bars

In the winter of 1861–62, Confederate soldiers in the field were already beginning to suffer from a lack of proper clothing. Some men still had bits and pieces of the garb they had worn when they marched off to war nine months earlier—few had thought the fighting would last longer than ninety days. Homemade replacements, acquired under the so-called commutation system, in which individual soldiers were made responsible for obtaining clothing from civilian sources with funds allotted for that purpose, often resulted in a variety of colors and materials within a single company.

For Southern troops compelled to fight in the damp and snow—as was the case with the defenders of Fort Donelson in February 1862—a shortage of overcoats was a particular concern. Fortunate was the man who could get an extra blanket or a captured Yankee greatcoat. But despite their hardships, the Confederate soldiers displayed a dauntless loyalty to their new country and flag.

The first national flag of the Confederacy was popularly known as "The Stars and Bars," its design reflecting its derivation from the Stars and Stripes of the former United States. Produced in large numbers, the flag had stars that symbolized the seceded states and sometimes contained additional stars for the border states, Kentucky and Missouri, that supplied men to Confederate armies even though they were officially still part of the Union. Patriotic slogans like "Liberty or Death," "Our Honor and Our Rights," and "In God We Trust" were often emblazoned on the colors.

In the smoke and confusion of battle the Stars and Bars were often mistaken for the Stars and Stripes of Federal banners—a problem that ultimately resulted in a modification of the Confederate national flag. But the ideals embodied in those flags would continue to motivate the Southern soldier through all the suffering and hardship that was to come.

PRIVATE COLLECTION

Men of Arkansas

Battle of Shiloh, April 6

The Confederacy had reason to expect great things of General Albert Sidney Johnston. Fifty-nine years old in the spring of 1862, Johnston could boast a military career that included service in the Black Hawk War of 1832, a stint as commander of the army of the Republic of Texas, and staff duty in the Mexican War. For five years the quiet, intellectual Johnston served on the western plains as colonel of the elite 2nd U.S. Cavalry. His efforts to quell a threatened rebellion of Mormon settlers in Utah had brought him the brevet rank of brigadier general. A senior and highly regarded officer of the Regular Army, Johnston's decision to join the Confederacy brought him command of the western theater of operations as the South's highest-ranking field commander.

But upright character and good credentials were not enough to ensure success as the war entered its second year. In the first months of 1862 the loss of Forts Henry and Donelson to the Federal forces of U. S. Grant gave control of the Tennessee and Cumberland Rivers to the Union. The city of Nashville was abandoned, Kentucky and Tennessee were occupied by the enemy, and Johnston's dispirited army withdrew to the strategic rail center at Corinth, Mississippi. Johnston's Civil War career changed dramatically in the first days of April, however, when he determined to challenge his seemingly complacent foe. In the early morning hours of April 6, Johnston's Army of Mississippi launched a surprise attack on the tented camps of Grant's Army of the Tennessee near Pittsburg Landing on the Tennessee River. Confederate soldiers swept through the Yankee encampments at Shiloh Church, and the majority of three Federal divisions were put to flight.

But after their initial success, the Southern forces began to lose cohesion, and a fateful delay as Johnston awaited General John C. Breckinridge's Reserve Corps permitted the battered Union troops to patch together a defensive position. The Federal stronghold rested on a sunken road, a scattering of timber, and a peach orchard—a bullet-swept perimeter that would come to be known as the "Hornets' Nest." Attack after attack advanced and recoiled, leaving the ground strewn with Southern dead and wounded.

Albert Sidney Johnston had been in the thick of the action since dawn, spurring his magnificent bay, Fire-eater, forward with the troops, savoring the victory that would affirm his men's devotion and his own military skills. "General Johnston was sitting on his horse where the bullets were flying like hail stones," a staff officer recalled; another observed, "His countenance gleamed with the enthusiasm of a great man who was conscious that he was achieving a great success." Johnston was flaunting a little tin cup, snatched up in an abandoned Yankee camp—what he called "my share of the spoils."

Shortly before noon, with the Southern offensive again picking up momentum, John-

> Research at the National Archives indicated that in addition to the ubiquitous bowie knives, the 9th Arkansas was armed with a variety of firearms, including flintlock muskets, Hall rifles, double-barreled shotguns, and squirrel rifles. Troiani's depiction of General Johnston's garb was based on the general's statue in New Orleans; its sculptor had consulted the original uniform in the possession of Johnston's son. A variety of accounts compiled by author and historian Wiley Sword supplied many of the details of this dramatic moment in the battle of Shiloh.

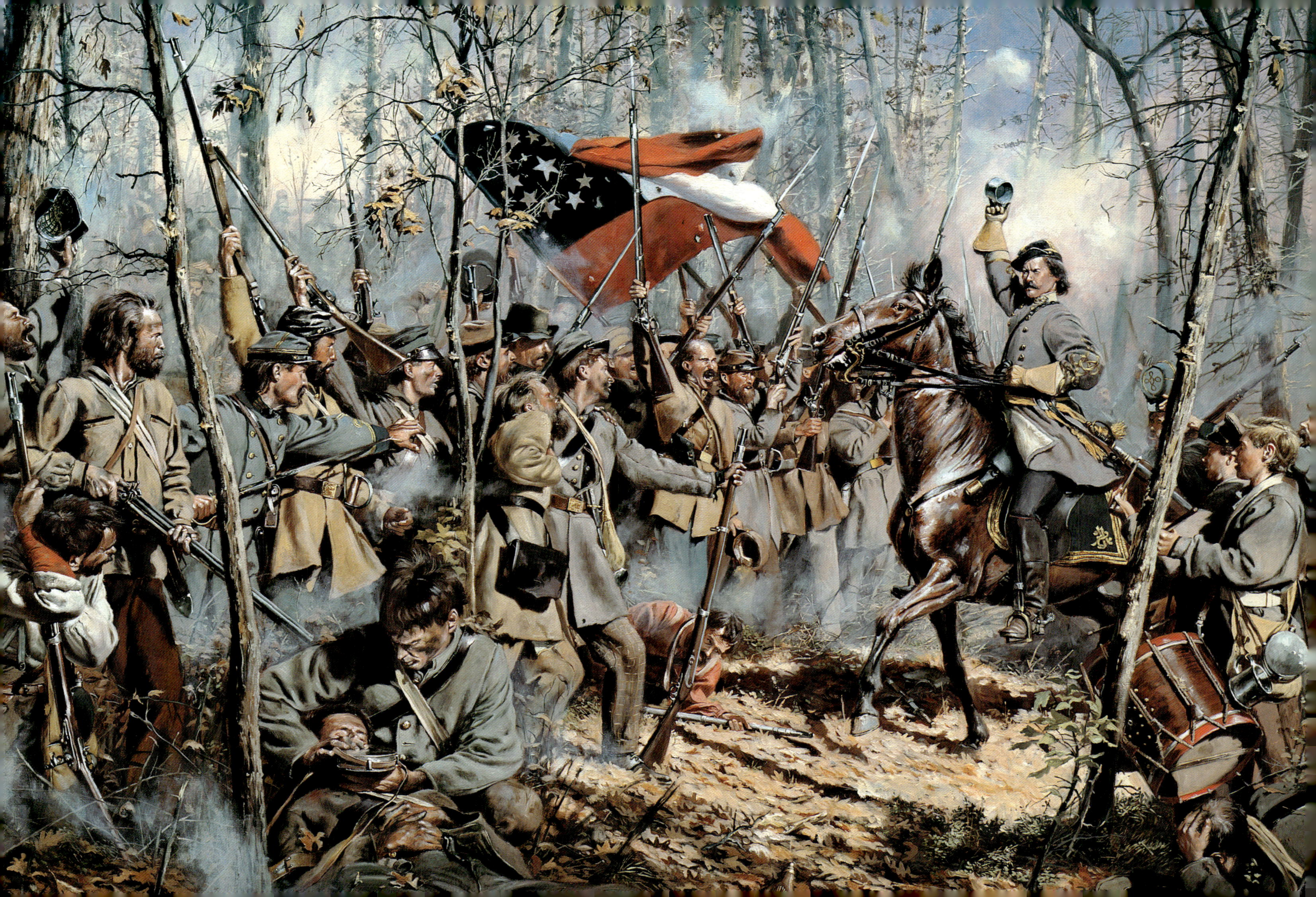

ston prepared to launch three brigades against the left flank of the Hornets' Nest. Riding up to Brigadier General John S. Bowen's brigade, formed in the timber and waiting the order to charge, Johnston addressed the men of the 9th Arkansas. "A few more charges and the day is ours!" he exhorted his troops. "His voice was persuasive, encouraging, and compelling," an officer wrote. "It was inviting men to their death, but they obeyed it."

The rough-hewn Arkansans, with their motley armament of flintlocks, shotguns, and bowie knives, greeted their commander with rousing cheers. "Men of Arkansas!" Johnston shouted, "They say you boast of your prowess with the bowie knife. Today you wield a nobler weapon—the bayonet. Employ it well."

Galloping on to the left, where Colonel Winfield Scott Statham's brigade was readying, Johnston rode along the line of the 45th Tennessee, tapping the fixed bayonets with his tin cup and repeating his injunction: "Men, they are stubborn; we must use the bayonet." When the general reached the center of the line, he swung his horse toward the enemy and shouted, "I will lead you!"

Shortly before 2 P.M. the three Southern brigades started forward, across a clearing and into a blizzard of musketry and artillery fire. On they pressed, driving the Yankees back through the peach orchard, blossoms falling upon the dead and wounded as the Confederate lines pushed on. Heartened by the successful charge, Johnston casually remarked to Tennessee Governor Isham Harris, a volunteer on his staff, "Governor, they came very near putting me *hors de combat* in that charge." Harris saw that a bullet had ripped across the toe of one of the general's high-top boots, though the projectile had not drawn blood.

In fact, Johnston had received a severe wound, though he seemed either not to notice or to consider it inconsequential. A second bullet had passed through the calf of his right leg, severing an artery, and even as the general shrugged off his injury, blood was steadily flowing into his right boot.

Some minutes later, Johnston suddenly swayed in the saddle. Governor Harris saw that he was "deadly pale," and when he asked, "General, are you wounded?" Johnston said deliberately, "Yes, and I fear seriously." At about 2:30 P.M., half an hour after leading his brigades in the charge, Albert Sidney Johnston died, and with his death, the battle at Shiloh began to turn in favor of the Union.

19th Tennessee Infantry

April 1862

The battle of Shiloh was the bloodiest engagement of the war to date, and the soldiers of the 19th Tennessee found themselves in the thick of the action. On April 6, 1862, the first day of the two-day clash, the 19th was called upon to join the assault on the Yankee strongpoint called the Hornets' Nest—a sunken road and patch of scrub from which the bluecoats hailed death upon the Southern attackers.

Like many troops in General Albert Sidney Johnston's army, the 19th Tennessee had marched to war armed with outdated Model 1816 flintlock muskets. Despite the Confederacy's seizure of U.S. arsenals, not until sufficient shipments of British Enfields began to arrive would the South be able to equip its forces with substantial numbers of modern percussion long arms.

Despite their primitive armament, the Tennesseans' fervor carried them through the early-morning onslaught that surged through the Union encampments near Shiloh Church. Though temporarily separated from their brigade, the 19th Tennessee joined the charge on the Hornets' Nest alongside other scattered units led by Colonel George Maney. Pushing through the demoralized survivors of early assaults, Maney's troops dropped prone to escape a Yankee volley, then rose up and stormed into the heart of the Hornets' Nest. By late afternoon the stubborn Union defenders were finally broken, and their stronghold was overrun.

Washington Artillery of New Orleans

Army of Northern Virginia Companies

THE OLDEST LOUISIANA MILITARY UNIT, AND one that drew its membership from the finest families of that state, the Washington Artillery went to war as a battalion of four companies, a fifth company being added early in 1862. They were trained and equipped to fight as infantry as well as to man the big guns. The four original companies would fight in the war's eastern theater, and from First Manassas to Appomattox they earned an honored place in the pantheon of Southern arms. "For efficiency, drill, and discipline," noted Lieutenant William Miller Owen, "it was not surpassed by any organization of citizen soldiery in the Southern States."

Originally uniformed in dark blue frock coats, sky blue trousers, and red kepis, the Louisianans by 1862 had received more traditional Confederate gray, though most retained their distinctive red caps. More than most Southern units, they tried to maintain a tailored, military uniformity befitting their elite status. Six twelve-pound Napoleons comprised the single largest component of their varied arsenal of sixteen guns, all of which had been captured from Federal forces.

It is indicative of the *esprit* of these gallant gunners that when defeat loomed, the Washington Artillery buried their guns and disbanded their companies rather than endure the indignity of the surrender at Appomattox Court House.

COLLECTION OF WILLIAM RODEN

8th Texas Cavalry

Terry's Texas Rangers

ALERT, VIGILANT, AND MOUNTED ON GOOD horseflesh, a trooper of the 8th Texas Cavalry reinforced his self-reliance with firepower. It was not at all unusual for one of Colonel Benjamin F. Terry's cavalrymen to carry a shotgun and up to four revolvers—two worn on the belt and two carried across the saddle. These were men who knew how to fight, and they intended to do just that.

Veterans of the fighting at First Manassas, Terry and his cousin, Thomas Lubbock, returned to their Houston home and raised ten companies, ostensibly for service in Virginia. But the unit decided to join Albert Sidney Johnston's army in Tennessee, and their wartime career would thereafter be in the rough western theater.

Their shotguns and pistols made the Texans a formidable force whether on foot or on horseback. Their horse equipments reflected their frontier heritage, generally being of the pattern dubbed "Mexian," and most of the Rangers omitted the saber as a useless appendage. For much of the war their clothing was supplied by their native state and varied in hue from gray to butternut, often trimmed in red. The spoils of war provided the horsemen with Yankee-made boots and accoutrements, and the favored slouch hat that they generally adorned with a handmade star, symbolic of the Lone Star State.

PRIVATE COLLECTION

THE RED DEVILS

Battle of Gaines's Mill, June 27

IT HAD BEEN NEARLY THREE MONTHS SINCE the 5th New York Volunteer Infantry had arrived on the Virginia Peninsula, and the once-gaudy red and blue Zouave regalia that made them one of the Union's most colorful regiments clearly showed the effects of hard campaigning.

In the year since they had been rallied to the colors by wealthy Manhattan businessman Abram Duryée—now a brigadier general—the 5th New York Zouaves had taken part in only one real engagement. That June 1861 clash at Big Bethel had won the flashy unit the sobriquet "Red Devils," and the subsequent months of garrison duty in occupied Baltimore had seen their new colonel, West Pointer Gouverneur Kemble Warren, bring their drill and discipline to a par with that of the Regular Army.

The Zouaves were eager to prove themselves, and on June 27, 1862, they got their chance. General George B. McClellan had commenced his change of base from the York to the James, and the series of battles known as the Seven Days was under way. The 5th Corps had been called upon to cover the Federal withdrawal, and as they took position on an open ridge above the wooded valley of Powhite Creek and Gaines's Mill, looming dust clouds and the firing of skirmishers heralded the advance of Robert E. Lee's army.

As artillery fire began to explode over and among the Zouave line, Colonel Warren, who was commanding the brigade, ordered Lieutenant Colonel Hiram Duryea to pull the New Yorkers back to the shelter of a sunken roadbed. The men hunkered down, some standing in knee-deep ditch water, while Rebel shells burst above them or tore into the earth, sending geysers of mud high in the air.

Finally the enemy made their appearance, with General Maxcy Gregg's South Carolina brigade deploying from the facing wood line and the 1st South Carolina "Orr's Rifles" in the vanguard. Lieutenant Colonel Duryea exclaimed to Colonel Warren, "They're in the open field where we want them!" At Warren's signal, Duryea ordered the Red Devils into line of battle, shouting "Now men, your time has come. Keep together and see that you do your duty!" The Zouaves followed their mounted commander forward, giving a mighty cheer as they swept down on Orr.

As the first bullets began to tear through the ranks, the charge briefly lost momentum. Gouverneur Warren spurred his gray horse to the color company and yelled, "Advance the colors! Advance the colors! Charge!" The Red Devils surged through the smoke of battle as men fell before the Confederate volleys.

Some opponents actually crossed bayonets before Orr's Rifles gave way. "The enemy was driven from the field in confusion," Hiram Duryea reported, "and the survivors nearly annihilated by our fire." But still more of Gregg's units had come into the fray, and the 5th New York was checked in turn, though they refused to retire. "Many of our little company lay scattered upon the ground with ghastly wounds, moaning in agony," Corporal Thomas Southwick recalled. Private Alfred Davenport commented, "Our boys fell in heaps."

When Color Sergeant Francis Spelman collapsed with heat stroke, the regimental flag was raised by Sergeant John H. Berrian, whose brother had been slain moments before. Anguished and enraged, Berrian carried the blue banner thirty paces in advance of the flaming battle line, planted the staff in the ground, and shook his fist at his Rebel foes.

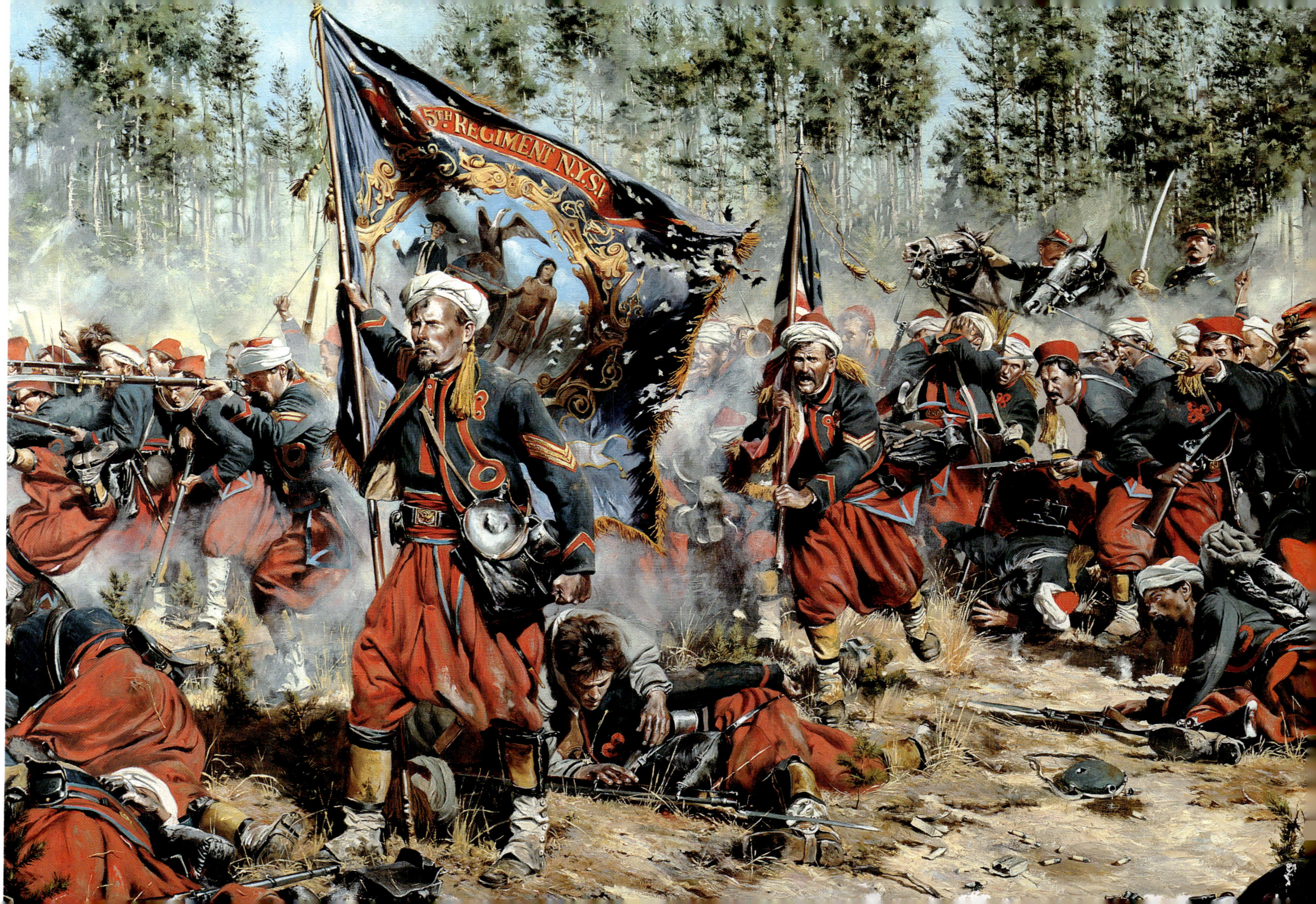

COLLECTION OF MICHAEL COPPOLA

Inspired by Berrian's gesture, Sergeant Andrew B. Allison joined him with the national colors. Watching from horseback, Duryea and Captain Cleveland Winslow shouted to the two men to come back. Instead, the rest of the regiment gave a terrible yell, and as Private Davenport wrote, "rushed like demons for the wood with the bayonet."

The South Carolinians held firm, and the Union charge dissolved in fire. The color guard was shot down almost en masse, men riddled and whirled about by flying lead. The ornamental tip of the regimental flagstaff was shot away, and both banners rent and torn.

By now many of the Zouaves were out of ammunition. Desperate, sweating, and powder-stained, they fumbled at the cartridge boxes of the dead and wounded and kept up

The gold chevrons of a corporal adorn the Zouave jacket of William C. Ryer, who served in Company F of the 5th New York Zouaves. Ryer was killed in action at the battle of Gaines's Mill. PHOTO COURTESY DON TROIANI COLLECTION

the fight. At last the 1st Pennsylvania Reserves came to their relief, and Duryea pulled his decimated companies out of the line. But before marching them rearward, the iron-willed commander ordered the Zouaves to halt and called them to attention. As Confederate shells exploded overhead, Duryea had his men count off and realign their ranks. Only then did he resume the retreat.

The battle of Gaines's Mill proved that the Duryée Zouaves were more than a colorful ornament on the parade ground. Of the 450 men who had entered the battle, 162 had fallen. But though the engagement had been a Federal defeat, the Southerners had gained a healthy respect for the colorfully clad New York Zouaves, and their proud reputation within the Army of the Potomac was assured.

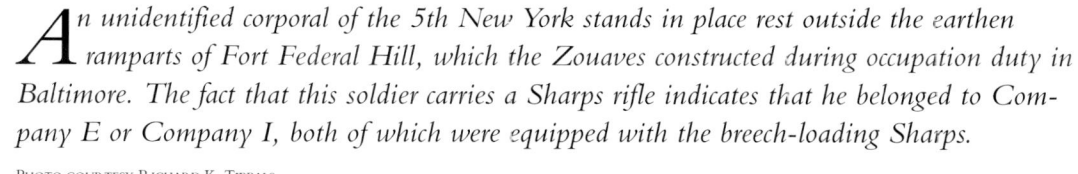

An unidentified corporal of the 5th New York stands in place rest outside the earthen ramparts of Fort Federal Hill, which the Zouaves constructed during occupation duty in Baltimore. The fact that this soldier carries a Sharps rifle indicates that he belonged to Company E or Company I, both of which were equipped with the breech-loading Sharps.

PHOTO COURTESY RICHARD K. TIBBALS

Southern Cross

Battle of Glendale, June 30

On the last day of June 1862, as McClellan's forces pursued their increasingly harried change of base from the York to the James, Robert E. Lee sought an opportunity to interdict the Federal move and destroy a large portion of the retreating enemy column. The opportunity came at a crossroads called Glendale, where the Union troops were funneled into a congested bottleneck that invited attack. In the late afternoon, as Lee strove to marshal his scattered columns for a decisive assault, another of the Seven Days battles erupted along the Long Bridge and Willis Church Roads, and on the fields of Frayser's Farm.

In the center of Lee's line, five Alabama regiments commanded by Brigadier General Cadmus M. Wilcox started forward, with little idea of what lay ahead. A graduate of the West Point Class of 1846 and a prewar Regular Army captain, Wilcox had led his brigade with distinction in earlier fighting on the Peninsula. Though the ranks of the Alabamians were thinned, their determination was strong, and as they passed through a pine thicket and into an open field beyond, they let forth a savage yell and pressed forward against the Yankees.

The troops facing Wilcox were men of the Pennsylvania Reserves, a division commanded by sixty-year-old Brigadier General George A. McCall. The Pennsylvanians, bloodied at Mechanicsville and Gaines's Mill, were at Glendale again destined to bear the brunt of the Rebel onslaught. The Union line was studded with artillery batteries, and when the enemy appeared, the guns roared.

When the 8th Alabama, on the left of Wilcox's line, tangled with Federal infantry, the 11th Alabama continued to advance across a level field some three hundred yards wide, toward a battery of bronze Napoleon guns and their infantry supports. This was Lieutenant Alanson M. Randol's Battery E, 1st U.S. Artillery, and the foot soldiers were the 4th and 7th Pennsylvania Reserves of Brigadier General George G. Meade's brigade.

As the 11th Alabama came howling across the field, Randol's guns cut bloody swaths through the Rebel lines. The Alabamians were staggered but kept on until their formation halted one hundred yards from the Yankee line. But although the Federal infantry added volleys of musketry to the deadly hail of fire, the Confederates rallied and charged again, "advancing in wedge shape, without order," General McCall recounted, "but with a wild recklessness that I never saw equalled."

The 11th Alabama came to within fifty yards of the Federal position, despite what Lieutenant Randol described as "frightful havoc" from the shotgunlike blasts of canister. General McCall watched as Randol's Napoleons "fairly opened lanes in the advancing host," and again the Southern infantry wavered. With the Rebels stalemated, the men of the 4th and 7th Pennsylvania Reserves could not be restrained, and with a cheer they precipitated themselves upon their enemy in a spontaneous and unauthorized counterattack.

The contesting lines crashed together in front of Randol's guns, firing into each other's faces at point-blank range and thrusting with fixed bayonets. Suddenly the Federals gave way; Randol reported that some "threw away their arms and rushed directly for the battery" rather than pass around the flanks of the artillery as he had cautioned. The soldiers of the 11th Alabama pursued them, sensing victory.

His field of fire blocked by the intermingled mob of Union and Confederate troops, Randol waited until he could see the grap-

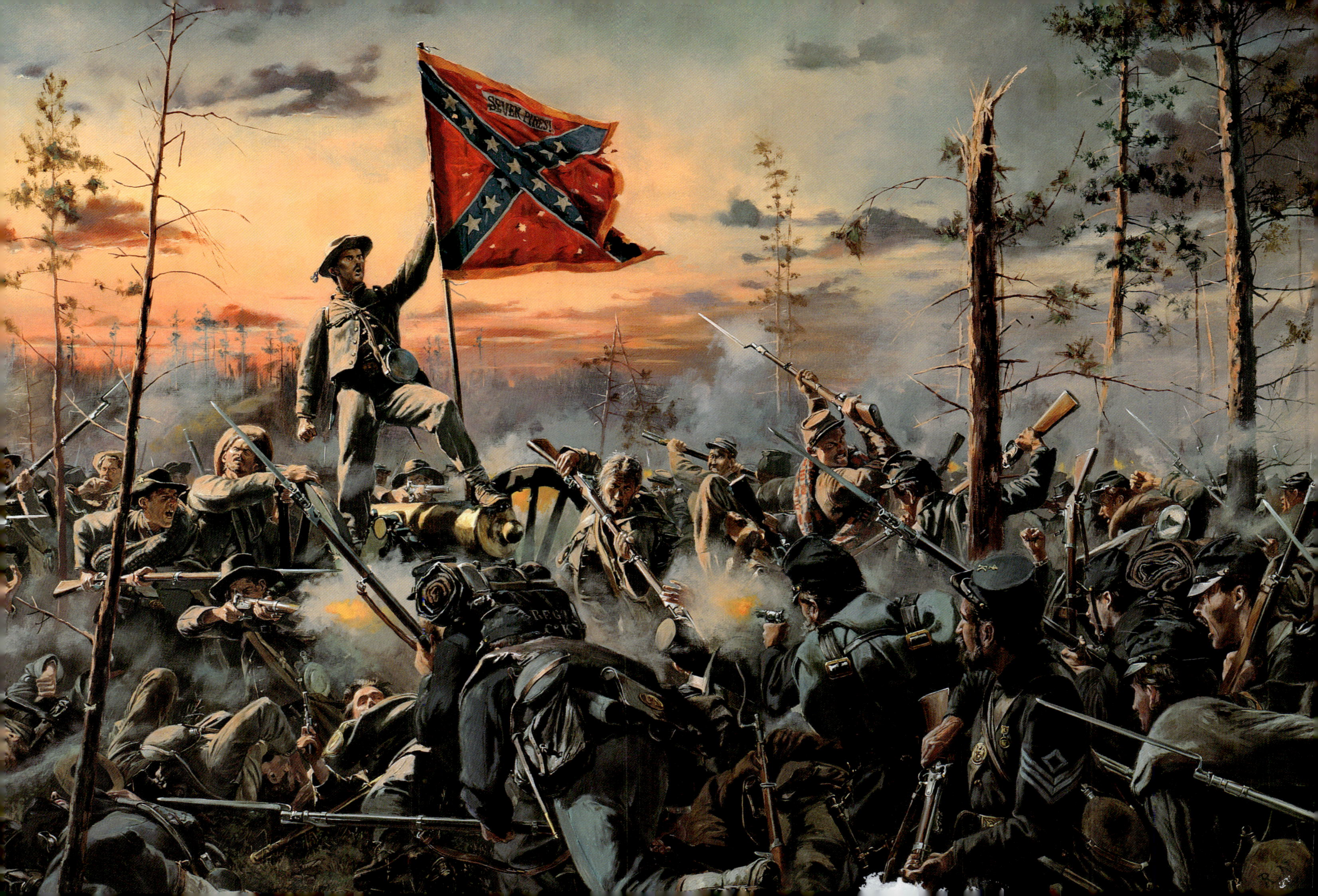
SEVEN PINES!

pling antagonists before firing a last murderous salvo of canister. There followed what Alabamian N. B. Hogan called "one of the most desperate, and sanguinary hand to hand conflicts ever recorded. . . . The scenes enacted in this horrible contest for mastery beggar description." Some men fought it out bayonet to bayonet, what General McCall described as "the desperate thrusts and parries of a life and death encounter." Others swung their weapons like clubs; McCall saw "skulls crushed by the heavy blow of the butt of the musket."

As the brutal grapple continued, the 11th Alabama shoved the Federal infantry back from the contested guns. "In this battle every man was a hero," claimed Private Hogan. Lieutenant W. S. Boyd had disabled two opponents when another Yankee ran him through with a bayonet. His skull laid bare by a saber cut, Lieutenant T. J. Michie thrust his sword into a Yankee captain, then fell dying with three bayonet wounds in the face and two in the breast.

Leaping into the battery, color bearer Charles McNeil of the 11th Alabama scrambled atop one of Randol's Napoleons and unfurled the Southern Cross above the frenzied melee. A Yankee bullet toppled McNeil from his perch, though the stricken soldier continued to wave his battle flag. The color bearer's nephew, William McNeil, attempted to raise the banner but was shot dead before he could do so.

Moments later the tide again turned in favor of the North as Lieutenant Randol led a desperate counterattack to retrieve his precious guns. Charley McNeil was bayonetted to death and the colors of the 11th Alabama

This pair of canvas and leather leggings from the Troiani collection was worn by a soldier of the 105th Pennsylvania. In the fight at Glendale many of the Pennsylvania Reserves wore leggings of the same pattern, the Federal government having made extensive contracts for them in early 1862. While far from popular with soldiers, who tended to view them as a superfluous decoration to the uniform, the leggings were issued as late as 1863, and there were plans to equip the entire 3rd Corps with them.

PHOTO COURTESY DON TROIANI COLLECTION

seized as a trophy, while another Pennsylvanian recaptured a Federal flag lost earlier in the fighting. Bleeding from a wound in the arm and side, General Meade rode up to Lieutenant Randol. "Fight your guns to the last," Meade commanded, "but save them if possible."

With his horses dead, gunners scattered, infantry support in disarray, and more Rebels advancing, Randol was forced to abandon all six Napoleons. For the rest of the day the guns lay amidst the heaps of dead and dying, and after dark they were irretrievably in the hands of the Confederates.

The Alabamians paid a heavy price for those guns. All four of Wilcox's regimental commanders had fallen. The 11th Alabama lost seven of ten company commanders, and one company was reduced from twenty-eight to three men. Lee failed to destroy McClellan's army, but the unparalled gallantry of his soldiers held forth the promise of ultimate victory.

The men of Company F, 7th Pennsylvania Reserves, participated in the desperate defense of Randol's Battery at Glendale. In the course of the Seven Days battles the regiment lost 294 men and would go on to play an important part in the campaigns that followed. PHOTO COURTESY MARK LEINAWEAVER COLLECTION AND THE U.S. ARMY MILITARY HISTORY INSTITUTE

"OLD JACK"

Major General Thomas J. Jackson

Stalwart and resolute, bodies toughened by a year of war, in the summer of 1862 the hard-marching infantrymen of Stonewall Jackson's "foot cavalry" had every reason to cheer the silent, determined commander they called "Old Jack." From his heroic stand on Henry Hill at First Manassas through the brilliant maneuvers of the Shenandoah Valley Campaign, Major General Thomas Jonathan Jackson had become a living legend to the men who wore the gray, a figure who elicited an almost mystical devotion. Though he never sought his troops' adulation and certainly never coddled them, Jackson's devout religiosity and stern adherence to duty was seen by his rugged soldiers as the moral strength of the Southern cause. As one discomfited Yankee prisoner expressed it, "Stonewall Jackson's men will follow him to the devil and he knows it."

In the pantheon of Southern heroes, there was no one quite like Jackson. The awkward West Pointer, Mexican War hero, and uninspiring VMI professor betrayed no obvious claim to greatness. And yet in the terrible crucible of Civil War he found the tangible expression of his innate strength. To his frustrated subordinates Jackson's uncommunicative nature and his refusal to discuss his strategy seemed quirky and unreasonable. "If silence be golden, he was a bonanza," Brigadier General Richard Taylor recalled. "Praying and fighting appeared to be his idea of the whole duty of man." Exasperated by his superior's penchant for pushing his soldiers to the limit of their endurance, General Charles Winder wrote, "Jackson is insane on these rapid marches." Winder's cousin and aide, the aristocratic Marylander McHenry Howard, recorded his impressions of the redoubtable Stonewall:

He was above middle height, compactly and strongly built but with no superfluous flesh. His eyes were a steel blue in color and well opened when he looked straight at one, which he did when addressing a general remark . . . and his mouth, half seen under the moustache was very firm and the lips usually compressed. The lower part of his face was tanned by exposure, but when his cap was off, the forehead, high and broad, was white. . . . The habitual expression of his face was that of one communing with his own thoughts and others seldom spoke to him without being first addressed.

Henry Kyd Douglas described his commander as a man of few words—a trait as much a part of Stonewall's character as his abiding religious faith, his moral rectitude, and his unwillingness to discuss his plans with subordinates. "His own words seemed to embarrass him," Douglas recalled.

Contrasting Jackson and his favorite horse, Little Sorrel, with Robert E. Lee astride Traveller, Douglas found his eccentric chief "the most awkward man in the army." "Walking or riding the general was ungainly," Douglas recalled. "He rode boldly and well, but not with grace or ease; and Little Sorrel was as little like a Pegasus as he was like an Apollo."

The pomp and circumstance of nineteenth century armies, with all their banners, brass bands, and parade ground pageantry, meant nothing to Jackson. His unostentatious frock coat and forage cap were a far cry from the gold braid and beplumed foppery of more colorful commanders. Everything about him seemed to evoke vigilance, self-reliance, and the grim business of war.

Artilleryman Robert Stiles, who caught his first glimpse of Jackson on the Virginia Peninsula, described the victorious but exhausted victor of the Valley campaign:

He sat stark and stiff in the saddle. Horse and rider appeared worn down to the lowest point of flesh consistent with effective service. His hair, skin, eyes, and clothes were all one neutral tint, and his badges of rank so dulled and tarnished as to be scarcely perceptible. The 'mangy little cadet cap' was pulled so low in front that the visor cut the glint of his eyeballs.

Those deep-set, spiritual eyes that gave Jackson another of his nicknames, "Old Blue Light," could flash with fire whenever a subordinate dared to challenge or contradict his judgment, or failed to live up to his standards of duty. "Don't say impossible" was a maxim that characterized Jackson's approach to the daunting challenge of war.

The hardworking staff officers who followed this stern taskmaster had to know their jobs and perform them well. Among them were the brilliant cartographer Jedediah Hotchkiss, whose grasp of terrain and detailed maps was crucial to the success of the Valley campaign, and youthful Alexander "Sandie" Pendleton, the efficient adjutant of whom Jackson once said, "Ask Sandie Pendleton. If he does not know, no one does." Their faith and devotion, like that of the "foot cavalry," was given unquestionably to "Old Jack."

Federal Infantryman

As the war entered its second year, many Union soldiers still carried smoothbore muskets. The percussion cap enabled the musket to fire in wet weather, but although deadly at close range, the "buck-and-ball" ammunition—one round lead ball and three buckshot—was much less effective at longer ranges than the conical .58 caliber bullet of more modern rifled muskets like the Model 1861 Springfield and Enfield.

The typical Federal field uniform was designed for function and serviceability, not show. The floppy forage cap, four-button sack coat, and sky-blue trousers were much plainer than the finery worn by most European armies but were easily manufactured in the numbers necessary to outfit hundreds of thousands.

Veteran soldiers had long since learned to lighten their burden as much as possible, and the knapsack was usually stripped of everything but the basic necessities: blanket, rubber poncho, shelter tent half, and a change of socks and underclothing. Rations were carried in the haversack slung on the left hip, along with a canteen. Still, when weighted down with all his traps and accoutrements and cartridge box filled with forty rounds of ammunition, the soldier found campaigning a strenuous test of physical endurance. Bolstered by their dedication to cause and country, the Yankee volunteers battled with a devotion equal to that of their Rebel foes.

PRIVATE COLLECTION

Corporal, 2nd Missouri Volunteer Cavalry

Merrill's Horse

In August 1861 General John C. Frémont authorized Captain Lewis Merrill of the 2nd U.S. Cavalry to organize a cavalry regiment at Benton Barracks, Missouri, for immediate service in the field. Merrill, an ambitious Pennsylvania-born West Pointer, bolstered a contingent of loyal Missourians with volunteers from Michigan, Ohio, and Indiana, and thus managed to recruit eight hundred men in less than a month. As colonel of the new organization, Merrill applied his strict sense of Regular Army discipline as he earnestly set about teaching the troopers their new profession.

The uniforms of the 2nd Missouri Cavalry—dubbed "Merrill's Horse" by General Frémont's wife, Jessie—were unusual in a number of respects. The troopers wore a sky-blue forage cap with an orange welt around the crown and the letter H near its lower edge. Although trimmed in regulation cavalry yellow, the pattern on its paneled front was unique. "All additions to or alterations of this uniform as prescribed are positively prohibited," Merrill ordered, "and will not be tolerated under any circumstances." Armament initially consisted of the Pattern 1843 hall carbine, the Model 1860 Colt army revolver, and Model 1840 cavalry saber.

For much of the war Merrill's Horse would face the ephemeral but ever-present host of Rebel guerrillas and bushwhackers that plagued Union forces in Missouri and Arkansas. It was generally unglamorous duty but one the proud troopers of the 2nd Missouri pursued with diligence and skill.

COLLECTION OF E. J. COATES

The Diehards

Battle of Second Manassas, August 30

It was nearing 3 p.m. on August 30, 1862. For two days the hard-bitten Louisianans of Colonel Leroy Stafford's brigade had helped Stonewall Jackson's corps stave off the advance of John Pope's Federal army on the fields of Manassas, and with the fighting on their front in a temporary lull, the soldiers sat near their stacked muskets, awaiting the next call to arms.

From the opening clash at Brawner's Farm on August 28, and through the attack and counterattack of August 29, the men from Louisiana had lived up to their fighting reputation. Colonel Stafford, a forty-two-year-old planter and Mexican War veteran, had assumed command on the 28th when Brigadier General William E. Starke took over the division from wounded General William Taliaferro. Stafford was no stranger to the Louisianans; although hot-tempered and fond of his liquor, he had performed gallantly in Jackson's Valley Campaign and in the Seven Days battles.

Stafford's regiments—the 1st, 2nd, 9th, 10th, and 15th Louisiana plus Lieutenant Colonel Gaston Coppens's former Zouave battalion—were positioned along a three-hundred-yard stretch of an unfinished railroad grade—a natural rampart that Stonewall Jackson's men had put to good use in their two days of fighting. Stafford's brigade held the left of General Starke's division, with the leftmost of the Louisiana units abutting on a gap in the grade known as "the Dump" because railroad workers had been in the habit of dumping loads of rock there.

At 3 p.m., three mighty cheers announced a resumption of the Yankee onslaught. In the most massive attack so far on Jackson's position, a division commanded by Brigadier General John Hatch, some ten thousand strong, emerged from a wood line and in column of brigades headed for the portion of the Southern line held by Starke's division and Stafford's Louisianans. Confederate artillery poured shells into the tight-packed blue formations, but the determined Union men came on, into the teeth of musketry that fringed the unfinished railroad grade with flame and smoke.

Stafford's men were in two lines, one along the grade, the other at the edge of the woods two hundred yards behind. Though they poured round after round into the charging Yankees, the Federals managed to gain a foothold on the earthen slope. Then the second wave came on, men sprawling at every step and the neat rectangular formations disintegrating, but still more soldiers joining those crowded onto the railroad fill. One Confederate recalled his opponents as "simply jammed up against the embankment. . . . They were so thick it was simply impossible to miss them."

At such close range dozens of Louisiana men were also cut down by the volleys of their foes. One heroic Federal officer, Major Andrew Jackson Barney of the 24th New York, spurred his horse up the railroad grade, shouting, "Come on! Come on!" to his

---

For his painting "The Diehards" Don Troiani was able to draw upon John Hennessy's detailed history of the battle of Second Manassas and that author's wealth of first-person accounts. The figure in the lower right is a Confederate ambulance corpsman, distinguished by his red hatband; several men wear carpets slung across their bodies in blanket rolls, the Confederate Quartermaster Department having purchased large amounts of ingrain carpet to augment the dwindling supplies of military blankets.

COLLECTION OF PAUL ORANGE

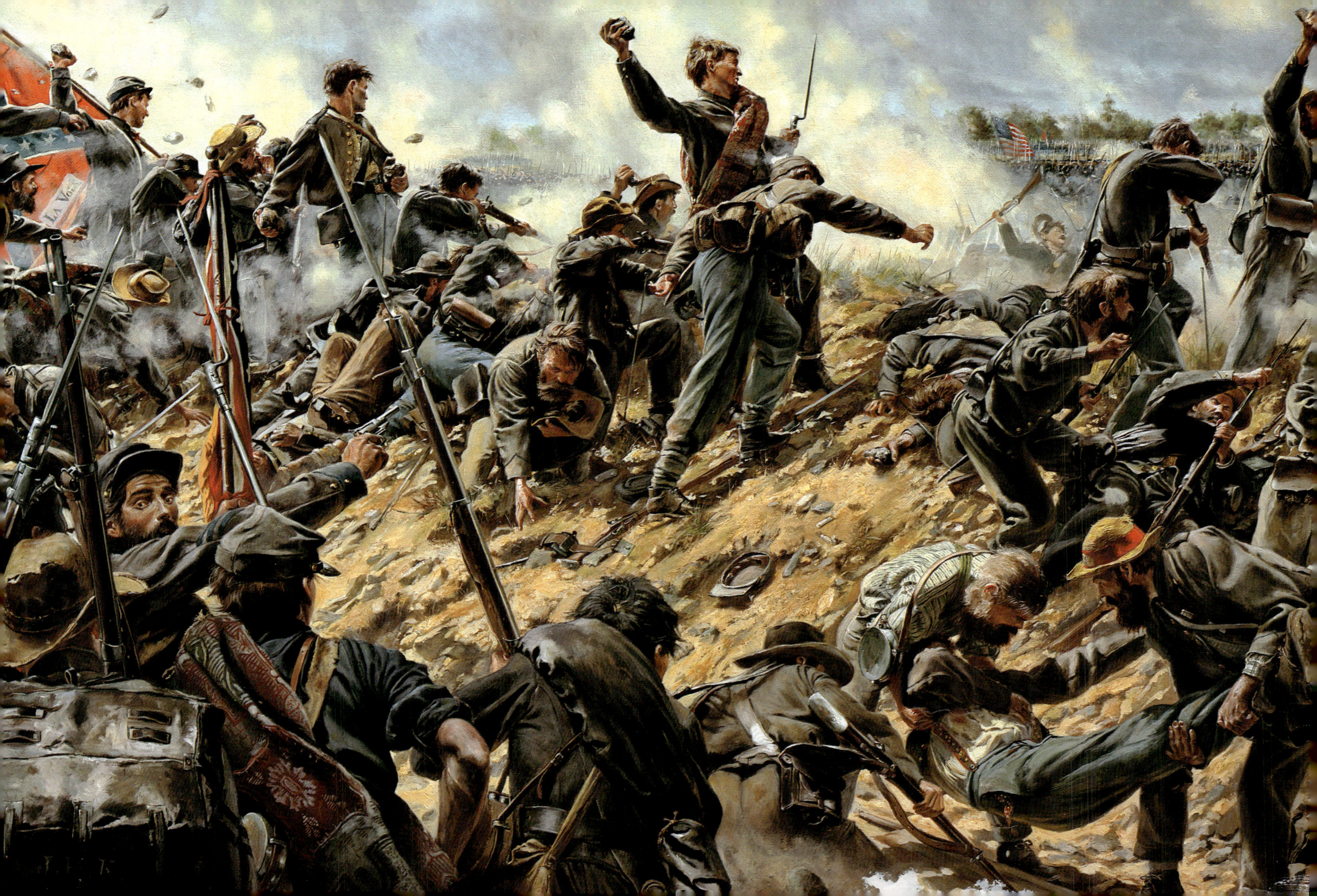

troops. Awed by such suicidal bravery, a Confederate cried, "Don't kill him! Don't kill him," but a Southern volley dropped Barney from the saddle, and his frenzied horse dashed into Stafford's lines.

For a full half hour the struggle continued at a range of fifteen yards or less. Those who dared not risk a fatal wound held their muskets overhead and fired blindly down upon the men on the opposite slope. The Stars and Stripes and Confederate battle flags were upraised only feet apart, the silk and bunting dancing with the tearing bullets. Soon Stafford's men exhausted their ammunition, as did Colonel Bradley Johnson's Virginia brigade on their right. The line quavered with apprehension—but before any break occurred a Louisiana soldier named Michael O'Keefe yelled out, "Boys, give them rocks," and the beleaguered Confederates began lobbing the stones scattered along the railroad grade and in the Dump onto the heads of their startled assailants.

At this critical moment, the arrival of reinforcements—Colonel J. M. Brockenbrough's brigade—sealed the Yankees' doom. Pelted with rocks and raked with the fire of fresh troops, the Union assault began to recoil. Those who preferred not to risk death in the mad dash rearward crawled over the embankment and surrendered to the exhausted but victorious soldiers of Stafford's brigade. When some exuberant Southerners from Starke's division emerged from their cover to pursue their retreating foe, they were checked by crisp volleys of Regular Army units deployed to cover the withdrawal.

The determined Confederates' stand along the unfinished railroad and the fact that some soldiers resorted to rocks when they exhausted their bullets entered into Confederate mythology as a sterling example of Southern fortitude. But tactically the stand of Stafford and Starke succeeded in checking the most threatening Federal incursion of the day and helped set the stage for General Longstreet's massive counterstroke, a blow from which General Pope's Yankee army would not recover.

2nd Wisconsin Volunteer Infantry

"Iron Brigade"

Of all the regiments in the Union Army, the 2nd Wisconsin volunteer Infantry sustained the greatest percentage of battle fatalities. Of the 1,203 men who served with the unit during its three years of service, 238 died in action or succumbed to wounds. One out of every five men who signed up with the 2nd Wisconsin would never return to the Badger State.

A month after fighting in the Federal debacle at First Bull Run, the 2nd Wisconsin joined three other units from Wisconsin and Indiana in a brigade commanded by Brigadier General John Gibbon. A tough Regular Army veteran, Gibbon forged his midwesterners into a superbly drilled and strictly disciplined force. The general saw to it that his men were uniformed in the style of the "Old Army," complete with frock coats and black dress hats, as well as the added touch of white canvas leggings. Gibbon was at first far from popular with his troops—at one point some wags affixed their leggings to the legs of the general's horse—but the hardy westerners soon came to admire their commander and appreciate his efforts to prepare them for battle.

On August 28, 1862, they would pay for their pride and devotion in blood on the fields of Brawner's Farm. In this opening clash of the great battle of Second Bull Run, Gibbon's brigade confronted Stonewall Jackson's troops in a stand-up fight at a distance of only seventy-five paces. Nearly three hundred men of the 2nd Wisconsin fell, eighty-six of them killed or mortally wounded. From Manassas, Gibbon's men marched on to glory in the Antietam campaign, winning immortality as the "Iron Brigade."

COLLECTION OF JOHN OCKERBLOOM

Colonel of the Confederacy

For all the battles, wounds, fame, and promotion that came his way in the terrible four-year war, John B. Gordon never forgot his crowded hour of combat at the May 31, 1862, battle of Seven Pines. As colonel of the 6th Alabama, it was Gordon's responsibility to see his men through their first great bloodletting. He recalled in his memoirs:

> Lieutenant-colonel, major, adjutant, with their horses, were all dead, and I was left alone on horseback, with my men dropping rapidly around me. My soldiers declared that they distinctly heard the command from the Union lines, "Shoot that man on horseback." In both armies it was thought that the surest way to demoralize troops was to shoot down the officers.

Gordon was a man who knew that only with skilled and dynamic leadership could the Southern Confederacy defend the rights of its people and secure its independence. At no level of command was leadership more important than for he who bore the stars—and the responsibility—of a regimental colonel.

Acceptance of the hierarchical and seemingly arbitrary distinctions of rank did not come easy to volunteer soldiers. Colonel Asbury Coward of the 5th South Carolina noted that some subordinates "refused to appreciate the fact that the wearing of a star, a bar, or a chevron made any change in the man they had known at home."

Any colonel worth his stars had to insist on tactical instruction of his junior officers. Recitations from the tactical manuals became standard procedure, whereby company-grade officers learned and mastered the complex choreography of battalion maneuvers. It was no easy task for a regimental commander to conceptualize and execute the series of commands that would deploy a column of ten companies into line of battle. Moreover, he had to have a grasp of the terrain and be able to quickly estimate distance in order to execute a given formation. Constant, repetitive practice on the drillfield was as essential for colonels as for privates.

Administrative ability, a level head, and a knack for dealing with differing personalities were all essential ingredients for regimental command. So too was the type of fearless

COLONEL OF THE CONFEDERACY 41

leadership that John Gordon displayed at Seven Pines. Civil War officers were expected to lead their men—in person—and the bravery of Confederate colonels was manifested through sacrifice on the field of battle. At Gettysburg forty-four colonels fell, fourteen of them fatally wounded.

A regimental commander whose persona exemplified pride, confidence, and military bearing and who appreciated and mastered the duties of his rank forged a bond with his men that enabled them to endure hardship and accomplish superhuman deeds. The unsurpassed valor of Southern arms was due in large degree to the self-sacrificing gallantry and military skills of the heroic colonels of the Confederacy.

PRIVATE COLLECTION

Lone Star

The Army of Northern Virginia contained many brigades whose soldierly skills and deeds of daring reflected the unsurpassed devotion of the Southern soldiers to their cause. The Virginians of Jackson's Stonewall Brigade, Kershaw's South Carolinians, Ramseur's North Carolina tarheels, "Rock" Benning's Georgians—all won immortal fame in those four terrible years of strife. But perhaps the finest fighting brigade of all was the men of the Lone Star State and their Georgia and South Carolina comrades who together made up John Bell Hood's famed Texas Brigade.

The epic events of 1862 saw the emergence of the Texas Brigade as Robert E. Lee's most effective shock troops, men who made up for what they may have lacked in the pomp and foppery of parade-ground ceremony with awe-inspiring, sledgehammer blows on the battlefield. At the battle of Gaines's Mill, Hood's Texans spearheaded the Confederate onslaught, smashing through the stubborn Yankee line and assuring victory in the bloodiest engagement of the Seven Days. The Southern triumph at Second Manassas found the Texas Brigade in the forefront of Longstreet's juggernaut, virtually annihilating Colonel G. K. Warren's Federal brigade and surging on to the bullet-swept plateau of Chinn Ridge, wreaking havoc on every enemy unit that tried to stand before them.

These actions had cost Hood's men dearly, and as Lee embarked on his daring invasion of the North in September 1862, Hood's entire division fielded less than two thousand men in ranks. Colonel William T. Wofford, who led the Texas Brigade across the Potomac into Maryland, mustered only 864 fighting men. The troops of the 1st, 4th, and 5th Texas; the 18th Georgia; and Hampton's South Carolina legion were lean and sun-browned, their uniforms and shoes generally in a sorry state of dilapidation. But hopes ran high, and the stalwart warriors of the Texas Brigade were determined to win new glory in the campaign every Rebel hoped would assure forever the integrity of the Southern Confederacy.

As Lee's forces prepared to meet George McClellan's Army of the Potomac north and east of the Maryland village of Sharpsburg, Wofford's tired soldiers settled down amidst the open timber called the West Woods to enjoy their first meal in three days. Each man was allotted a half ration of beef and green corn, hardly an adequate repast. Their grit and pride would have to see them through the unprecedented strife that would erupt on the morrow, the terrible 17th of September 1862.

Just before daylight, the incoming salvos of Federal artillery announced the beginning of the enemy offensive. The regiments of the Texas Brigade hastened into formation, not far from the little Dunker Church that stood at the edge of the West Woods. As they awaited the call to battle, the Yankees emerged from the cover of the North Woods, advanced through the tasseled stalks of farmer David Miller's cornfield, and slammed into General Alexander Lawton's brigade. The battle was roaring in full fury when Colonel Wofford crossed the Hagerstown Pike at double-quick to bolster Lawton's crumbling line.

Deploying across the open field south of Miller's cornfield, the Texas Brigade surged forward, mingling with the survivors of Lawton's decimated units, and unleashed a deadly hail of musketry on the blueclad masses to their front. Fielding fewer men than a regulation company, the Hampton Legion—which held the left of the brigade—was staggered by

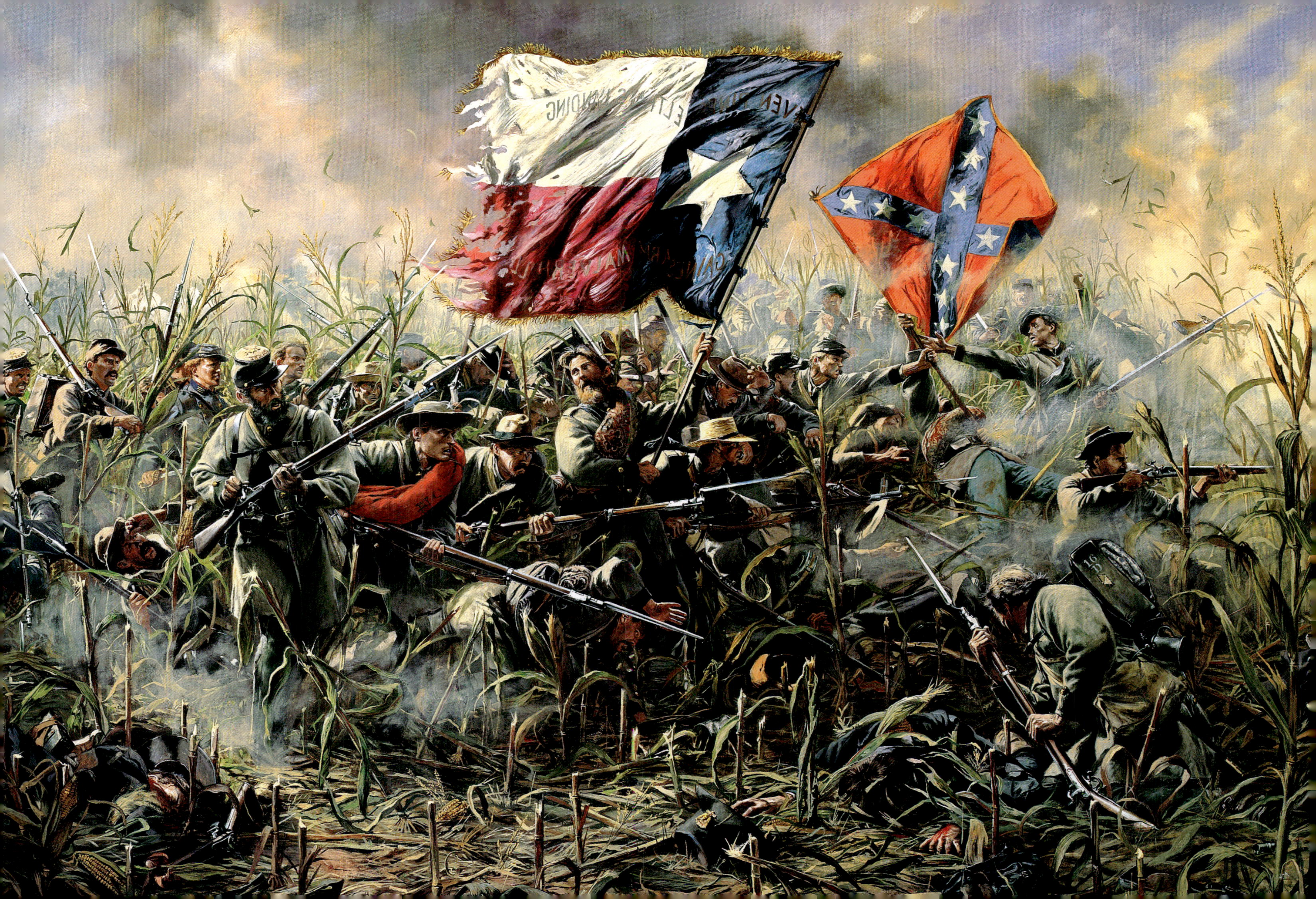

shotgun-like blasts of canister from Battery B, 4th U.S. Artillery, and the 18th Georgia to their right fared little better. But at the center of the brigade, Lieutenant Colonel Philip A. Work and the 226 soldiers of his 1st Texas pressed forward against the wavering Yankee line. When the Federals gave way, Work led his Texans over the dead and writhing wounded of the famed Iron Brigade and into the carnage of the forty-acre cornfield.

With the troops on their left stalemated, the men of the 1st and 4th Texas veered in that direction as they charged through the trampled, bullet-riddled cornstalks. Canister came shrieking into their flank, splintering the fence rails along the pike and tearing through the flesh and bone of those unfortunates who were nearest the flaming mouths of the Napoleon guns. As the Texans struggled through the corn, volleys from the unseen Yankees in their front scythed through the ranks. But screaming the Rebel Yell, Work's 1st Texas continued to forge ahead, following the gallant men who bore their colors—the Confederate battle flag and the faded silk of the "Lone Star" banner.

Time and again the colors fell, to be raised again and carried on. The 1st Texas had lost contact with the units to their left and right, and as they pressed on to the cornfield's Northern edge, fire ripped into their left and rear. Lieutenant Colonel Work realized his troops were at least 150 yards in front of the rest of the brigade. Major Matthew Dale, Work's second in command, ran up to confer with the colonel but was shot dead as he spoke. Moments later, counterattacking Federals from General George Meade's Pennsylvania Reserve division unleashed a terrific volley from the fence line in front, as one Texan put it, "cutting us down almost like grain." Lieutenant Colonel Work decided "it was madness to advance with the few men left me."

Work ordered the fragments of his unit to pull back with their colors. As the desperate knots of men staggered rearward through the roiling smoke, the cheering Yankees hot on their heels, both Texas flags were again shot down. All those who rushed to rescue the banners were felled around the bullet-torn colors and their splintered staffs. In the confusion of the retreat, no one realized the flags had been lost until the shattered wreck of the 1st Texas emerged from the cornfield's southern edge. By then it was impossible to rescue the colors; both banners had been snatched up as trophies by Private Samuel Johnson of the 9th Pennsylvania Reserves.

The Confederate lines reformed near the Dunker Church and checked the Union onslaught. But the cost had been unbearably high. When Lee asked General Hood where his troops were, the grieving commander responded, "They are lying on the field." For no unit was that more true than for the 1st Texas: Of their 226 men, 186 had fallen—a staggering 82 percent loss. Company F had been annihilated; Company A fielded one man; the largest company remaining mustered only eleven men. Never had the Texans fought more gloriously, and never had so much pain been mingled with so much pride.

Until Sundown

Sunken Road, Battle of Antietam, September 17

INSPIRED BY THEIR SECOND VICTORY OVER Federal forces on the plains of Manassas, in early September 1862 General Robert E. Lee's Army of Northern Virginia marched northward, crossed the Potomac, and forged into Union-held Maryland. In less than three months the revered commander, known to his admiring soldiers as "Marse Robert," had defeated two Yankee armies and shifted the field of operations from the outskirts of Richmond to a position that threatened the capital at Washington. Even if Marylanders failed to flock to Southern ranks, every soldier in Lee's army sensed that the dramatic offensive might turn the war in favor of the Confederacy. They knew that if anyone could achieve Southern independence on the battlefield, Lee was the man.

In an era when many officers affected a swashbuckling bravado replete with plumes, gold braid, and jangling spurs, Lee's plain and serviceable attire seemed to emphasize his natural dignity. One staff officer remembered the general as "always well dressed in gray sack-coat of Confederate cloth, matching trousers tucked into well-fitting riding boots—the simplest emblems of his rank appearing, and a large black felt army hat." The officer remarked that Lee "rarely wore his sword, but his binoculars were always at hand."

At the outset of the Maryland campaign Lee had suffered a painful mishap. When his favorite horse, Traveller, was startled by a map flapping in the wind, Lee grabbed for the animal's reins but stumbled and fell on his hands. A doctor found that Lee had "a serious ligamentous strain" in both limbs and suspected that the general's right arm was fractured. The doctor applied splints to both injuries, and for much of the campaign the general was forced to wear a sling on his more severely injured right arm. Managing Traveller was difficult, and for a time Lee was forced to take to an ambulance. Still, when the summons to battle came, the great commander was sure to be found in the saddle.

Revitalized by the return of their cautious but beloved commander George B. McClellan, the Army of the Potomac moved northwestward from the defenses of Washington to confront Lee's invasion. On September 14, Major General D. H. Hill's division waged a stubborn defense of the three gaps leading through the South Mountain range, delaying McClellan's superior forces long enough for Stonewall Jackson's men to besiege and capture the Federal garrison at Harpers Ferry. Both armies then converged on the town of Sharpsburg, where on September 17 a great battle would rage along the banks of Antietam creek. It would be the bloodiest day in the history of the United States.

The struggle began at early dawn with the Yankees striking at Lee's left flank. As the roar of battle reverberated through the rolling hills and thousands of desperate soldiers fought on the carnage-strewn cornfield and surrounding woodlots of the Miller farm, the Confederate center braced for the inevitable onslaught. The sector was defended by D. H. Hill's troops, bloodied three days earlier in the fight at South Mountain. The hardened veterans of the 6th Alabama Regiment, part of General Robert Rodes's brigade, were among the units deployed in a sunken farm lane that provided a natural entrenchment.

Worn from rough service on the Virginia Peninsula and bearing four different types of firearms, the Alabamians were nonetheless confident that they could hold their position in the sunken road. Their fortitude in large part reflected the personality of their iron-willed commander, Colonel John B. Gordon.

Gordon was the very embodiment of the Southern warrior. Thin and ramrod straight, Gordon was a man whose presence elicited courage and devotion from those entrusted to his care. He habitually led in the very forefront of the charge, and no officer displayed more grit on the defensive. The colonel had been the only field officer to escape unscathed from the bloodbath at Seven Pines, and at Malvern Hill seven bullets had passed through his clothing. Gordon's apparent invincibility boosted the morale of the soldiers of the 6th Alabama, and Gordon noted "a sort of blind faith possessed my men that I was not to be killed in battle."

As the battle of Antietam began to shift inexorably toward the Sunken Road, Robert E. Lee rode along the line, accompanied by Generals Hill and Rodes. When Lee came to Gordon's position, the colonel stepped forward and said so all could hear, "These men are going to stay here, General, till the sun goes down or victory is won!"

A scant fifteen minutes later, troops of the Federal 2nd Corps launched the first of a desperate series of attacks against the Sunken Road. When the Yankees crested the rise in front of the road, Gordon's men rose up and delivered a volley that decimated the leading ranks. Gordon said, "The entire front line, with few exceptions, went down in the consuming blast." Two more brigades of General William H. French's division swept forward, only to be savaged and checked by the Rebel fire. Then another Union division, the hard-fighting troops of General Israel Richardson, was put into battle.

Though the ridge to their front was carpeted with dead and wounded Yankees, the Federals were taking a toll of the Southern brigades as well. Pacing back and forth along his line, shouting encouragement to his men, Gordon's seeming invulnerability to enemy fire was sorely tested. Shot twice in the right leg, as well as in the left arm and shoulder, he staggered on until a fifth bullet tore into his left cheekbone just under the eye. The colonel sprawled unconscious, his face resting in his kepi. A sixth round had ripped through the cap, and only this prevented him from drowning in his own blood.

A misunderstanding in orders caused many Confederate troops to evacuate their natural stronghold, and when a Union regiment managed to flank the Rebel position, they raked the line with fire that transformed the Sunken Road into "Bloody Lane," carpeted from one end to the other with dead and wounded. Lee's center seemed on the verge of collapse, but by a desperate effort the Yankee breakthrough was stopped, and the battle of Antietam flared out in gory stalemate.

Historian John Hennessy, and Dr. Joseph Harsh both noted authorities on the Second Manassas campaign, discovered many rare accounts that elaborate on General Lee's injuries. The jackets of the 6th Alabama are based on an original worn at Antietam by Thomas M. Murfree of Company A, the Independent Rifles.

Borne to the rear, John Gordon would survive his terrible wounds, nursed back to health by his devoted wife, who followed him to the seat of war. Seeking to diffuse her shock at seeing his bandaged limbs and swollen, disfigured face, the colonel quipped, "Here's your handsome husband; been to an Irish wedding."

Gordon would return to battle, his scars a badge of honor and his gallantry a byword to every soldier in the Army of Northern Virginia down to the last sad day at Appomattox. He had indeed held until sundown.

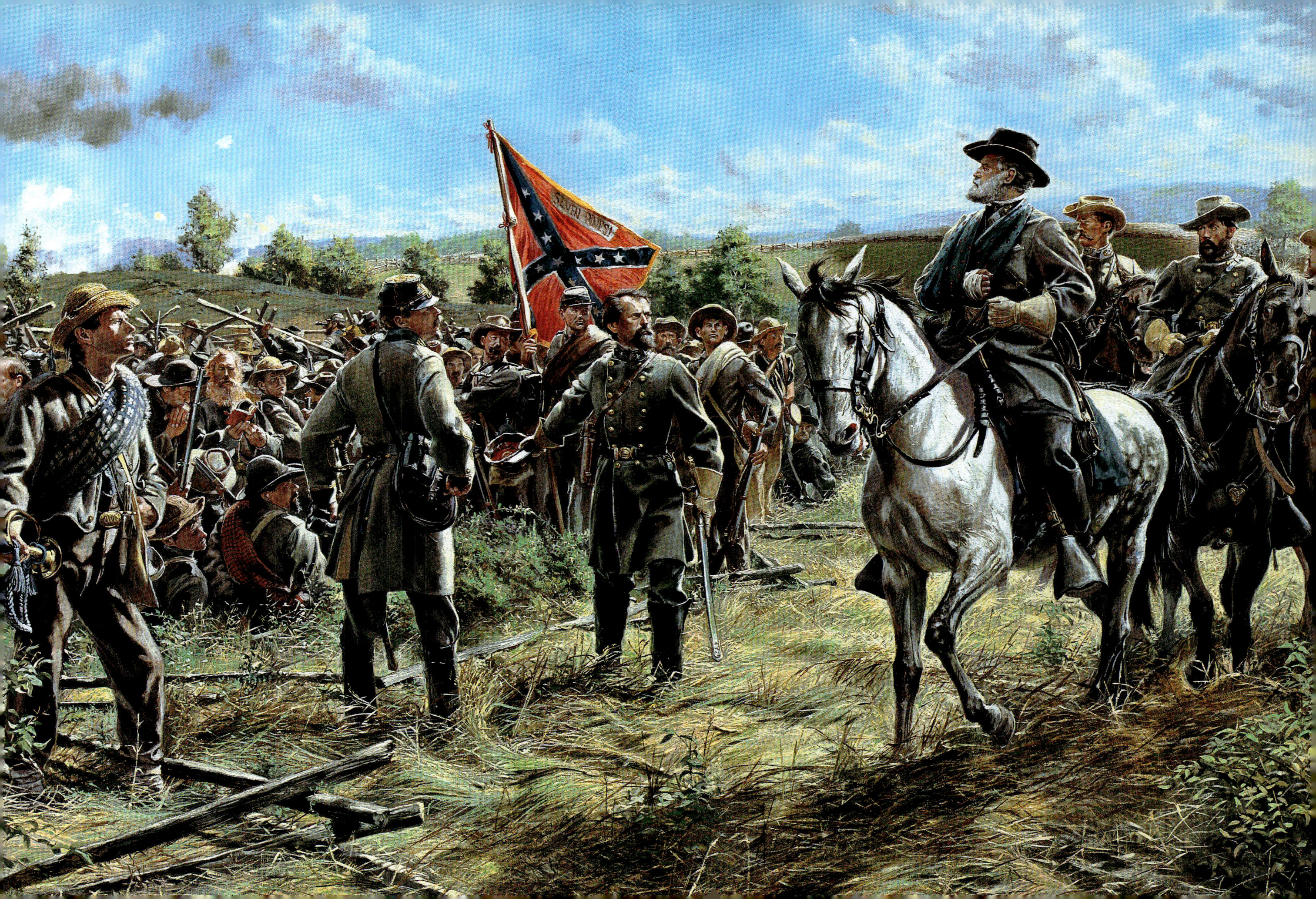

9th New York Volunteer Infantry

"Hawkins's Zouaves"

Sweeping forward like an incoming tide, wave after wave of Union soldiers battled their way toward the town of Sharpsburg, only to find their valor matched by that of their Southern opponents. When General A. P. Hill's hard-marching column arrived to shore up the Southern line, the battle of Antietam, the bloodiest single day in American history, ended as a draw.

The Zouaves of the 9th New York Volunteer Infantry managed to get closer to Sharpsburg than any other Federal unit that day, having crossed Antietam Creek and ascended a steep ridge in the face of determined resistance. The commander of the 9th New York, Lieutenant Colonel Edgar Kimball, reported, "The infantry fire was like hail around and among us, producing the most dreadful carnage." Eight companies totalling 373 men began the charge, and 240 of their number fell. "The men retired in good order," Kimball noted, "with tears in their eyes at the necessity which compelled them to leave the field they had so dearly won."

The 9th New York had been one of the first regiments in Manhattan to answer President Lincoln's call. The unit's founder was a dashing young military enthusiast named Rush C. Hawkins, whose dreams of glory were matched by a fondness for rare books. Hawkins had his troops outfitted in a dark blue Zouave uniform that was retained for the regiment's two-year term of enlistment. Other units, including the 17th and 164th New York, would also be issued the distinctive Hawkins's Zouave uniform, which by war's end had become the most common variation of the exotic French-inspired regalia supplied by Federal quartermaster departments.

9TH NEW YORK VOLUNTEER INFANTRY 49

One of Colonel Rush Hawkins's Zouaves penned this illustrated letter on shipboard, while the unit was en route to Roanoke Island, North Carolina. Because of their colorful garb, the 9th New York received a great deal of press coverage for their part in General Burnside's operations on the Carolina coast—a fact that caused some degree of grumbling among their less flamboyant comrades. But at the battle of Antietam the Zouaves more than lived up to their romantic image. PHOTO COURTESY JOHN GUNDERSON

CONFEDERATE DRUMMER

IN BOTH THE FEDERAL AND CONFEDERATE armies the company musicians—fifers and drummers—performed a service that went beyond supplying a rhythmic musical accompaniment to the marching infantry. From reveille to lights out, the roll of drum and squeal of fife relayed the calls that structured the soldiers' routine. When officers' shouts were lost amidst the roar of battle, the beat of the drum could convey the order to aim and fire. Long after the armies disbanded most of their brass bands as inspirational but superfluous trappings to war's realities, the drummers and fifers stayed on, an integral part of the military machine.

A chronic shortage of medical orderlies necessitated another important aspect of service for the musicians. When battle seemed imminent, they were often detailed to assist the regimental surgeons as stretcher bearers. Stacking their drums, they would await the grim task of carrying their stricken comrades from battlefield to hospital.

Many Confederate drums lacked the colorful patriotic emblems and devices painted on the drums of their Yankee counterparts, but the role of the Rebel drummers shared their combination of military pomp and practicality.

PRIVATE COLLECTION

These Civil War–era drumsticks and their holder, from Troiani's collection, are of a French design. They were usually attached to the musician's shoulder belt or the drum hoops.

PHOTO COURTESY DON TROIANI COLLECTION

Corporal, 2nd Regiment United States Sharpshooters

In the last months of 1861, with the war clearly shaping up to be a protracted encounter, thousands of Northern recruits answered their country's call. Perhaps the most unusual of the newly organized regiments were two units comprised of marksmen handpicked from a number of Northern states by an ambitious inventor and celebrated rifleman named Hiram Berdan.

Colonel Berdan required each of his prospective recruits to attempt to place ten shots within a ten-inch circle at a range of two hundred yards. Those who passed the test were mustered into Berdan's 1st U.S. Sharpshooters. In the end, so many men proved their proficiency with a rifle that a second unit was organized—the 2nd U.S. Sharpshooters, which was placed under the command of Colonel Henry A. V. Post.

Both units were issued dark green uniforms of the regulation pattern, which reflected the traditional garb of European riflemen and were a practical attempt at providing camouflage for soldiers whose duties would habitually see them fighting in skirmish order, each man five paces from his comrades and making available use of natural cover.

In June 1862 the 2nd Sharpshooters belatedly received the Sharps New Model Rifle 1859, specially fitted with double-set triggers. With these breech-loading weapons, a Sharpshooter could fire up to ten rounds a minute. But accuracy, not speed, was the nature of skirmish duty, and the Green Coats were deadly proficient at their task.

COLLECTION OF JOHN SIRLIN

J. E. B. Stuart

From his first thundering charge on the plains of Manassas to his last desperate battle at Yellow Tavern, no commander more epitomized the dash, ambition, and unbounded success of the Confederate mounted arm than that quintessential cavalryman, James Ewell Brown Stuart.

Broad-shouldered and powerfully built, with a flowing red-brown beard, Jeb Stuart's love of war's panoply and glory made him the very incarnation of the cavalier. His high boots, jangling spurs, and plumed hat evoked images of Prince Rupert, the flashy British cavalier of the English Civil War, or Napoleon's great cavalry commander, Joachim Murat. Eager, undaunted, and brave, but also fun-loving, Stuart was all that many daring troopers aspired to be.

A graduate of the West Point Class of 1854, the Virginian had seen hard service on the western frontier and by 1861 was one of the most experienced Indian fighters in the Regular Army. Severely wounded in a battle with the Southern Cheyennes, Lieutenant Stuart's gallantry had early brought him to the attention of Robert E. Lee. The young officer's participation in quelling John Brown's 1859 raid on Harpers Ferry, during which he served as Lee's aide, further endeared him to the man who would become his superior officer in the Army of Northern Virginia.

While it is true that Stuart's thirst for glory and wholehearted confidence in his hard-riding troopers at times led him into perilous situations, those who would fault him for his crucial absence during the Gettysburg campaign would do well to remember General Lee's tribute: "He was always cheerful under all circumstances," Lee wrote, "and always ready for work, and always reliable." Stuart's energy and unbounded confidence in his horsemen and in the Southern cause was a manifestation of that hope of ultimate victory that saw Lee's army through many a trying hour.

As he emerged as the preeminent Confederate cavalry leader in the Civil War's eastern theater, Stuart took full advantage of the South's superiority in horseflesh and riding skills. The success of his June 1862 circumvention of McClellan's Army on the Virginia Peninsula was repeated in his August 1862 raid behind John Pope's Army of Virginia, and again around McClellan following Antietam.

Stuart coupled his repeated humiliations of the Yankee cavalry with a firm grasp of the mounted arm's traditional role as advanced scouts, gathering information of enemy numbers and troop movements and relaying that vital information to the high command. In addition, Lee knew he could rely on his flamboyant cavalry commander to effectively screen the infantry's movements from Federal cavalry probes. At no point was this more ably manifested than during the dangerous march toward the Potomac in June 1863. Although facing a much-improved Yankee cavalry, Stuart repeatedly thwarted his counterpart, General Alfred Pleasonton, when the Union horsemen attempted to locate Lee's northward-marching army.

It was perhaps fitting that a man who so embodied the promise of Confederate victory would give his life at a point when the tide had at last begun to turn irrevocably in favor of the Union. A new generation of Federal cavalry leaders—Sheridan, Custer, Merritt, Wilson, and others—had at last taken advantage of the North's innate superiority in numbers of men, horseflesh, and armament. When a dismounted Yankee trooper fired a fatal

For his depiction of Jeb Stuart astride his bay, Virginia, Troiani consulted both contemporary accounts of the famed cavalry commander and the general's surviving uniform and equipage at Richmond's Museum of the Confederacy. His study of the actual artifacts enabled Troiani to correctly portray Stuart's French saber, riding boots, gauntlets, and famous plumed hat, and to avoid a common error made by other modern-day painters of Civil War themes, who often depict the turned-back lapels of Stuart's short jacket as yellow. In fact the lapels were, like the rest of the jacket, Confederate gray.

round into Stuart's side, he spared the great trooper the ultimate heartbreak and tragedy of a cause that was all but lost.

Bronze Guns and Iron Men

Battle of Fredericksburg, December 13

Whenever discussion turns to the subject of Civil War artillery, one cannot help but invoke the name of John Pelham. Boyish, modest, brave, and a master of his profession, to his comrades in Lee's army and to his Northern foes, he was what he yet remains: "The gallant Pelham."

Born in northern Alabama on September 7, 1838, the son of a country doctor and cotton planter, the tall, blond-haired youth resigned from West Point two weeks before he would have graduated in May 1861. Pelham had stayed on at the academy after his native state seceded—his commission as lieutenant in the Confederate artillery was dated March 16, 1861—but his course was plain.

Though a solid supporter of the Southern cause, Pelham was by all accounts one of the most popular young men at the military academy, and his friendships transcended sectional divisiveness. Years later one of Pelham's classmates, Medal of Honor recipient and distinguished Union General Adelbert Ames, recalled, "He was a gentleman in the highest sense of the term. A discourteous act was wholly foreign to his nature. His kindly heart, sweet voice, and genial smile carried sunshine with him always . . . we heard with secret pride of his gallant deeds on the field of battle."

Pelham's bravery in his very first engagement—the Confederate victory at First Manassas—brought him to the attention of J. E. B. Stuart, who saw to it that the handsome Alabamian was given command of the horse artillery attached to Stuart's cavalry. Commissioned a captain in May 1862 and promoted to major that August, Pelham shared in the triumphs of the glory days of the Confederate mounted arm. In the Seven Days battles, at Second Manassas, and at Antietam he displayed a keen sense of terrain, an utter fearlessness under fire, and a rare ability to manage men. Modest, even shy in social situations, as a leader in battle he was an inspiration. "His most remarkable feature was his eyes," one veteran recalled. "In social life they were gentle and merry, laughing eyes; but in battle they were restless and flashed like diamonds."

In a record replete with daring deeds, John Pelham's performance at the battle of Fredericksburg on December 13, 1862, stands out as a sterling example of his gallantry and skill.

As Robert E. Lee's forces braced to meet the massive onslaught of Ambrose Burnside's Army of the Potomac, Major Pelham's five batteries were called upon to support the right wing of the Confederate line. Several divisions of Federal troops had crossed the Rappahannock River and were preparing to advance in strength toward the wooded ridge held by Stonewall Jackson's troops.

Realizing that the Yankee left flank was exposed, Pelham seized the opportunity to disrupt the enemy advance before it could reach the main Confederate line. With Captain Mathias W. Henry, his trusted subordinate and West Point classmate, Pelham maneuvered two guns—a Blakely and a Napoleon—into a position from which they rained death on the Yankee masses a mere four hundred yards away. With shells plowing through the blue-clad infantry, the Union artillery sought to destroy the daring Rebel gunners, and Pelham was forced to gallop his guns from point to point in order to avoid the deadly iron hail of counterbattery fire.

When his Blakely gun was disabled, Pelham and Captain Henry continued the fight with the remaining Napoleon. Ignoring the incoming fire, the major sat his horse beside

PRIVATE COLLECTION

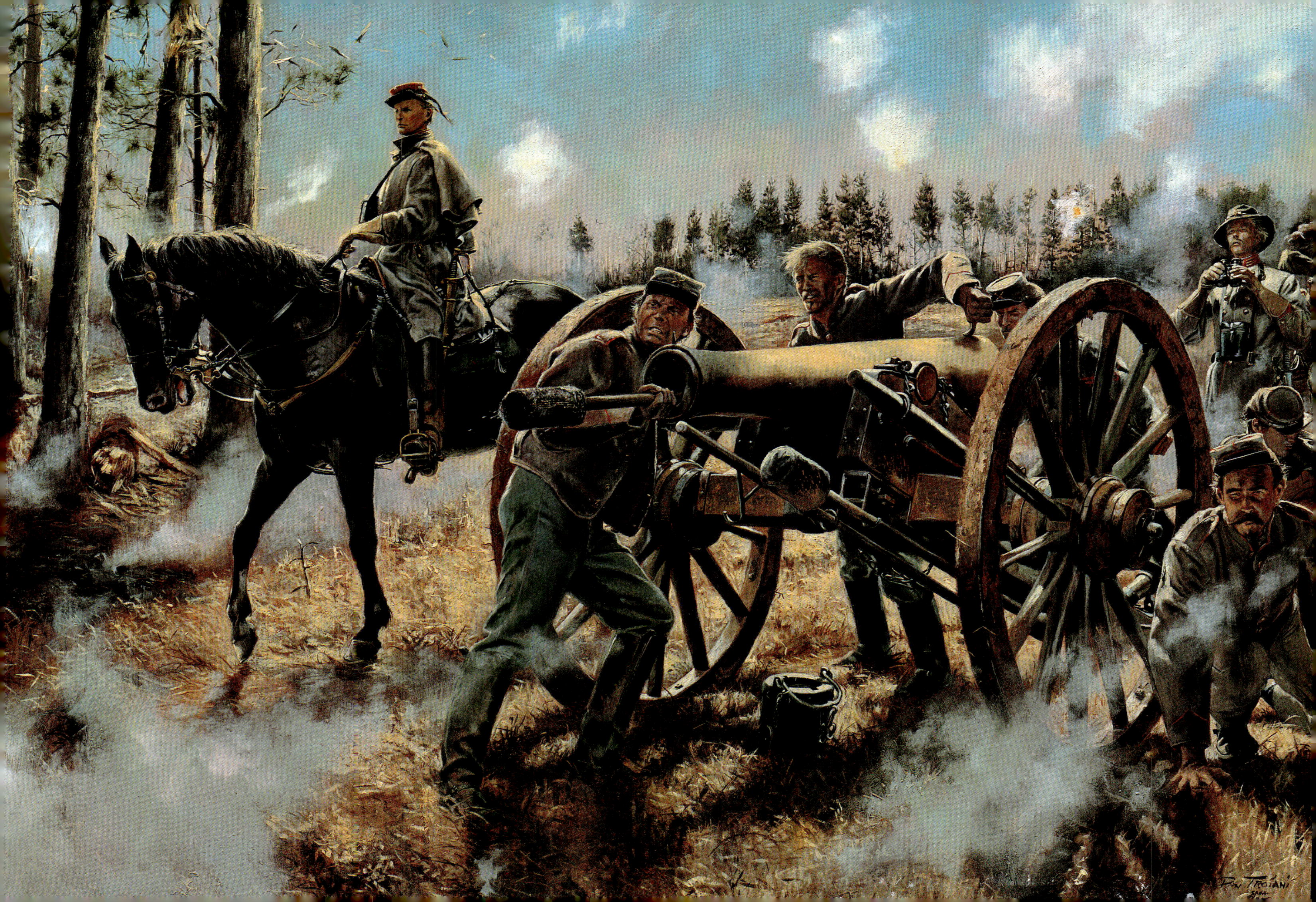

the gun, shouting orders to his men. Solid shot was hurled at the blue ranks, knocking over scores of men, and when one Federal battery came into range, the Confederate gunners exploded a limber chest with a well-aimed shell. Watching Pelham's courageous performance, Robert E. Lee is said to have remarked, "It is glorious to see such courage in one so young."

After his initial success, Pelham took charge of a line of guns that continued to embarrass the Federal advance. As morning passed toward afternoon, the enemy managed to amass considerable artillery support, and the Southern gunners were themselves hard-pressed. Major Pelham fought on energetically, reminding one comrade of "a boy playing ball," so enthused was the young commander by the challenge and excitement of battle. When General Lee, in his postbattle report, referred to the major as "the gallant Pelham," the young officer's fame was assured throughout the army as in the hearts of the Southern people.

John Pelham survived his day of glory at Fredericksburg a scant three months. On March 17, 1863, with characteristic daring he joined a Confederate cavalry charge at Kelly's Ford on the Rappahannock. A Federal shell exploded above the thundering horsemen, and one of its shards struck the twenty-four-year-old major in the head. When he died that evening, the South lost a soldier whose name has ever after remained a byword for all that was gallant and romantic in that great and terrible war.

Clear the Way *(Faugh-a-Ballagh)*

Battle of Fredericksburg, December 13

For thousands of Irish-Americans who answered the call of their adopted country, service under the Stars and Stripes was viewed as a precursor to the war of independence they hoped one day would free the Emerald Isle from British rule. The fighting prowess and martial enthusiasm of the Army of the Potomac's famed Irish Brigade was fired by this dual motivation. These sons of Erin were keenly aware of the close ties between Britain and the Confederacy, a point Irish Brigade commander Thomas Francis Meagher sought to impress upon his men. "Every blow you strike in the cause of the Union is aimed at the allies of England," Meagher told one volunteer, "the enemy of your land and race."

Meagher's colorful reputation had won him command of the brigade, which he led through the Peninsula campaign and in the charge on the Sunken Road at Antietam. Two months after that bloodiest day of the war, with ranks sadly thinned and green flags hanging in shreds from their staffs, brigade morale was bolstered by a double dose of good news.

The torn banners would soon be replaced with new Irish colors, and the only native Yankee unit in the Irish Brigade—the 29th Massachusetts—would exchange places with the 28th Massachusetts, an Irish-American outfit in the 9th Corps. Led by Colonel Richard Byrnes, a strict disciplinarian, the Massachusetts men still bore the green flag emblazoned with the harp and sunburst symbolic of their native land.

On November 23 Byrnes reported for duty with the 28th Massachusetts, joining the 63rd, 69th, and 88th New York and the 116th Pennsylvania. Though the 28th fielded fewer than 450 men, it was still twice as large as most regiments in the brigade. With General Burnside preparing to launch the Army of the Potomac against Lee's defenses at Fredericksburg, Meagher's five units together numbered only 1,200 men—little more than regulation regimental strength. But the tough, idealistic veterans were determined to maintain their proud record in Major General Winfield Scott Hancock's 1st Division of the 2nd Corps.

On the chill, fog-shrouded morning of December 12, 1862, the Irish Brigade filed across a pontoon bridge spanning the Rappahannock River and stacked arms on a street in the war-ravaged town of Fredericksburg. The bodies of Union and Confederate soldiers lay amidst the wreckage, a reminder of the grim house-to-house fighting that had secured a crossing for the Federals.

The next day Burnside commenced his ill-fated assault on Marye's Heights. The commanding ridge bristled with Rebel artillery and infantry, many of the latter deployed in a sunken road behind the cover of a thick stone wall. It was a desperate undertaking, and as Meagher inspired his overcoated troops with a fiery oration, the general's staff officers handed out clumps of boxwood so that every man would go into action with a sprig of green tucked into his forage cap.

Formed in column, the Irish Brigade passed through the city to their staging area below the heights. "The aspect was already terrible," wrote brigade historian Captain D. P. Conyngham. "Noon-day was turned to dusk by the smoke and storm of battle." The assault of General William H. French's division had already been torn to pieces, as had the charge of Hancock's leading brigade, commanded by Brigadier General Samuel K. Zook. The bodies of the dead and wounded, along with hundreds of dazed survivors, lay in irregular lines on the bullet-swept slope.

Before they could deploy, the five regiments of the Irish Brigade had to cross the canal that lay at the foot of Marye's Heights, filing across a narrow bridge and millrace as shellfire continued to savage their congested columns. The 69th New York was first across, and the other units came into line of battle alongside—the 88th New York, 28th Massachusetts, 116th Pennsylvania, and the 63rd New York, on the left of the brigade. Perhaps because of their conspicuous green flag, Colonel Byrnes' Baystaters were given the post of honor in the center of the brigade.

Packs and blanket roles were unslung, and for ten anxious minutes the men awaited the inevitable. Finally General Meagher, on foot and nursing an injured knee, waved his sword and shouted, "Irish Brigade, advance! Forward, double-quick, guide center, march!" Muskets at a right shoulder shift, the brigade surged forward. Amidst the deafening cacophony of battle could be heard the old Irish cheer *"Faugh-a-Ballagh!"*—"Clear the Way!" —the motto of the 28th Massachusetts.

As Brigadier General John C. Caldwell's brigade came on in support, the Irish Brigade passed over the heaps of the fallen and into the smoke and flame that engulfed the deadly heights. Blasts of artillery mowed gaps through their formations, but the ranks closed up and pressed on. When the Rebel infantry opened up the carnage was even greater. Captain Conyngham called it "a perfect slaughter-pen" in which "whole regiments melted away."

Over two fences they went, but the charge sputtered out before the stone wall in tangled heaps of dead and writhing wounded. Major James Cavanaugh of the 69th New York yelled, "Blaze away and stand it, boys!" and the survivors—kneeling or laying prone amidst the human wreckage—poured round after round into their tormentors. The color sergeant of the 116th Pennsylvania shook his banner at the enemy until he was riddled with five balls. Major William Horgan led a group of men from the 88th New York to within yards of the wall and sunken road, but all were shot down—the major was felled by a bullet through his open mouth and head.

Caldwell's brigade came up into the embattled line but fared no better. Those who

Two 1864 images of the Fredericksburg battlefield were of immense value in reconstructing the wartime appearance of Marye's Heights and the town's churches and residences. One view shows the open nature of the terrain over which the Irish Brigade and the other Federal units had to advance. The strip of trees near the horizon marks the position of the famous sunken road and stone wall, above which rises the crest of Marye's Heights. The other image looks toward the town of Fredericksburg from a line of Southern earthworks. The square brick house, visible in both images, was surrounded with Union casualties and shaken survivors who vainly sought cover behind it. PHOTOS COURTESY MASSACHUSETTS COMMANDERY, MILITARY ORDER OF THE LOYAL LEGION, AND THE U.S. ARMY MILITARY HISTORY INSTITUTE

could made their way to the rear and rallied around their unit colors. Many others were caught there through the night. The valorous charge had failed, at a cost of 545 of the 1,200 men in the Irish Brigade. "Their devotion transcended anything I ever saw or even dreamed of," one observer wrote. "Men walked right up to their deaths as though it were to a feast."

Only a portion remains of the original flag of the 28th Massachusetts, the only Irish color carried in the charge at Fredericksburg. Troiani had to reconstruct the banner's appearance by comparing the surviving fragment with the colors of the 69th New York, which was of an identical pattern. Both flags were embroidered rather than painted. Troiani obtained actual Virginia boxwood in order to correctly portray the sprigs in the men's caps.

Period photographs supplied details of the Fredericksburg skyline and the landscape, which today has been altered by postwar development. One of the town steeples, today, was bare brick at the time of the battle and is thus shown in the painting.

COLLECTION OF JOHN OCKERBLOOM

Federal Cavalry Picket in Winter

Cavalry pickets, or "videttes" as they were known in the mounted branch, furnished the alert eyes that screened the army from enemy observation. "The vigilance of cavalry protecting an army in position is always of most vital importance," wrote Union General William W. Averell; "the lack of it has sometimes led to great and humiliating surprises." The mounted videttes were the first line of defense against a sudden enemy move, the outermost ring in a series of human alarm bells, without which an army commander would be at the mercy of his foe.

Through the long winter months, when the foot soldiers settled down in their rough-hewn cabins and active campaigning gave way to a period of rest and recuperation, the cavalry was never idle. Shivering on their lonely posts, the videttes were ever on the qui vive, conscious of the importance of their role as the "eyes of the army."

PRIVATE COLLECTION

The Advance Picket

Muffled against the cold, Federal cavalrymen enjoy a steaming pot of coffee at their picket post on a Tennessee mountainside. Grand campaigns were rare in the winter months, but the danger of Rebel cavalry forays was ever present.

PRIVATE COLLECTION

Emblems of Valor

All that the Confederate soldier was fighting for was embodied in his regimental battle flag. It seemed only natural that these precious banners, torn with bullets and often stained with the blood of fallen bearers, be adorned with the names of the engagements in which the unit had served. It is somewhat surprising that it was not until the summer of 1862 that the practice of adding battle honors to the regimental flags received the official sanction of the government in Richmond.

On July 23, 1862, the Confederate War Department directed that army commanders in the field "cause to be entered in some conspicuous place on the standards the names of

In this earlier version of "Emblems of Valor," a soldier-artist of the 8th Georgia applies honors to his unit's battle flag in white paint. When research by historian Howard Madaus revealed that the honors in blue were the last to be added, although the engagements predated the ones applied in white, Troiani painted a second version of the scene.

COLLECTION OF DOUGLAS KILLIAN

the several battles in which their regiments, battalions, and separate squadrons have been actually engaged."

In practice, numbers of flags had already been adorned with the names of engagements. A year prior to the official decision to add battle honors, citizens of Mississippi had donated a banner to that state's 11th Infantry regiment emblazoned with "MANASSAS," and in June 1862 General James Longstreet had authorized units that served under his command in the defense of Richmond to add a strip of cloth lettered "SEVEN PINES!" to their flags.

In the wake of the War Department directive, units hastened to decorate their banners with an impressive list of battles. When it was found that the imprinted strips of cloth awkwardly weighed down the bunting, some soldiers stitched the honors on, letter by letter, while others contracted civilian artists to paint them on by hand.

Not long after the battle of Fredericksburg, it was determined that whenever new flags were issued to replace those lost or destroyed, the battle honors of Lee's Army of Northern Virginia would be standardized—the names of engagements applied in small letters with blue paint at the Richmond Quartermaster's Depot.

Beginning in early 1863, Lee's troops began receiving these new flags a division at a time, but the effort proved short-lived. Perhaps because of a shortage of bunting, not long after the battle of Gettysburg it fell again to the individual units to decorate their banners.

Such was the case with the 8th Georgia Infantry, a regiment that commenced its proud career on the plains of Manassas and by early 1863 was serving with Brigadier General George "Tige" Anderson's brigade of Hood's division, Longstreet's corps. The men of the 8th Georgia had added a number of battle honors to their flag in white paint, concluding with "FREDERICKSBURG" in large letters across the top of the banner. By the time it was noticed that the artist had omitted the engagements at Rappahannock and Thoroughfare Gap—clashes that occurred in the campaign of Second Manassas—there was no more white paint to be had. But blue paint was available, and as officers and enlisted personnel looked on, the honors were applied to the crimson symbol of their cause.

1 8 6 3

General Robert E. Lee

No veteran of the Army of Northern Virginia would ever forget his first sight of General Robert E. Lee. For Major Robert Stiles the encounter came during the Peninsula campaign, not long after Lee had assumed command of the army he would lead to immortality. "A magnificent staff approached from the direction of Richmond, and riding at its head, superbly mounted, a born king among men," Stiles recalled. The awestruck officer thought "General Lee was one of the handsomest of men, especially on horseback, and that morning every detail of the dress and equipment of himself and horse was absolute perfection."

Virginia Military Institute cadet John S. Wise agreed with Stiles's assessment. "It is impossible to speak of General Lee without seeming to deal in hyperbole," Wise wrote; "Robert E. Lee was incomparably the greatest-looking man I ever saw. . . . the impression which that man made by his presence, and by his leadership, upon all who came in contact with him, can be described by no other term than that of grandeur."

Colonel Garnet Wolseley, a British military observer, was one of many contemporaries who saw in Lee's dignified simplicity a striking resemblance to the strengths traditionally ascribed to George Washington. The Englishman was pleasantly surprised at the absence of the sort of pomp and circumstance that he had observed around the headquarters of European armies. Lee and his staff lived simply, in regulation canvas tents, and there was "no crowd of aides-de-camp loitering about," as would have been the case with European commanders. Wolseley, who ultimately attained knighthood, the rank of field marshal, and command of the British Army, considered Robert E. Lee "one of the two greatest men" he ever knew—the other being Charles Gordon, the British defender of Khartoum.

As Lee rode through the streets of a Southern town, accompanied by Generals Longstreet and A. P. Hill and his loyal staff officers Walter Taylor and Charles Marshall, the regal bearing of the man known to his admiring troops as "Marse Robert" made his handsome figure the center of attention. When a Confederate band serenaded Lee, they vested their patriotic air with the essence of their hearts and souls—for this man seemed the very embodiment of the cause for which they almost happily risked their lives.

Lee's innate dignity, aristocratic reserve, and quiet determination elicited an almost instinctive respect from his subordinates. "The fear of incurring his displeasure at all times enforced implicit obedience," wrote Alabama Colonel William Oates. Indeed, the slightest hint of disapproval from Lee could be far more devastating than the stinging rebukes or profane tantrums of other generals.

But there was more to Lee than his dignified image and management skills. He was a consummate campaigner, a skilled tactician, and a daring strategist. Knowing the odds the

---

In addition to incorporating portraits of several of General Lee's senior subordinates and staff officers in the mounted entourage, Don Troiani needed to locate a variety of 1860s era instruments for the military band. To that end the artist consulted collector and historian Mark Elrod, who has assembled an impressive number of period instruments. It should be noted that most horns played by mid-nineteenth century military bands were held over the shoulder, so that their sound projected rearward to the troops marching behind them.

time service encompassed the triumphs and tragedies of the Army of Northern Virginia, noted, "I am sure there can never have been an army with more supreme confidence in its commander than that army had in Gen. Lee. We looked forward to victory under him as confidently as to successive sunrises."

In his wartime memoirs Porter Alexander described the "wave of sentiment" that swept through the ranks at an 1864 review of the artillery of Longstreet's corps. "Each man seemed to feel the bond which held us all to Lee," Alexander wrote; "the effect was that of a military sacrament, in which we pledged anew our lives." When a Confederate chaplain asked Lee's aide, Colonel Charles Venable, "Does it not make the general proud to see how these men love him?" Venable replied, "Not proud, it awes him."

In the spring of 1863, as Lee prepared to wage one his most brilliant campaigns against a strong and ambitious foe, both he and the Army of the Northern Virginia were at the apex of their self-confident abilities. But even at the bitter end, as defeat closed about the defiant remnant of Lee's army at Appomattox, those bonds of reverence and love between the soldiers and their leader remained, firm and insoluble.

Confederacy faced, he was ever willing to risk defeat to attain victory. Until the advent of U. S. Grant, few Federal commanders could match his daring. Lee's willingness to divide his forces in the face of a numerically superior foe, then to fall on his enemy's flank or rear— as he did at Second Manassas and Chancellorsville—rank him among history's great commanders. As Staff Captain Joseph Ives put it, "Lee is audacity personified."

The Confederate artillerist General E. Porter Alexander, whose distinguished war-

165th New York Volunteer Infantry

2nd Battalion "Duryée's Zouaves"

LATE IN 1862, VETERANS OF THE 5TH NEW York, "Duryée's Zouaves," began offering cash bounties at their recruiting office in Manhattan in order to replenish the ranks of their war-worn unit. So many volunteers responded to the call that a new eight-company battalion was raised and uniformed in the full Zouave regalia made famous by the original outfit. The only distinction between the two regiments was that the 165th New York Zouaves sported a blue, rather than yellow, tassel on their fezzes.

With the removal of General George McClellan from command, plans to create a "Zouave Brigade" in the Army of the Potomac were temporarily abandoned, and the members of the 165th found themselves sent to Louisiana, where they joined General Nathaniel Banks's forces in the siege of the Confederate Mississippi River stronghold, Port Hudson.

On May 27, 1863, the Zouaves participated in a desperate but doomed assault on the Rebel earthworks. More than a third of the battalion was cut down; both color bearers died, and the battalion's commanding officer, Lieutenant Colonel Abel Smith, Jr., was mortally wounded.

PRIVATE COLLECTION

1st South Carolina Infantry, U.S.

In May 1862, months before President Lincoln's Emancipation Proclamation officially sanctioned the recruitment of African Americans for the Union Army, General David Hunter organized a company of black soldiers for service in his Department of the South. In November, following the proclamation, prominent Boston abolitionist Thomas Wentworth Higginson expanded Hunter's unit and assumed the colonelcy of the 1st South Carolina Volunteer Infantry. One of the first regiments of United States Colored Troops, the former slaves and their white officers would battle for the cause of freedom on the Carolina coast.

On New Year's Day 1863, Colonel Higginson's soldiers proudly received a set of regimental colors, resplendent in blue frock coats and forage caps and red trousers reminiscent of those worn by the French Army. But many of the black troops apparently felt set apart by the red pants, and early in 1863 the unit was resupplied with regulation U.S. Army sky blue trousers. Although Higginson had promised his men that their mixed lot of .69 caliber French and Belgian and U.S. Model 1842 muskets would be replaced with up-to-date Springfield rifled muskets, it was January 1864 before new long arms arrived, and those were of French manufacture.

On March 26, 1864, the regiment was redesignated the 33rd Regiment, United States Colored Troops, and served as such to the last months of the war. While not as distinguished in battle as many other black units, these brave men of color had helped blaze a path that tens of thousands of others were to follow. As Colonel Higginson noted, "It was their demeanor under arms that shamed the nation into recognizing them as men." By 1865, one out of every ten Union soldiers was of African descent.

COLLECTION OF W. GLADSTONE

Before the Storm

Stonewall Jackson at Chancellorsville, May 2

ON THE CHILL EVENING OF MAY 1, 1863, the Confederacy's two greatest commanders, Robert E. Lee and Thomas J. "Stonewall" Jackson, encamped with their staffs at a rustic bivouac in the scrub oak and pine forest called the Wilderness. After months of inactivity both the Army of Northern Virginia and Major General Joseph Hooker's Army of the Potomac were on the move. And, though often foiled in the past, this time the revitalized, well-equipped, and confident Yankees seemed to have superiority.

Pursuing a brilliantly conceived strategic plan, "Fighting Joe" Hooker had marched the bulk of his army—some seventy thousand men—northwest from their winter camps at Falmouth, then struck south across the Rappahannock and Rapidan Rivers to threaten the left and rear of Lee's force. Had the Federal commander kept moving, his strategy might well have succeeded. But upon reaching the Wilderness crossroads of Chancellorsville, Hooker had unaccountably gone on the defensive. Like so many other failed Union commanders, he had yielded the initiative to his formidable opponent. Though the Federals outnumbered him by some thirty thousand men, Lee was never one to shy from the danger of attacking a numerically superior foe.

On May 1, as a series of heavy skirmishes flared along the fronts of both armies, Jackson had accompanied Jeb Stuart's cavalry on a reconnaissance that revealed Hooker's right flank to be open and vulnerable to assault. Further scouting by Stuart's troopers confirmed that the Federal right was indeed "in the air." As night fell, the challenge facing Jackson and Lee was how to get at the beckoning flank through the junglelike tangle of the Wilderness.

Shortly before dawn Jackson awakened his chief topographical engineer, Major Jedediah Hotchkiss, and dispatched him on an exploring expedition to pinpoint a potential route of approach. He rode to the home of Charles C. Wellford, owner of the nearby Catharine iron furnace, who told Hotchkiss of a new road that he had recently cut through the woods to the Brock Road—a natural avenue of approach that would lead the Confederates north to the Orange Plank Road, along which Hooker's troops were believed to be posted. Hotchkiss penciled the track on his map, and after Wellford agreed to act as a guide, he hastened back to Lee and Jackson's bivouac with the information.

Several times that night Lee and Jackson had conferred beside the campfire. When Hotchkiss joined his commanders they were seated atop hardtack boxes beside the fire, deep in thought. Jackson was quick to seize upon the promising route of march and suggested a daring gambit—that Lee divide his force and march the bulk of it, some twenty-six thousand troops, across the Federal front to assault Hooker's exposed right in flank. "Well," Lee said, "go on." The course was set.

Jackson's men got under way shortly after 7 A.M., a winding column of silent tramping figures some ten miles in length that would have to cover between nine and fourteen miles to arrive at the position from which they would launch their attack. Nursing a cold, his arms and shoulders covered by an oilcloth raincoat, Jackson rode along the column, seeing that the files were closed up and the pace maintained. "Press forward!" he urged, "Press on, press on!"

Reporting for orders, one of Jackson's young staff officers, James Power Smith, recalled his chief's determined and resolute

COLLECTION OF MR. AND MRS. ALBERT BLACK

mien: "His cap was pulled low over his eye, and, looking up from under the visor, with lips compressed, indicating the firm purpose within, he nodded to me, and in brief and rapid utterance, without a superfluous word, as though all were distinctly formed in his mind and beyond question, he gave me orders for our wagon and ambulance trains."

Jackson's famed "foot cavalry" trudged on, down the Furnace Road and Wellford's track to the Brock Road, then north toward the Orange Plank Road. Tired though they were, the men's spirits were high. "Tell Old Jack we're all a-comin'," the old soldiers said to staff officer J. P. Smith, "Don't let him begin the fuss till we git thar!" When General Fitzhugh Lee's cavalry reported that the position of Hooker's right wing was farther north than anticipated, Jackson accompanied Fitz Lee to a vantage point from which Jackson silently scanned the unsuspecting troops of the 11th Corps through his field glasses. The cavalryman remembered how Jackson's eyes "burned with a brilliant glow, lighting up a sad face."

Pushing his troops farther north to an assembly point on the Old Orange Turnpike, Jackson sat down on a stump and scrawled a dispatch to Robert E. Lee. "I hope as soon as practicable to attack," Jackson wrote. "I trust that an ever kind Providence will bless us with success."

It was after 5 P.M. and the sun was going down when Jackson's troops were ready to strike. Jackson was with the men of Robert Rodes's brigade as Major Eugene Blackford of the 5th Alabama deployed a line of skirmishers in advance. After consulting his watch, Jackson turned to his subordinate and asked, "Are you ready, General Rodes?" When the handsome young commander responded yes, Jackson said, "You can go forward then." Rodes nodded to Blackford and the skirmish line advanced, followed by Rodes's and Colston's divisions.

"Never did troops move forward with more enthusiasm," recalled Jackson's aide and brother-in-law, Captain J. G. Morrison. When the startled Federal pickets were swept aside, the men let loose what Morrison called "that peculiar yell characteristic of the Southern soldier."

Lee and Jackson's daring gambit had succeeded. The storm had been unleashed, and Jackson's greatest and final battle had begun.

"Charge"

The 8th Pennsylvania Cavalry at Chancellorsville, May 2

At the end of April 1863, Major General Joseph Hooker embarked on a skillfully planned campaign intended to flank and destroy the Army of Northern Virginia. With the bulk of Hooker's cavalry away with Brigadier General George Stoneman on a sweeping raid behind Lee's army, the remaining division of mounted troops under Brigadier General Alfred Pleasonton worked hard to screen the Army of the Potomac as it crossed the Rapidan River and moved toward the strategic crossroads of Chancellorsville.

On May 2, as Hooker's forces deployed in the tangled woodland known as the Wilderness, the horses and men of the 8th Pennsylvania Cavalry were enjoying a well-earned rest from the previous few days of slogging down muddy roads, splashing across treacherous fords, and skirmishing with enemy outposts. Until late in the afternoon, the Pennsylvanians rested in the clearing beside the Chancellor house with the other units of Colonel Thomas Devin's brigade. At 4 p.m. the commander of the 8th Pennsylvania, Major Pennock Huey, was ordered to saddle up his troopers and, along with two other cavalry units and a battery of horse artillery, to report to Major General Daniel Sickles at Hazel Grove. The combative Sickles had located an enemy column marching through the woods and was preparing to lash out at what appeared to be a Confederate retreat. In reality these were Jackson's men, moving to strike Hooker's flank.

Jackson's troops smashed into Major General Oliver O. Howard's 11th Corps, and pressed on, driving the demoralized Yankees in their path. At 6:30 p.m. the 8th Pennsylvania was dispatched from its position at Hazel Grove to join the 11th Corps on the Orange Plank Road. The cavalrymen turned north along a narrow track that forced the riders into a slender column, two abreast. In the lead was Major Huey, along with his second in command, Major Peter Keenan. Captain Charles Arrowsmith of Company B, Lieutenant James E. Carpenter of Company K, and Regimental Adjutant J. Haseltine Haddock rode close behind. Unaware of the disaster that had befallen the 11th Corps, the troopers rode with swords sheathed and pistols holstered.

As Huey's men approached the Orange Plank Road, they suddenly found themselves riding between a Rebel skirmish line and a larger body of enemy infantry. Instantly deciding to gallop onto the Orange Plank Road and turn eastward for Chancellorsville, Major Huey shouted, "Draw saber and charge."

When the horsemen defiled onto the road they saw the route to Chancellorsville blocked by a mass of Confederate infantry. Wheeling to the left, Huey and his officers spurred their horses into another body of Rebel troops, hacking and slashing with their sabers as the troopers thundered behind. At

Federal-issue cavalry spurs and straps were worn by the troopers of the 8th Pennsylvania at Chancellorsville. Photo courtesy Don Troiani Collection

first the enemy soldiers—men of General Robert Rodes's division—were too startled to resist. "We cut our way through," Major Huey recalled, "trampling down all who could not escape us." But a hundred yards farther along the Orange Plank Road the Southerners poured a deadly volley into the charging column.

Flourishing his sword in the vanguard, Major Keenan was riddled with bullets and killed, as were Captain Arrowsmith and Adjutant Haddock. Major Huey and Lieutenant Carpenter escaped the fusilade and turned their horses into the woods north of the road, followed by the shattered and confused remnant of their command. Behind them nearly thirty men and ninety horses were shot down or captured, while others were taken prisoner in the wild ride back to Chancellorsville. The tail end of the cavalry column had meanwhile steered clear of the melee on the Orange Plank Road and escaped by a different route.

Gallant as the 8th Pennsylvania had been, the incident was of minor import to the course of the battle. The sudden appearance of Yankee cavalry on their flank did, however, put many Confederates on the alert. And later that evening it was Southern fire that cut down Stonewall Jackson when the general and his staff were mistaken for Federal horsemen.

Following the war General Pleasonton authored a highly embroidered account of what he called "Keenan's Charge," representing the tragic affray as a glorious martyrdom that saved Hooker's army. Besides ignoring Major Huey's role as commanding officer, Pleasonton claimed personal credit for almost single-handedly shoring up the crumbling Federal line. Nevertheless, the charge of the 8th Pennsylvania Cavalry stands as one of the relatively few times in the Civil War that mounted troops took on massed infantry.

This frock coat, trousers, swordbelt, sash and shaving mug belonged to Major Peter Keenan, who perished in the charge of the 8th Pennsylvania Cavalry at Chancellorsville. The son of Irish immigrants, Keenan was immortalized as the hero of the doomed attack, though he was actually second in command of the regiment.

PHOTO COURTESY RON WEAVER

Manufactured by the firm of Stratton and Foote, this regulation Federal bugle bears a yellow cord, indicating its use by the cavalry arm. Most U.S. government–contracted bugles were copper with brass trim, though some all-brass and German-silver styles were also used. Each instrument was supplied with three different mouthpieces and was slung across the musician's back when not in use. PHOTO COURTESY DON TROIANI COLLECTION

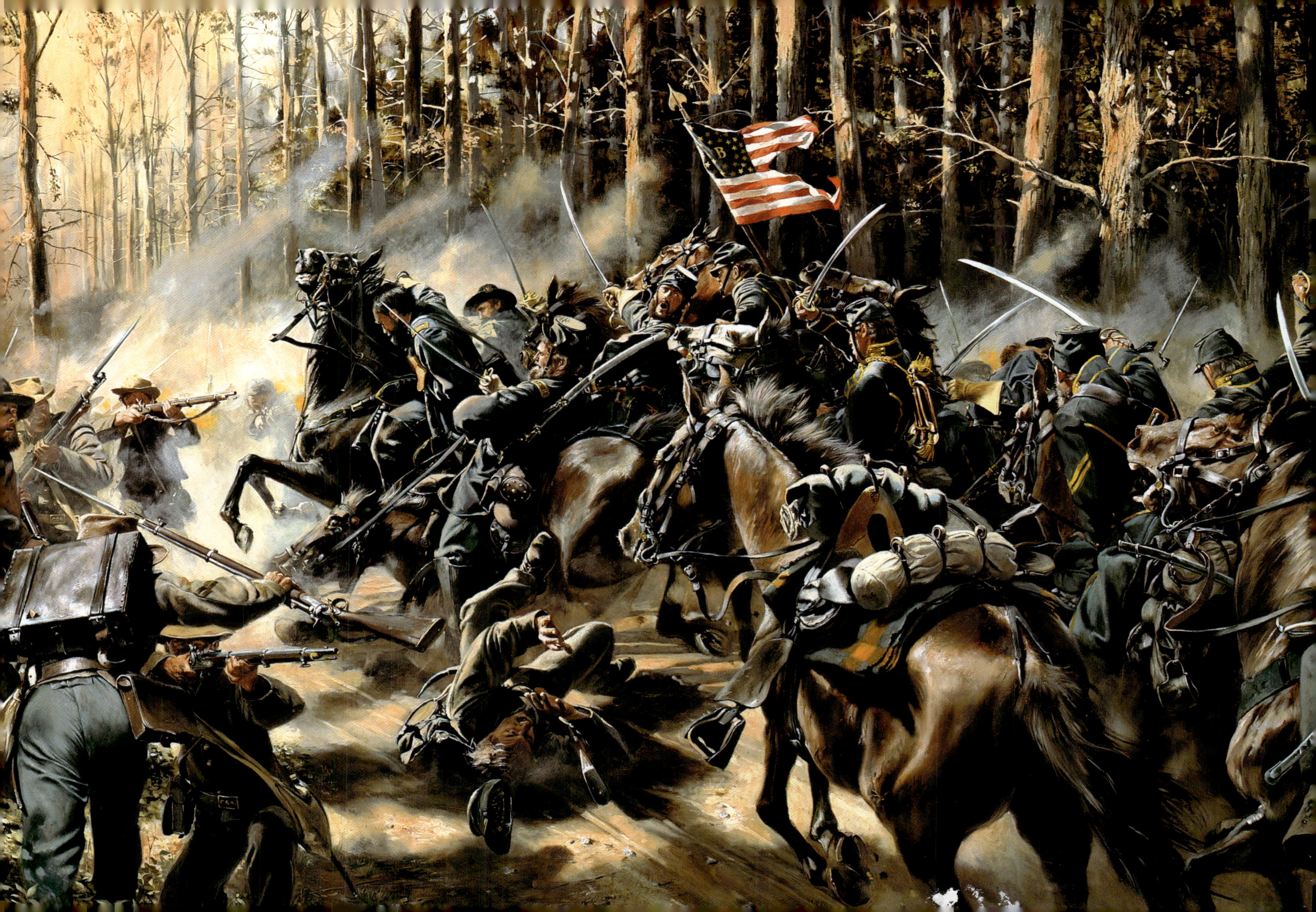

Eagle of the 8th

Siege of Vicksburg, May 22

Throughout time soldiers have been in the habit of acquiring mascots, and the Civil War was no exception. Hundreds of dogs shared the danger of the battlefield, many were photographed, and at least one was memorialized on a regimental monument. Some men had pet raccoons or badgers, a Confederate outfit brought a young wildcat to war, and two Federal western units had bears as mascots. But the most unusual—and symbolic—of all these animal auxiliaries was "Old Abe," the Bald Eagle of the 8th Wisconsin Volunteer Infantry.

Just prior to the outbreak of war, the bird that was to become famous as "Old Abe the Battle Eagle" was acquired by a farming family named McCann from a Chippewa Indian who had killed the eaglet's mother. The powerful young bird was difficult to care for, so its owner, Dan McCann, decided to sell it to one of the local companies mustering for the volunteer service. He found a buyer in Captain John E. Perkins's Eau Claire Badgers, an outfit destined to become Company C—the color company—of the 8th Wisconsin Infantry. It was Captain Perkins who named the mascot after of the embattled Union's president.

The 8th Wisconsin was mustered into service in September 1861 and began its initial period of training at Camp Randall, near Madison. Old Abe attracted a great deal of attention to the new unit. Regimental Quartermaster Francis L. Billings constructed a wooden perch to which the young eagle was tethered, and during the next years of battle it would be the special duty of four successive bearers to carry their mascot in the front rank of the color guard, between the national and regimental banners.

The 8th Wisconsin headed for the front in October 1861. While en route Old Abe broke loose from his perch and flew off when taunted by pro-Southern agitators in Saint Louis, but he returned to the unit. The regiment met its first fire in a clash near Farmington, Mississippi, on May 9, 1862, an action that claimed the life of Captain Perkins. During the far bloodier engagement at Corinth on October 3, a bullet severed the cord that held Old Abe to his perch, and the young eagle flew along the flaming battle line, losing several of his tail and wing feathers to enemy fire. At the risk of his life, eagle bearer David McLain scooped up his charge and carried it back when the unit retreated.

In the late spring of 1863, as U. S. Grant prepared to attack the Mississippi River stronghold of Vicksburg, Old Abe was entrusted to his third bearer of the war, former blacksmith Edwin Homaston. Like the soldiers of the 8th Wisconsin, Abe was now a veteran, and in the chaos of battle his flapping wings and fierce cries seemed to echo the cheers of his human comrades. The bird's fame had spread throughout General William T. Sherman's command; the 8th was now known as the Eagle Regiment, and their brigade, commanded by Brigadier General Joseph A. Mower, was the Eagle Brigade.

Through the morning and afternoon of May 22, 1863, Grant had hurled assault after assault on the formidable Confederate earthworks at Vicksburg. Despite gallant efforts, every attack had been repulsed, with heavy losses. But when word came that some of

EAGLE OF THE 8TH ~ 77

> Although Don Troiani was able to make use of several photographs of Old Abe, in order to properly capture the appearance and mannerisms of an immature male bald eagle, he photographed a comparable bird at the Bridgeport, Connecticut, Zoo. From military historian Howard Madaus, a noted authority on wartime flags and Wisconsin units, Troiani borrowed an accurate reproduction of the eagle perch carried by the 8th Wisconsin. ~

General E. J. McClernand's corps had gained a foothold in the Rebel lines, Sherman was ordered to renew his attacks. The reports of a breakthrough were in fact erroneous, and when Mower's Eagle Brigade moved forward, it entered a veritable inferno at one of the strongest sections of the Vicksburg defenses—the northeast angle of the Confederate line called the Stockade Redan.

Mower's line of approach was down a narrow artery with the ominous name Graveyard Road, from which the troops would deploy into line of battle and charge Stockade Redan. The third regiment in order of attack, the 8th Wisconsin started down the sunken

PRIVATE COLLECTION

roadway in a compact column, four men abreast, officers and file-closers at intervals on the right of the shuffling column. The leading units had drawn heavy fire even before leaving the roadway, and as the 8th Wisconsin picked up their pace to a jogging double-quick, they were forced to trample over the fallen bodies of their comrades.

As the bullets and shells ripped through the air and men began to drop, the 8th Wisconsin filed right and came into line of battle, directly in front of the Stockade Redan and the shambles of the units that had preceded them. As the color company began to deploy, its ranks were savaged by canister shot. Old Abe rocketed from his perch at the rear of the color company and his bearer, Private Homiston, stumbled and fell against a stump. Stunned by the blow, Homiston was actually dragged a short distance by the muscular eagle before regaining control of his charge.

The assault was a failure, Mower's units cut up and fragmented, and all they could do was hunker down until nightfall. As the color guard huddled beside their riddled flags, one soldier managed to capture a terrified rabbit, which he offered to Old Abe as consolation.

The eagle of the 8th Wisconsin would experience and survive many other battles before returning to Wisconsin, where he found a home in the capitol building at Madison and was occasionally displayed at patriotic gatherings. A celebrated subject for songs, poetry, and statues, eleven years after the close of hostilities Old Abe traveled to the Centennial Exhibition in Philadelphia. Five years later he died from the effects of smoke inhalation sustained during a fire in the Wisconsin capitol. His mounted remains were lost in a second fire, in 1904.

Pioneer, Army of the Cumberland

In the late spring of 1863, Major General William S. Rosecrans was preparing to take the field in middle Tennessee. The ambitious and self-confident Federal commander of the Department of the Cumberland was a good organizer and motivator of men, generally admired by the soldiers in his command. One of "Old Rosy's" innovations was the creation of a Pioneer Corps—men detached from their units to form a mobile workforce. Organized into battalions, the principal duties of the Pioneers were road and bridge construction, both of which were crucial to the movement of a large army through hostile territory. Among other incentives, Pioneers received an extra forty cents a day.

On May 29, 1863, a recently appointed Pioneer named Isaac Raub described the benefits of his distinctive insignia to a friend: "We wear a badge on our left arm. The badge has two hatchets on it and that badge is the same as a pass. We can go anywhere and the guards don't trouble us any." His morale clearly boosted by his uncommon status, Pioneer Raub concluded, "I think by present indications that this war will soon be settled up." In that, however, the cocky Pioneer could not have been more mistaken.

PRIVATE COLLECTION

Confederate Infantry Corporal

PRIVATE COLLECTION

The Gray Comanches

Battle of Brandy Station, June 9

With some seventeen thousand riders engaged, the battle of Brandy Station was the largest and most spectacular cavalry clash ever waged on American soil. The swirling combat, the flashing sabers, and the thundering charge and countercharge of horsemen in blue and gray awed every participant with the terrible pageantry of war. Beyond its epic scale, the fight on the rolling hills of Culpeper County, Virginia, confirmed once and for all that the Yankee cavalry had finally come on a par with Jeb Stuart's vaunted Confederate horsemen. Though Union commander Alfred Pleasonton was forced to relinquish the field, the savage day-long battle had seen Stuart surprised and very nearly beaten by a foe once scorned as hopelessly incompetent.

Stuart's men were already heavily engaged with Brigadier General John Buford's troopers when, shortly before noon, Colonel Percy Wyndham approached the strategic elevation of Fleetwood Hill with his brigade, the vanguard of Brigadier General David McMurtrie Gregg's division. Seizing the opportunity to crush the Rebel horsemen between the two arms of the Union strike force, Wyndham led the 1st New Jersey, 1st Pennsylvania, and 1st Maryland cavalry regiments uphill toward what had been Stuart's headquarters. Three guns of Captain Joseph W. Martin's 6th Battery New York Light Artillery crossed Flat Run and rumbled forward in support.

When word of the threat at Fleetwood Hill reached Stuart, the Confederate commander extricated two of his brigades from the fight with Buford and sent them galloping southward to meet the assault. Brigadier Generals William E. "Grumble" Jones and Wade Hampton hurled their troopers against Wyndham's riders.

The 12th Virginia Cavalry, lead element in the Confederate counterattack, was struck head-on by the 1st New Jersey and brushed aside. As the crest of Fleetwood Hill was submerged in blue, the 35th Battalion of Virginia Cavalry plowed into the Yankees and in a confused melee of slashing sabers and cracking pistols began to fight their way through Wyndham's column.

Ahead of the 35th Battalion rode their impetuous leader, Lieutenant Colonel Elijah V. White. With his plumed hat, gold-braided uniform, and gray warhorse, "Lige" White was the very image of a Southern cavalier. His troopers had a jaunty swagger and devil-may-care attitude that gained them a reputation for indiscipline, but their ferocity in battle—accompanied by shrieking war cries—won for them the name "Comanches" and a place in the first rank of the Confederate cavalry arm.

White's Comanches found their fighting prowess tested when Colonel Judson Kilpatrick's Yankee brigade slammed into their flank and Captain Martin's New York battery

---

Although Captain Martin later implied that his stubborn gunners had been virtually annihilated by the 35th Virginia battalion, Don Troiani's research in the New York State Adjutant General's report and historian Earl J. Coates's examination of pension records in the National Archives showed that none of the batterymen were killed. Most of the gunners received minor saber wounds or avoided contact with the impetuous Comanches by scurrying under their limbers and gun carriages. Archival records also provided information on the color of White's horse and the fact that his battalion was armed in part with Mississippi rifles. Also, many troopers were equipped with caps and shoes in addition to cavalry boots.

82 ~ THE GRAY COMANCHES

began to rake the gray-clad troopers with deadly salvos of canister. Infuriated by the hail of lead balls spewing from the three rifled guns, White shouted a command to charge and spurred his gray horse toward the battery.

Martin's gunners held their ground as the Comanches surged down on them, riding into the very mouths of the flaming cannon. With White in the leading rank, the Southern troopers swept over and through the embattled artillery and, as Captain Martin reported, "It became a hand-to-hand fight with pistol and sabre." But despite their valor, the artillerymen could not withstand the mounted onslaught. The guns were lost, and though nearly one hundred men of the 35th Virginia lay dead and wounded on the field, White's charge had been a crucial turning point in the battle of Brandy Station. When Wade Hampton's men came roaring behind the Virginians, Fleetwood Hill was back in Confederate hands for keeps, and victory on that hard-fought day lay with the South.

COLLECTION OF LARRY PAGE

THE FIGHT FOR THE COLORS

Battle of Gettysburg, July 1

NO ORGANIZATION HELD A MORE HONORED place in the ranks of the Army of the Potomac than the 1st Brigade, 1st Division, 1st Corps. Bearing with pride the name the "Iron Brigade," the soldiers of the 2nd, 6th, and 7th Wisconsin, the 19th Indiana, and the 24th Michigan had purchased their fame in blood—at Brawner's Farm, South Mountain, and Antietam. The distinctive black dress hats and white leggings issued to them had set them apart from other volunteers, and they were conscious of the fact that they were the only all-western brigade serving in the great eastern army.

Their band playing "The Campbells are Coming," the 6th Wisconsin marched toward battle on July 1, 1863, under the command of Lieutenant Colonel Rufus Dawes, who would be celebrating his twenty-fifth birthday three days later. Picking up the pace, the Iron Brigade double-quicked for the wooded flank of McPherson's Ridge, where General John Buford's cavalry troopers had been bearing the brunt of the fight against the Rebel infantry advancing toward Gettysburg. As 1st Corps Commander John Reynolds personally led the other four units of the Iron Brigade against General James Archer's Confederates in McPherson's Woods, a hard-riding staff officer brought orders for Lieutenant Colonel Dawes to double-quick the 6th Wisconsin to the right, toward the sunken bed of an unfinished railroad.

A brigade of Mississippi and North Carolina troops led by Brigadier General Joseph R. Davis had swept down upon the right flank of the 1st Corps, breaking the 147th New York and moving into the railroad cut. Panting with exertion, the 6th Wisconsin raced to plug the widening gap before Davis's soldiers could move south from the railroad to the Chambersburg Pike. Rufus Dawes was unhorsed by enemy fire and his men began to fall, but there was only one thing to do—cross the fence-lined pike and charge the Rebels before they emerged from the natural trench. To the left of the 6th Wisconsin the 95th New York was coming forward, as were the red-legged chasseurs of the 14th Brooklyn. To halt was to risk disaster, and Dawes gave the command, "Forward, charge!"

Dawes tried to keep his men in formation with shouts of "Align on the colors! Close up on the colors!" But as the troops sprinted forward their formation broke up into a wedge-shaped, cheering mob. "With the colors at the advance point," Dawes wrote, "the whole field behind streamed with men who had been shot, and who were struggling to the rear or sinking in death upon the ground."

Surging up to the lip of the railroad cut, the Wisconsin soldiers could see the red battle flag of the 2nd Mississippi, silhouetted against the smoke-shrouded line of gray-clad troops. Possessed by what Rufus Dawes called "A heroic ambition to capture it," a cluster of Iron Brigade men rushed toward the Confederate color bearer, Corporal W. B. Murphy, whose bullet-riddled banner and splintered staff became the focus of what Murphy later called, "one of the most deadly struggles that was ever witnessed during any battle in the war."

Lieutenant William Remington was racing for the flag, sword in hand, when bullets in the neck and shoulder brought him down. As Remington later noted, "Flag-taking was pretty well knocked out of me." Corporals Cornelius Okey and Lewis Eggleston ran past the wounded officer and began grappling with the Rebel color bearer; though both Okey

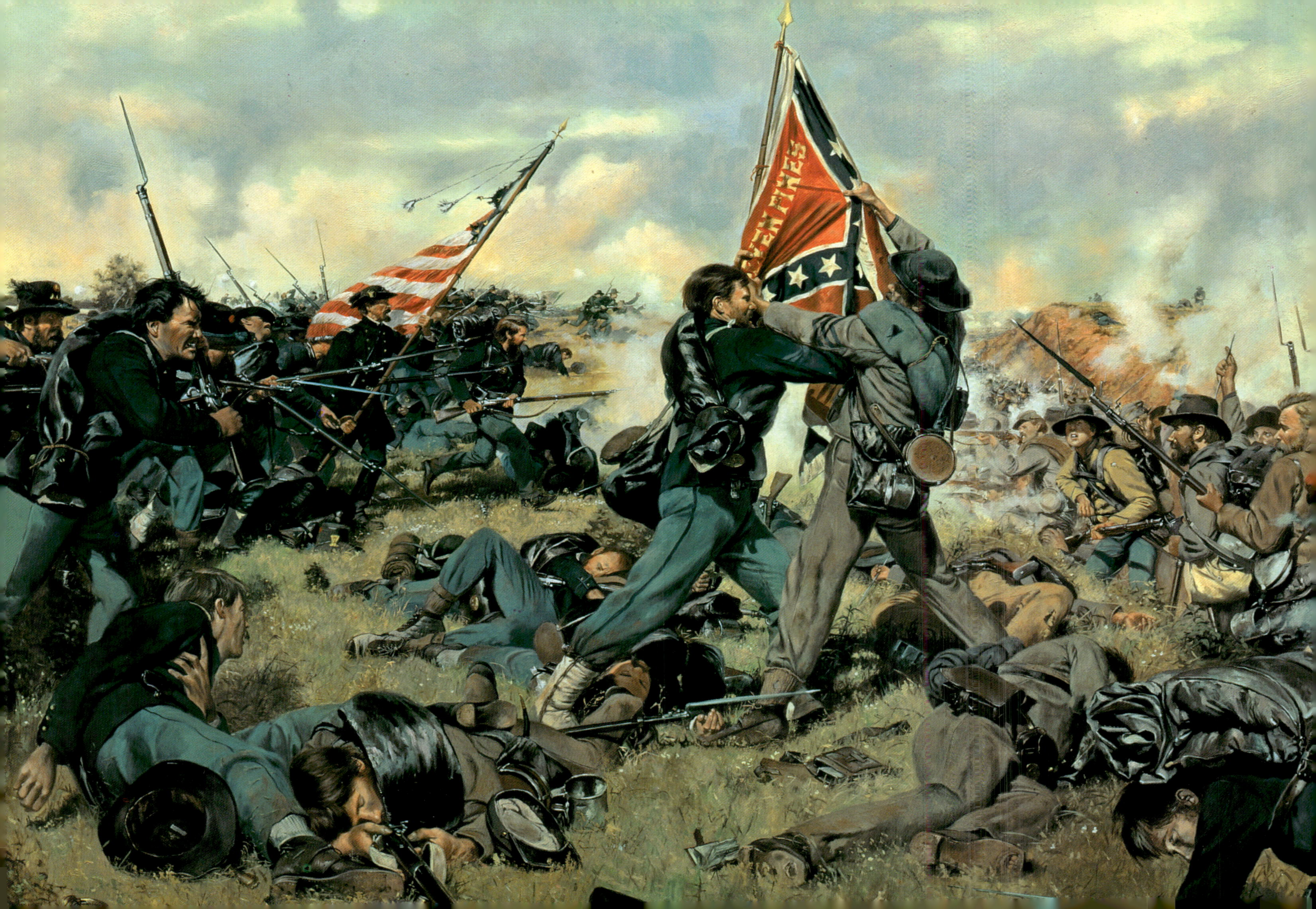
PINES

THE FIGHT FOR THE COLORS   85

and Eggleston seized the flagstaff, Color Corporal Murphy had driven the staff so deep in the earth that the Wisconsin men were unable to get control of it before they too were felled by enemy fire.

With Okey wounded and Eggleston dying, Private Bodley Jones clutched at the bunting of the flag but was shot dead. At the same moment, Private David Anderson—nicknamed "Rocky Mountain" because of his burly build and wild shock of hair—plunged into the fight and with a mighty swing of his musket crushed the skull of the Rebel soldier who had shot his friend Eggleston.

As brothers Francis and Samuel Wallar of Company I raced into the fight, Sam Wallar knocked aside the muzzle of a Confederate musket aimed at his brother and felled the Rebel with his musket butt. Frank Wallar closed with Color Corporal Murphy, and the two men wrestled for control of the flag. Murphy tried to tear his precious banner from its staff, but Wallar, a muscular farmer, finally overpowered the determined color bearer. As Murphy was seized and captured, Corporal Wallar threw down the flag and stood upon it as he fired several more shots into the defenders of the railroad cut.

While the fight for the flag was raging, all along the edge of the cut the men of the 6th Wisconsin were compelling the unfortunate soldiers of Davis's brigade to surrender. The unfinished railroad bed had become a cul-de-sac from which there was little chance of escape. "The coolness, self-possession, and discipline which held back our men from pouring in a general volley saved a hundred lives of the enemy," Rufus Dawes remembered, "and as my mind goes back to the fearful excitement of the moment, I marvel at it." While his excited troops yelled "Throw down your muskets! Down with your muskets!" Dawes pushed his way through the jostling crowd to Major John Blair, commander of the 2nd Mississippi, and accepted his sword; more than two hundred other Confederates likewise gave up their arms and joined the major in captivity.

Decisive as the charge of the 6th Wisconsin was, the fortunes of war were soon to turn against the 1st Corps. After a lull in the fighting, by afternoon a full-scale Confederate assault began shoving the Iron Brigade back toward Gettysburg, even as the 11th Corps collapsed north of the town. The survivors of the 6th Wisconsin held together through the mounting chaos, Lieutenant Colonel Dawes at one point bearing the regimental colors to steady his men. The battle of Gettysburg cost the 6th Wisconsin 168 of their 340 men, but their bravery at the railroad cut won them imperishable renown.

In painting the struggle between Corporal Wallar of the 6th Wisconsin and the 2nd Mississippi color bearer, Corporal W. B. Murphy, photographs of the disputed banner enabled Troiani to accurately render the battlehonors and bullet holes of the bunting that was at the center of the hand-to-hand fight. The captured color was taken to Milwaukee when the 6th Wisconsin returned on veteran furlough in 1864.

PHOTO COURTESY STATE HISTORICAL SOCIETY OF WISCONSIN

76th Pennsylvania Volunteer Infantry

"Keystone Zouaves"

One of Pennsylvania's most colorful units, the 76th Volunteer Infantry, or "Keystone Zouaves," spent much of their term of service on the Carolina Coast. Their battle honors included two unsuccessful assaults on Fort Wagner, the Confederate bastion that guarded Morris Island and the approaches to Charleston Harbor. Remembered chiefly as the trial by fire of the 54th Massachusetts, the war's most famed black regiment, Fort Wagner also witnessed desperate gallantry on the part of the Pennsylvania Zouaves.

On July 11, 1863, the Zouaves along with other units of Brigadier General George C. Strong's brigade battled their way onto the parapet of Fort Wagner but were hurled back with a loss of 180 men, more than 50 of whom were killed outright or died of wounds. A week later the 76th participated in a second charge on the fort, during which General Strong was fatally wounded alongside the unit's bullet-riddled flag.

The Keystone Zouaves' unique garb, including blue fez and trousers and a false vest front stitched to the short Zouave jacket, was manufactured by Philadelphia's Schuykill Arsenal. Don Troiani's collection includes a complete 76th Pennsylvania uniform, which he consulted in this rendition of a Keystone Zouave practicing a bayonet exercise adapted from a French text in 1851 by Captain—later General—George B. McClellan.

COLLECTION OF RICK AND JOAN DAVIES

The Boy Colonel

Battle of Gettysburg, July 1

It was 2 p.m. on July 1, 1863. Since the initial clash that morning, the fighting north and west of Gettysburg had intensified until now it was clear to every soldier that a great battle was at hand. Robert E. Lee's Army of Northern Virginia was on the offensive, and fresh troops were moving forward to drive their blue-clad foes from ridgelines that commanded the town beyond.

No officer felt the urgency of the hour more keenly than Colonel Henry King Burgwyn, Jr., commander of the 26th North Carolina. His was one of four North Carolina regiments in Brigadier General J. Johnston Pettigrew's brigade, which since noon had been waiting to enter the fray. Yankee shells and occasional spatters of musketry had been striking among Burgwyn's position on Herr Ridge, and the colonel was eager to fight. Now at last it was time. Burgwyn called his men to attention, drew his sword, and took position on foot at the center of the regiment, ready to lead them forward.

Burgwyn's zeal was fueled by the impetuosity of youth. At age twenty-one, he was the youngest colonel in Lee's army, having risen to field grade while still in his teens. But Harry Burgwyn was something more than a "boy colonel." In two years of war he had forged a reputation as a firm disciplinarian, skilled drillmaster, and unsurpassed leader of men. At first he was viewed as something of a martinet, but by August 1862, when he assumed the colonelcy of the 26th, Burgwyn had won his men's affection as well as their respect.

As the Army of Northern Virginia marched into Maryland and across the Mason-Dixon Line into Pennsylvania, the soldiers noticed that their young commander was uncharacteristically subdued. Some thought he had a premonition of approaching death. "God alone knows how tired I am of this

PRIVATE COLLECTION

war," Burgwyn had written his family; "I am sure that no day in my life will be hailed by me with the same degree of delight as that on which I hear the blessed tidings of peace assured."

Whatever his forebodings, the boy colonel advanced bravely into the first day's fight at Gettysburg. "His eye was aflame with the ardor of battle," recalled Burgwyn's second in command, Lieutenant Colonel John R. Lane. "At the command Forward March," Lane wrote, the nearly nine hundred soldiers of the 26th, well clad in recently issued uniforms, "to a man stepped off apparently as willingly and as proudly as if they were on review." Opposing them were some of the finest troops in the Union Army: the tough westerners of the Iron Brigade.

Men struck down at every step, the 26th North Carolina swept on toward the enemy position on McPherson's Ridge. Their ranks were disordered by the tangled undergrowth that bordered Willoughby Run, but under heavy fire the men splashed across and reformed on the opposite bank. Already four soldiers had fallen while bearing the regimental battle flag—a newly issued banner, now torn with bullets. Screaming the Rebel yell, the Tarheels charged uphill, driving the 24th Michigan and a portion of the 19th Indiana into the shelter of McPherson's Woods.

There the Yankees stood their ground, bringing the North Carolinians to a standstill in a deadly slugging match, the opposing forces a scant twenty yards apart. Four more times the flag of the 26th went down, only to be raised again.

In the thick of the fighting, Captain W. W. McCreery galloped up to Colonel Burgwyn with a message from General Pettigrew: "Your regiment has covered itself with glory today!" Then, leaping from his horse, McCreery picked up the banner and fell, shot through the heart. Second Lieutenant George Wilcox pulled the flag from under McCreery's body, stood up, and was also shot.

Now Burgwyn himself snatched up the flag from a heap of fallen men. Seeing that the color company and those on its flanks were all but annihilated, the colonel bore the colors to First Lieutenant Thomas Cureton of Company B and asked if he could furnish a man to carry them. Private Frank Hunneycut stepped forward, took the flag, and went down.

Again Burgwyn raised the bloodstained banner. Bullets tore at his clothes and struck the scabbard that hung at his side. Pointing his sword at the enemy line, the boy colonel turned to his embattled soldiers and urged them forward. At that moment a bullet ripped through his lungs, and Burgwyn went down, the flag enfolding him as he fell.

Lieutenant Colonel Lane ran to the side of his stricken commander and with the words, "It is my time to take them now," snatched the flag from the hands of its thirteenth bearer and led the regiment on. The ravaged Yankee line gave way, and as Lane scrambled in their wake he was shot in the back of the head, the bullet emerging from his open mouth. For the final time that day, the flag of the 26th went down.

Lane would live to fight another day, but at least 95 of his men had died in the charge. By the final day of Gettysburg, 697 of the North Carolinians had been killed, wounded or captured. Of these 174 were killed outright or later succumbed to their wounds.

For two hours Henry Burgwyn's life ebbed away as he lay in the arms of Lieutenant J. J. Young. He left messages of love for his family and words of praise for his men. Just before the end, the boy colonel's mind drifted back to the eve of battle and he whispered, "I know my gallant regiment will do their duty . . . Where is my sword?"

45th New York Volunteer Infantry

The 45th New York Volunteer Infantry was among the many German-American units serving in the ranks of Major General Oliver O. Howard's 11th Corps at Gettysburg. The 45th New York was commanded by Colonel Georg Karl Heinrich Wilhelm von Amsberg, a forty-two-year-old veteran of the Hungarian Revolution who prior to the war was a riding instructor in Hoboken, New Jersey. Organized in the fall of 1861 as the 5th German Rifles, Amsberg's unit retained its German identity as well as its short New York-state issue jackets and Model 1841 Mississippi rifles with fearsome saber bayonets.

The fact that many Union soldiers had lost their knapsacks at the battle of Chancellorsville resulted in soldiers limiting the practice of removing packs before entering combat. The bulky knapsack carried by this soldier reflects a directive by Major General Carl Schurz, the 45th New York's division commander, that required every man to carry an extra pair of shoes and set of underwear, as well as an overcoat, blanket, rubber blanket, and shelter half. The only regulation item the 45th seems to have lacked was its division's blue crescent moon corps badge; unlike most of the Army of the Potomac, the 1st Brigade, 3rd Division, 11th Corps does not seem to have received its insignia prior to Gettysburg.

Engaged on all three days of the battle, the 45th New York lost 324 of its 447 men, many of them captured in the streets of Gettysburg on July 1.

PRIVATE COLLECTION

COLLECTION OF FRED AND NANCY EDMUNDS

Battle in the Streets

Baltimore Street, Gettysburg, July 1–3

THE BATTLE OF GETTYSBURG CAUGHT HUNdreds of civilians—and their homes—in the deadly crossfire of contending armies. Just as the Southern town of Fredericksburg had been ravaged by war, so the once peaceful Pennsylvania village was transformed into a death-strewn battleground.

Following the collapse of the Federal 1st and 11th Corps on July 1, Confederate troops established a foothold in the southern portion of the town from whence they could fire on the Union stronghold on Cemetery Hill. On July 2, the 73rd Pennsylvania Regiment attempted to clear the Rebels from their positions, but the Georgia and Louisiana defenders were cleverly concealed and stymied the Federals with well-aimed shots. Firing from windows and rooftops, and from the cover of an improvised barricade on Baltimore Street, the Southern infantry easily repulsed the Yankees.

The deadly sniper's duel continued on July 3, and it was a stray bullet from this action that took the life of twenty-year-old Jennie Wade, the only Gettysburg civilian killed.

Cemetery Hill

Battle of Gettysburg, July 1

By late afternoon, the first day's battle at Gettysburg looked to be a Union disaster. Pressured from three directions by superior Southern forces, the 1st and 11th Corps were giving way in a retreat that in places bordered on panic. While some units waged a fighting withdrawal toward the town, others fell back through the streets of Gettysburg, demoralized.

Those who managed to escape the bullets and elude capture by the victorious Rebel troops began to gather atop the commanding elevation known as Cemetery Hill. There, just south of town, a modicum of order remained as sweat-soaked, panting soldiers clustered about bullet-torn colors, and officers shouted themselves hoarse in an attempt to patch together a defensive position near the brick archway of the Evergreen Cemetery gatehouse.

With the bulk of General Meade's Army of the Potomac yet to arrive, the senior Federal officer on the field was Major General Oliver Otis Howard. The one-armed general, whose 11th Corps had been shattered by the Confederate onslaught, worked with 1st Corps commander Abner Doubleday to prepare for a continuation of the Rebel advance. Doubleday's superior officer, Major General John Reynolds, had fallen early in the action, and the loss of that highly esteemed leader had hampered his successors' efforts.

George Meade was headquartered at Taneytown, Maryland, thirteen miles south of Gettysburg, when word of Reynolds' death prompted the Army commander to make an unorthodox decision. Meade, who had neither expected nor planned to fight a battle at Gettysburg, thought it best that he remain with the main body to hasten their approach to the scene of combat. In the interim, he decided to send one of his most trusted subordinates ahead to assess the crisis.

The daunting task was assigned to thirty-nine year old Major General Winfield Scott Hancock, who had assumed command of the Army's 2nd Corps in late May, following the defeat at Chancellorsville. Meade instructed Hancock to take charge of the 1st and 11th Corps, as well as the 3rd, which was camped at nearby Emmitsburg, Maryland. Hancock questioned the wisdom of the order, as he was junior in rank to both General Howard and Major General Daniel E. Sickles, commander

Six-foot-two and powerfully built, Winfield Scott Hancock not only looked the part of a fighting general but also was able to transfuse his strength and fortitude to those around him. Hancock's adjutant, Lieutenant Colonel Francis A. Walker, aptly assessed his chief's impact on Gettysburg's first day: "As the sun shining through a rift in the clouds may change a scene of gloom to one of beauty, so did the coming of this prince of soldiers. . . . At his call the braver spirits flamed to their heights, the weaker souls yielded gladly to the impulse of that powerful, aggressive, resolute nature." Photo courtesy U.S. Military History Institute

of the 3rd Corps. But Meade was adamant. He trusted Hancock and could rely implicitly on his judgment. Above all, Meade knew that Hancock possessed a rare ability to galvanize men by his stalwart, soldierly demeanor. If Hancock judged the position at Gettysburg to be defensible, Meade would continue the battle there.

Ordering several of his staff to ride ahead, Hancock took some time inside an ambulance to study maps of the Gettysburg area before mounting his own horse and spurring toward the scene of combat. It was about 3:30 P.M. when Winfield Scott Hancock made his dramatic appearance on Cemetery Hill.

Captain Eminel P. Halstead, one of General Doubleday's staff officers, was beside Howard when Hancock approached at a gallop. Halstead overheard the brief, acrimonious exchange that took place between the two corps commanders, a confrontation that would become a source of controversy after the battle.

According to Captain Halstead, Hancock saluted Howard "and with great animation, as if there was no time for ceremony, said General Meade had sent him forward to take command of the three corps." When Howard objected, pointing out that he was the senior in rank, Hancock said, "I am aware of that, General, but I have orders in my pocket from General Meade which I will show you if you wish to see them." Howard replied, "I do not doubt your word, General Hancock, but you can give no orders while I am here."

Hancock acceded to his superior's wishes but was not about to be cowed by his petulant colleague "I think this the strongest position by nature upon which to fight a battle that I ever saw," Hancock stated, "and if it meets your approbation I will select this as the battlefield."

On this point, at least, both generals were in full agreement, and Hancock rode off to see to the troops' deployments. "His bearing was courageous and hopeful," Captain Halstead recalled, 'while his eyes flashed defiance." Tall, broad-shouldered, and spotlessly uniformed, Hancock quickly demonstrated the appropriateness of his sobriquet "The Superb"—bestowed upon him for his gallantry in the May 1862 battle of Williamsburg.

The guns of Battery E, 5th Maine Light Artillery, came rumbling into the chaos on Cemetery Hill, where Lieutenant Edward N. Whittier reported to Hancock for orders. "I shall never forget," Whittier wrote, "the inspiration of his commanding, controlling presence, nor the fresh courage he imparted; his very atmosphere, strong and invigorating."

---

*F*ervently devout and an ardent abolitionist, Major General Oliver O. Howard displayed great courage in earlier campaigns and lost his right arm at the battle of Fair Oaks. But his 11th Corps—comprised largely of German-American volunteers—was routed both at Chancellorsville and Gettysburg, and his bickering with Hancock on Cemetery Hill cast Howard in a negative light that still clouds his distinguished war record. PHOTO COURTESY U.S. ARMY MILITARY HISTORY INSTITUTE

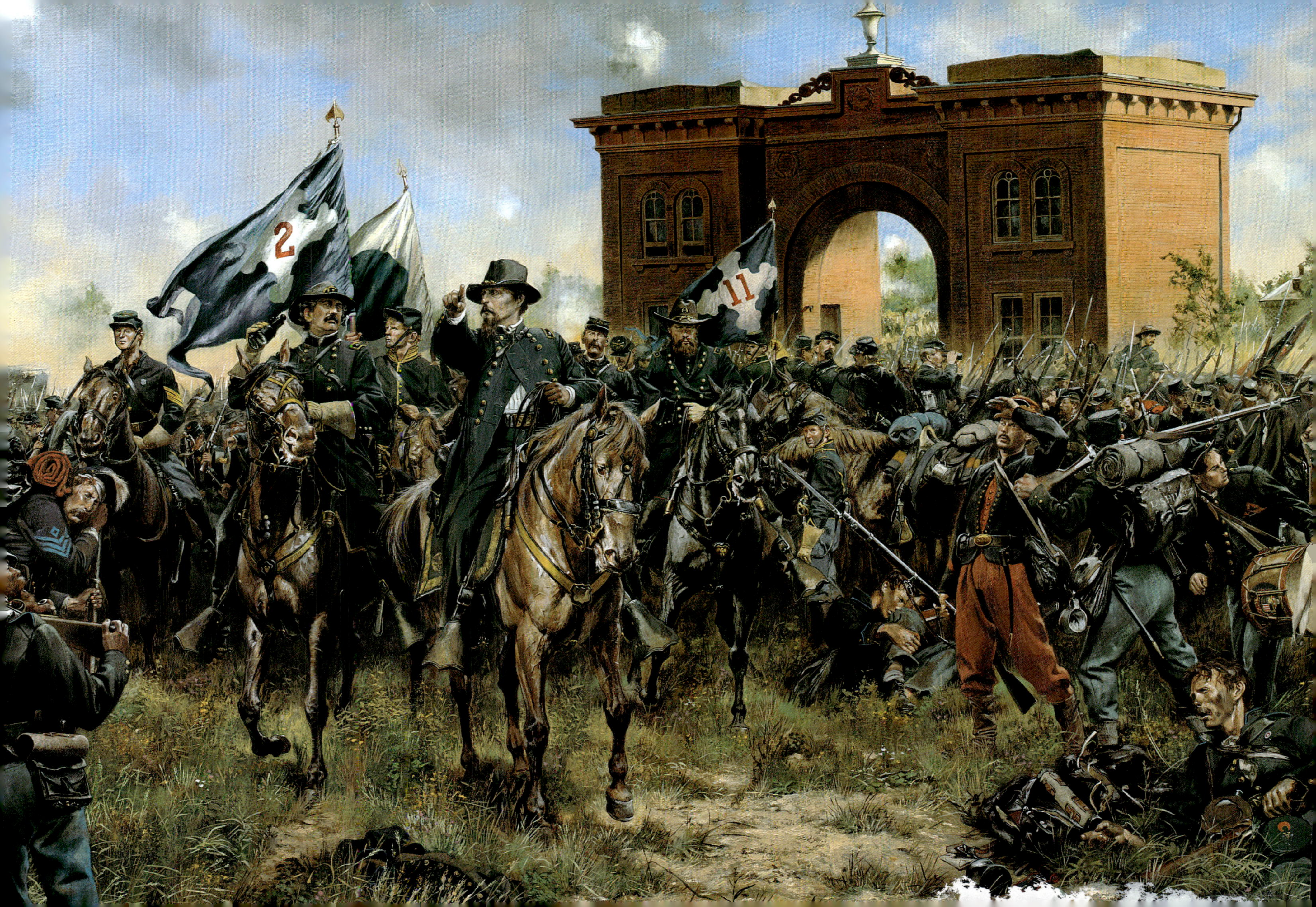

Whittier was awed by Hancock's composure, "on horseback, erect, unmoved by all confusion among the thousands of retreating and well-nigh worn out soldiers." The general seemed "born to command . . . cool, calm, self-possessed."

General Meade's instincts had proven to be correct. Disaster was averted, and for the next two days the inspiring presence and heroic deeds of Winfield Scott Hancock would prove instrumental to Union victory at Gettysburg.

Major General Abner Doubleday, best known for his erroneous attribution as the inventor of baseball, was a twenty-one-year-veteran of military service who had fired the first Union shot in response to the Confederate bombardment of Fort Sumter. He performed capably at Gettysburg but lacked the fiery spirit so conspicuous in Hancock and never achieved the greatness of his fellow corps commander. PHOTO COURTESY U.S. ARMY MILITARY HISTORY INSTITUTE

Decision at Dawn

Gettysburg, July 2

Robert E. Lee rose well before the sun that humid summer morning. The great commander's thoughts were focussed on the daunting challenge that lay ahead, and he had slept neither long nor well. The battle at Gettysburg had come upon Lee's Army of Northern Virginia unexpectedly, and while the savage combat of July 1 had gone in favor of the Confederates, it would clearly require a second day of fighting if a decisive victory was to be won on Northern soil.

At his headquarters, located on the western slope of Seminary Ridge not far from the Lutheran theological seminary that gave the slope its name, Lee carefully pondered his next move. The previous day's combat had inflicted grievous loss on the Federal army, with the better part of two corps smashed and hurled back through the streets of Gettysburg in near rout. But Southern losses had also been heavy, and when General Richard Ewell's 2nd Corps had failed to dominate, the enemy had been able to regroup atop the strategically crucial high ground south of town.

Lee was still handicapped by the absence of J. E. B. Stuart's cavalry, which under normal circumstances would have kept him informed of Federal deployments, lines of march, and the lay of the land. It was clear, however, that the greater part of General George Meade's Army of the Potomac had arrived on the field and that the battle of the second day would be far more severe than that of the first.

Ever the military gambler, Lee began to consider striking on the Union left flank, where the topography was less favorable to Federal defense. In order to get a sense of the ground, in the predawn hours Lee dispatched Engineer Captain Samuel R. Johnston to survey the terrain. Lee was fully determined to maintain the offensive, by whatever means seemed to promise success on the battlefield.

General James Longstreet, stalwart commander of the 1st Corps, arrived at Lee's headquarters accompanied by several of his staff officers. Longstreet was opposed to what he considered a risky and potentially fatal offensive action; it was far better, he argued, to pass around Meade's army, assume an impregnable position, and lure the Yankees into a bloody head-on assault reminiscent of Burnside's fiasco at Fredericksburg. But Lee was adamant. As he had told Longstreet the previous evening, "If the enemy is there tomorrow, we must attack him."

As the impromptu council of war continued, a number of other senior officers joined the group gathered beside a fallen tree near Lee's headquarters. Major General John B. Hood, the blond-bearded, big-framed division commander, seated himself beside his corps commander, Longstreet, who glumly whittled on a stick. Lieutenant General A. P. Hill, whose 3rd Corps had taken heavy losses on July 1, arrived in company with Major General Henry Heth, whose bandaged head testified to a grazing from a Yankee bullet.

All eyes were focused on their gray-bearded commander as he paced before the assembled officers, deep in thought. General Hood noted that Lee halted "now and then to observe the enemy" with his field glasses, and that despite the hot and humid weather, the general wore his coat "buttoned to the throat." Another who remembered Lee's appearance at this trying hour was British Lieutenant Colonel Arthur Fremantle, who was scanning the Federal position from the branches of a nearby tree along with another foreign observer, Prussian Captain Justus Scheibert.

Fremantle, a member of the elite Coldstream Guards, considered Lee "the handsomest man of his age I ever saw," and "a perfect gentleman in every respect." The Englishman commented that neither Lee nor Longstreet was in the habit of carrying a sidearm, and that despite Lee's martial appearance, he never seemed to wear a sword slung from his belt.

Other foreigners who joined the large array of generals and staff officers were Francis Lawley, war correspondent of *The Times* of London, and Captain Fitzgerald Ross, whose gold-braided blue uniform and waxed moustaches denoted his membership in the 6th Austrian hussar regiment.

Still fixed in his opinion that an assault was unwise, Longstreet explained to Hood that with Major General George Pickett's division still at least half a day's march from the field, a premature move would mean going into battle "with one boot off." Lee put great weight in the words of his "Old War Horse" and undoubtedly grappled with Longstreet's disturbing reluctance as he shaped his plans for the day.

When Captain Johnston finally returned and reported the results of his scout of the Federal left, Lee made up his mind to attack. The orders were issued: As Ewell's Corps tied down the heavily defended Federal right, Longstreet would swing his corps southward, then lash out at the exposed Union left, driving northward up the Emmitsburg Road. If the god of battles smiled upon them, the Army of Northern Virginia would add the name of Gettysburg to those of Second Manassas, Fredericksburg, and Chancellorsville. The decision had been made.

ALWAYS WANTING TO INCLUDE INDIvidual portraits in his work, Troiani consulted period photographs and descriptions of Generals Longstreet, Hood, Heth, and others, including the members of Lee and Longstreet's staffs. Contrary to legend, there is no evidence that A. P. Hill wore a solid red shirt at Gettysburg or at any other time. Accounts of his dress in the Peninsula campaign mention a "figured or red calico shirt," which was prominent when he removed his uniform coat during the heat of battle. Though propagated by modern artists and others, this myth needs to be laid to rest. In the case of the foreign observers, we know that while the Prussian Scheibert wore civilian clothing, Arthur Fremantle was garbed in a gray shooting suit rather than a British redcoat. Determining the uniform of the Austrian Fitzhugh Ross proved a particular challenge, but Troiani's research in the Anne S. K. Brown Collection and Austria located the correct pattern of the officer's colorful undress hussar outfit.

PRIVATE COLLECTION

"The Men Must See Us Today"

Battle of Gettysburg, July 2

The battle of Gettysburg was well into its second day and the opposing armies had strengthened their forces for a decisive engagement. There had as yet been little fighting that day, but this would change dramatically, as it neared 4 P.M., when Major General John Bell Hood's division would initiate a massive Confederate offensive on the Federal left and center.

After a circuitous march and nagging delays, General James Longstreet's corps was finally poised to begin a series of attacks, each timed to step off one after the other in the Napoleonic stratagem known as an assault *en echelon*. By the time Longstreet was ready to strike, the Union 3rd Corps had shifted its line westward, directly in the Confederates' path. Hood's division would have to deal with a new Yankee line that angled south from a peach orchard to a jumbled heap of massive boulders known as Devils Den.

Worn, weary, and sweltering in the summer's heat, the men of the 124th New York braced themselves for the onslaught, taking what cover they could behind the stone wall that bordered a triangular-shaped field near the Devils Den. They were veterans now, commanded by a colonel as strict as he was brave, and they knew their business. They held the left of their brigade line, and the four Parrott guns of Captain James Smith's New York battery needed their support.

In the nine months since their departure from Orange County, bullets and disease had winnowed the ranks of the 124th, and war was becoming an all-too-familiar ordeal. The hell of Chancellorsville, where more than two hundred comrades had been shot down or fallen into Rebel hands a month earlier, was seared into their souls.

These sons of Orange had willingly answered President Lincoln's call for recruits to fill the vacant ranks of an army bled white on the Virginia Peninsula. On September 6, 1862, they had departed the Goshen railroad depot to the cheers and tears of loved ones left behind. Many of them wore orange ribbons looped in the buttonholes of their uniform blouses—tokens of remembrance and symbols of pride. Atop their forage caps they bore the blue diamond, symbol of the 3rd Division of the 3rd Army Corps. And though the 3rd Division had been recently disbanded and the 124th reassigned to Major General David Birney's 2nd Division, the "Orange Blossoms" had chosen to retain the blue lozenge so resonant with memories of the slaughter at Chancellorsville. The other units of their brigade, commanded by brawny, hard-drinking General Hobart Ward, sported the red diamond, and they would be watching to see if these Orange Blossoms proved themselves worthy of membership in the division immortalized by the dashing one-armed daredevil, General Phil Kearny.

No man was more determined to show the mettle of the 124th New York than the unit's commanding officer, Colonel Augustus Van Horne Ellis. Of distinguished lineage and educated at New York City's Columbia College, Ellis had forsaken his genteel upbringing and aspiring law career to seek his fortune in the California Gold Rush. In the decade preceding the war, the lean and intense commander had been a real estate broker, lumberman, clipper ship captain, and pearl fisherman. One of his last assignments prior to returning to New York was the post of captain in the Hawaiian Navy. Van Horne Ellis was an adventurer, and his varied experience had imbued him with an iron will and made him familiar with the challenges of command.

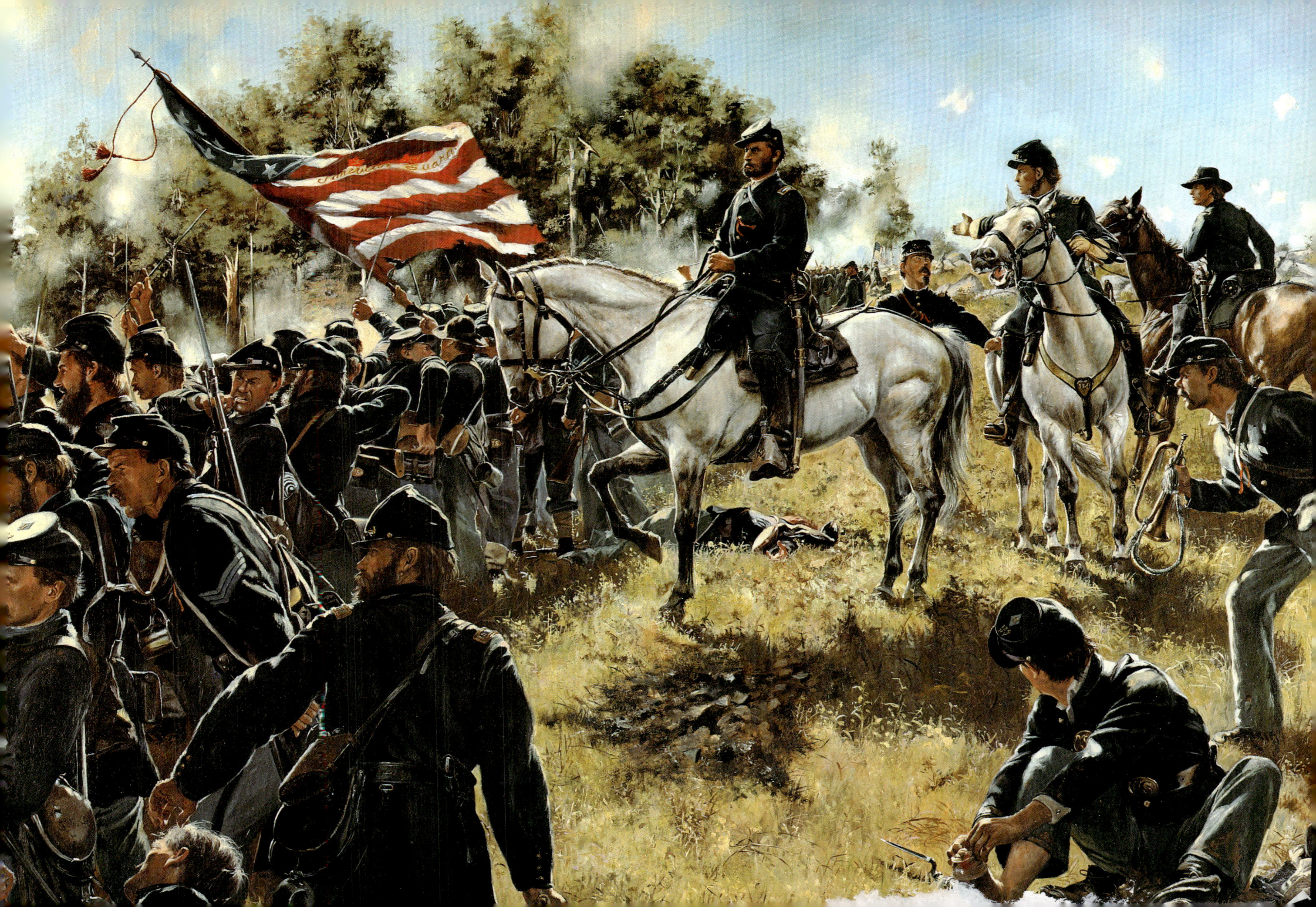

Captain Smith's rifled guns were thundering from atop the ridge alongside the 124th New York as the blood-curdling Rebel yells drew closer and closer to Colonel Ellis's position. As soldiers of the famed Texas Brigade came surging across the triangular field, Ellis shouted a command and the New Yorkers unleashed a deadly volley into the ranks of the 1st Texas regiment, barely two hundred feet to their front. The Confederate line was staggered but pressed on, men dropping on all sides as their comrades returned fire.

Thirty-six-year-old Colonel A. Van Horne Ellis, commander of the 124th New York, had experienced a colorful and varied career as a California prospector and ship's captain. A friend of Hawaii's King Kamehameha IV, he was tendered command of the Hawaiian navy but abandoned the task when sufficient funds for the purchase of naval vessels failed to be forthcoming.

Ellis accepted command of the Orange Blossoms following a stint in the 71st New York, with whom he fought in the first battle of Bull Run. "Colonel Ellis was a rather cold, harsh ambitious man, and sometimes chilled us with his terrible bursts of profanity," Captain Charles Weygant recalled, "But he was every inch a soldier." A swarthy six-footer, Ellis cut an impressive figure: "As trim as an arrow," Weygant noted, "and so straight that he seemed to bend backward."

PHOTO COURTESY LIBRARY OF CONGRESS

Seeing the Rebel line waver, young Major James Cromwell approached Colonel Ellis, who stood with Regimental Adjutant Henry Ramsdell, and urged his commander to launch a counterattack. Twice the colonel refused, but finally he yielded to his subordinates' entreaties and called for their horses to be brought up so that they might lead the charge in person. When Captain William Silliman begged Cromwell not to make a target of himself on horseback, the major replied, "The men must see us today."

As the Southerners came within fifty feet of the embattled Union line, bugler Moses Ross sounded the charge, and with mad cheers the Orange Blossoms surged downslope into the oncoming Rebels. The gray line gave way, but more Southern troops were on hand, and the New Yorkers were forced back. As Major Cromwell flourished his sword and urged on his men, a bullet pierced his heart and he dropped lifeless from the saddle.

Seeing his young subordinate go down amidst the chaos, Colonel Ellis spurred his gray horse forward and yelled, "My God! My God, men! Your major's down; save him!" The Yankees rallied and battled their way through the zipping bullets, back to the fallen officer. Wreathed in the smoke and flame of battle, Ellis stood erect in the stirrups of his charger, his sword upraised, and began to shout an order. His voice was cut off in mid-sentence when a bullet slammed into his forehead.

Dragging the bodies of their officers to the rear, the Orange Blossoms laid their corpses atop a large boulder and continued the fight. But brave as they were, they could not stop Hood's men. Slowly, grudgingly, the men of Ward's brigade yielded the crest above Devils Den and the battle swept on, toward the valley of Plum Run and the rocky slopes of Little Round Top.

The Texas Brigade

Tough and reliable veteran soldiers, the men of the Texas Brigade were perhaps the finest shock troops in the Army of Northern Virginia. At Gaines's Mill, Second Manassas, and Antietam they had been in the forefront of the attack, charging into the teeth of artillery fire, smashing a way through Yankee lines, and battling fiercely.

At Gettysburg the Texas Brigade was led by Brigadier General Jerome B. Robertson, their former commander, John Bell Hood, having been elevated to division command the previous year. The brigade played a conspicuous part in the fight for Devils Den and the rocky slope of Little Round Top, and 597 of their number were killed, wounded, or missing in action.

The four units of the Texas Brigade are shown here in the uniforms worn at Gettysburg (left to right): the 1st Texas, many of whom stripped to their shirtsleeves before attacking Devils Den, carrying .69 caliber muskets; a noncommissioned officer of the 5th Texas, armed with a short version of the Enfield Rifle, with saber bayonet; the 4th Texas, with a tarred cover on their caps; a musician from the band of the 3rd Arkansas.

PRIVATE COLLECTION

20th Georgia Infantry

Wearing a frock coat with a large patch pocket, a soldier of the 20th Georgia Infantry marches to destiny in the war's greatest confrontation. As part of Brigadier General Henry L. Benning's brigade, the 20th Georgia took part in the assault on Devils Den. There they engaged the 124th New York and helped capture several guns of Smith's New York battery.

"Don't Give an Inch"

Little Round Top, Battle of Gettysburg, July 2

More than any other engagement of the Civil War, the battle of Gettysburg called for immediate and decisive action on the part of junior officers. With such large armies contending on so wide a front, it was impossible for Robert E. Lee and George Meade to exercise personal control of their respective armies. The situation was complex and constantly changing, and neither commander was fully aware of what was happening on the regimental, brigade, or even corps level. Though some subordinates failed to rise to the challenge, many others were quite competent, and particularly in the ranks of the Army of the Potomac, the manner in which officers met and resolved the crises of battle was crucial to the ultimate Union victory.

One Federal officer who rose to the challenge of battle was Colonel Strong Vincent, commander of the 3rd Brigade, 1st Division, 5th Corps. Born in Erie County, Pennsylvania, in 1837, Vincent was an 1859 graduate of Harvard University, a fervent supporter of Abraham Lincoln's presidential campaign, and a practicing lawyer in Erie when war began. After a brief stint as private in a militia unit, Vincent helped to recruit and train the 83rd Pennsylvania Volunteers, of which he was commissioned lieutenant colonel. Wholeheartedly devoted to the Union, Vincent wrote his young wife, Elizabeth, "If I live, we will rejoice over our country's success. If I fall, remember you have given your husband a sacrifice to the most righteous cause that ever widowed a woman."

By the summer of 1863, Strong Vincent's grit and ability had brought him promotion to colonel and command of a brigade. By the time his hard-marching regiments arrived at Gettysburg with Major General George Sykes's 5th Corps, the four understrength units numbered a scant thirteen hundred officers and men.

As General James Longstreet's massive Confederate assault began on the afternoon of July 2, the 5th Corps was ordered to support the exposed line of General Daniel Sickles's 3rd Corps, which lay in the path of the Rebel advance. Strong Vincent was on horseback at the head of his brigade, stationed on the lower reaches of Cemetery Ridge, when a mounted staff officer came galloping up in search of Vincent's division commander, Brigadier General James Barnes. "What are your orders?"

Gifted with a sharp mind and a powerful physique, Colonel Strong Vincent's earnest sense of duty led him to reject romantic notions of chivalry. For him, war against the Confederacy was war to the death. "We must fight them more vindictively, or we shall be foiled at every step," he wrote of his Southern foes. "The life of every man, yea, of every weak woman or helpless child in the entire South, is of no value whatever compared with the integrity of the Union." Photo courtesy Massachusetts Commadery, Military Order of the Loyal Legion, and the U.S. Army Military History Institute

Vincent barked. "Give me your orders."

"General Sykes told me to direct General Barnes to send one of his brigades to occupy that hill yonder," the courier replied, pointing at the rocky elevation called Little Round Top.

"I will take the responsibility of taking my brigade there," Vincent stated. As his troops began marching for the conspicuous hillock, Vincent and his brigade standard bearer, Oliver Willcox Norton, rode ahead.

Little Round Top was a topographical feature of utmost importance. Situated at the southern end of the Federal position, it commanded much of the Yankee line, including the strategically vital Cemetery Ridge. During a tour of Union positions, Brigadier General Gouverneur Kemble Warren, Meade's chief engineer, had been shocked to find Little Round Top unoccupied, save for a handful of signalmen. Realizing that an enemy advance was imminent, Warren sent his staff officers scurrying for troops to seize the hill before the Confederates did. Fortunately for the fate of the Union, Strong Vincent had unhesitatingly responded to the call.

Dodging Confederate shellfire, Vincent and Private Norton were forced to dismount as they scouted a path to the summit. By the time the four regiments came up, the colonel had located a route that took his brigade behind the crest to what he deemed the most likely avenue of enemy approach: a relatively level spur that commanded Little Round Top's southern approaches.

Vincent placed the 20th Maine, commanded by college-professor-turned-soldier Joshua Lawrence Chamberlain, on the left of the line and extended his position to the right with the 83rd Pennsylvania, 44th New York, and 16th Michigan. They had arrived none too soon. As the escalating roar of battle gave evidence that the Confederates had begun their great assault, gray-clad troops of General John Bell Hood's division came sweeping toward Little Round Top, driving Vincent's skirmishers before them. The 4th Alabama and 4th and 5th Texas struck at Vincent's right, and the 15th and 47th Alabama engaged his vulnerable left, where Chamberlain's 20th Maine found themselves beleaguered on front and flank.

Taking what cover they could find on Little Round Top's boulder-strewn flank, Vincent's men unleashed a devastating volley on their assailants, and charge after charge recoiled before the defiant Federals. Vincent climbed atop a large rock near the right flank of his embattled line, brandishing a riding crop, and shouted encouragement to his troops—he had left his sword with his horse behind the hill.

When the 48th Alabama which had taken part in the successful attack on Devils Den, moved forward to join in the attack on Vincent's right, the 16th Michigan, which bore the brunt of the onslaught, began to abandon their crucial toehold. Colonel Vincent ran to the threatened point, flourishing his riding crop and yelling, "Don't give an inch!" At that moment a Rebel bullet slammed into his groin, and Vincent crumpled in agony.

The Southerners' chances for victory were snatched away when the 140th New York, led by their gallant colonel, Patrick O'Rorke, arrived to shore up the threatened right of Vincent's brigade. O'Rorke's men were the vanguard of General Stephen Weed's brigade, which had been alerted to the crisis on Little Round Top and, like Vincent before them, had hastened to the scene. Colonel O'Rorke was killed, but his New Yorkers secured the crest of the hill.

Vincent clung desperately to life—his wife was seven months into her pregnancy—but realized his wound was a mortal one. On July 3 he was promoted to the rank of brigadier general, though it is doubtful that word of the promotion reached him before his death on July 7. He did, at least, have the satisfaction of knowing that his courageous action at Little Round Top had contributed mightily to the great Union victory at Gettysburg.

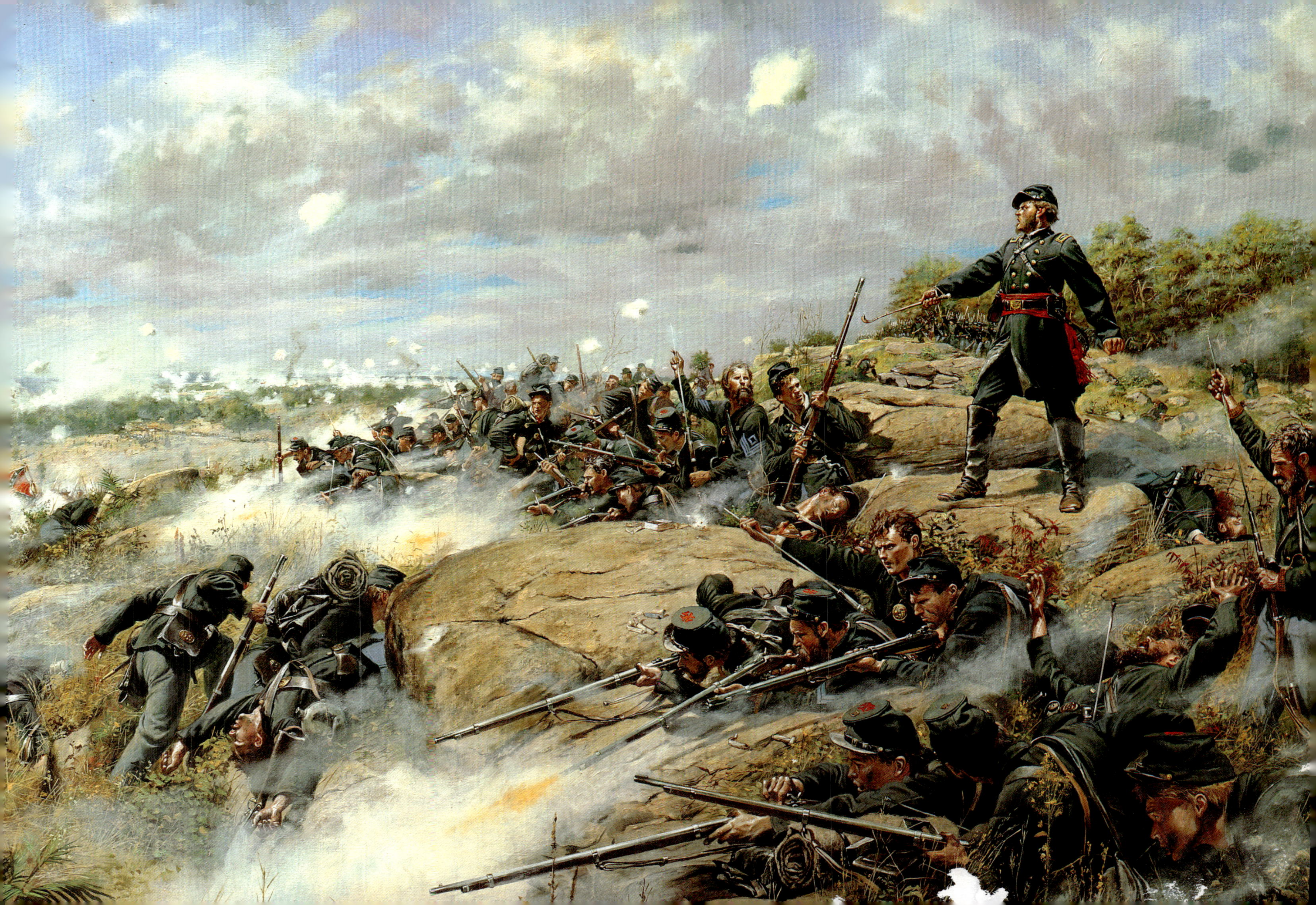

Lions of the Round Top

Battle of Gettysburg, July 2

No Union officer at Gettysburg has been more venerated by students of the epic conflict than Colonel Joshua Lawrence Chamberlain, and no unit is more renowned than his regiment, the 20th Maine. In the fight for Little Round Top the thirty-four-year-old Bowdoin College professor proved himself to be a charismatic and unsurpassed leader of men in battle.

When Strong Vincent brought his four regiments to the threatened height, the 20th Maine double-quicked up the slope and came into position on the left of the brigade. Colonel Chamberlain received Vincent's stern injunction, "I place you here! This is the left of the Union line. You understand. You are to hold this ground at all hazards!"

Chamberlain deployed his 358 men atop a rocky, wooded ledge, on the right by file into line, and dispatched the 50 men of Captain Walter G. Morrill's Company B still farther to his left, joining a detachment of the 2nd U.S. Sharpshooters behind a stone wall at a point that enabled them to fire upon the right flank of any Rebel advance. "The air was filled with fragments of exploding shells and splinters torn from mangled trees," recalled Theodore Gerrish of Company H, "but our men appeared to be as cool and deliberate in their movements as if they had been forming a line upon the parade ground in camp."

The men from Maine did not have long to wait. Over the crest of Big Round Top and down toward the saddle between the higher hill and Little Round Top to its north, came Colonel William C. Oates's 15th Alabama. The 47th Alabama was to Oates's immediate left, with the 4th Alabama still farther to the left and west. Chamberlain gave the command to open fire. "Our regiment was mantled in fire and smoke," Theodore Gerrish later wrote. "How rapidly the cartridges were torn from the boxes and stuffed in the smoking muzzles of the guns. How the steel rammers clashed and clanged in the heated barrels. How the men's hands and faces grew grim and black with burning powder."

As his men blazed away at their assailants, Chamberlain became aware of still more Confederate troops maneuvering toward his left and rear. In order to cover the threatened point, he extended his regimental front and refused the left wing, commanded by Captain Ellis Spear, so that it was nearly at right angles with the five companies of Captain Atherton Clark's right wing. Again and again the Confederates came, were repulsed, rallied, and renewed the attack.

As the battle raged across the front of Vincent's brigade and the 47th Alabama was caught in a crossfire that mowed men down "like grass before the scythe." Colonel Oates led his 15th Alabama in a sweeping charge on the 20th Maine, only to have his line staggered by a hail of bullets "so destructive that my line wavered like a man trying to walk against a strong wind." Undaunted, Oates again exhorted his men to the charge.

"The two lines met and broke and mingled in the shock," Chamberlain recalled. "The crash of musketry gave way to cuts and thrusts, grapplings and wrestlings." At such close quarters, tactical order dissolved in a chaotic melee, what Chamberlain described as "wild whirlpools and eddies" of firing, flailing combatants. "At times I saw around me more of the enemy than my own men: gaps opening, swallowing, closing again with sharp convulsive energy; squads of stalwart men who had cut their way through us, disappearing as if translated." All but the stern resolve of duty

PRIVATE COLLECTION

LIONS OF THE ROUNDTOP ~ *107*

IN PREPARING HIS SECOND VERSION of the 20th Maine's fight for Little Round Top, Don Troiani took into consideration the fact that the wartime terrain was altered by grading and road construction following the creation of the Gettysburg Battlefield Park. Moreover, Troiani's painting incorporates recent research by historian William B. Styple that contradicts the traditional view of Chamberlain's counterattack as carefully choreographed. It was in fact a desperate, spontaneous reaction, largely precipitated by the audacity of young Lieutenant Holman Melcher, commander of the color company, who figures prominently in the artist's depiction. Details of the uniforms and equipment of the contending forces were verified by archival research—about one-third of the regiment carried Springfields, the rest Enfields—and the fragile remnants of the flag of the 20th Maine, preserved at the Maine State Museum, was unrolled so that its pattern and design could be verified.

was forgotten amidst the slaughter; when a hole opened in his line, the colonel did not hesitate to commit his younger brother, Adjutant Tom Chamberlain, to plug the gap, and once more the enemy recoiled.

"It did not seem possible to withstand another shock," Chamberlain reported. "One-half of my left wing had fallen, and a third of my regiment lay just behind us, dead or badly wounded." Color Corporal Elisha Coan recalled, "Our line was melting away like ice before the sun." With the ammunition supply perilously low, the colonel decided on a desperate stratagem—a counterattack that he hoped would catch the Confederates off guard and ensure victory.

As Chamberlain assessed the situation, twenty-two-year-old Lieutenant Holman S. Melcher of Company F—the 20th Maine's color company—appealed to the colonel for permission to lead a foray to cover and reclaim a number of wounded men who lay in front of the battle line. Chamberlain gave his assent and moments later shouted "Bayonet!" As the colonel reported, "The word was enough. It ran like fire along the line, from man to man, and rose into a shout." Those who could not hear the order above the din and crash of battle saw their comrades fixing the deadly steel at the muzzles of their muskets and emulated them, in preparation for the final onslaught.

Possibly taking Chamberlain's shout as a command to begin his foray after the wounded, Lieutenant Melcher sprang ten paces in front of the line, and with a flash of his sword yelled out, "Come on! Come on! Come on boys!" Color Sergeant Andrew Tozier leapt forward in the wake of the lieutenant, the surviving color guard and company followed, and as Theodore Gerrish described it, "with one wild yell of anguish wrung from its tortured heart the regiment charged." When Captain Spear heard the shouts of "Forward!" and saw the colors moving through the smoke, he ordered his left wing to join the rush. The 150 men of the 20th Maine still standing plowed into the startled Rebels with lowered bayonets and tore the enemy line asunder.

Charging down the rocky slope with his soldiers, Joshua Chamberlain came face to face with a Confederate officer, "coming on fiercely, sword in one hand and big navy revolver in the other." The Southerner fired and missed. Chamberlain put the point of his sword at the officer's throat, and the Rebel reversed his arms, yielding sword and pistol to the intrepid Yankee commander.

The Southern assault had at last run out of steam, and the 20th Maine's unexpected counterattack was more than Colonel Oates's Alabamians could stand. As the Confederates began to give way, they were raked with fire from Captain Morrill's Company G. "While one man was shot in the face, his right or left hand comrade was shot in the back," Oates stated. "Some were struck simultaneously with two or three balls from different directions.... The dead literally covered the ground. The blood stood in puddles on the rocks." Finally, as Oates confessed, "we ran like a herd of wild cattle."

After breaking the Rebel line, Chamberlain's men wheeled to the right. As many as three hundred Confederates were captured; some eighty Alabamians fled eastward, were trapped in the Weikert farm lane, and were taken prisoner well behind Union lines. The crucial southern flank of Little Round Top was saved, and with it the left of the Federal army.

Joshua Lawrence Chamberlain, seen here in the uniform of lieutenant colonel of the 20th Maine, used his well-honed intellectual abilities to become the quintessential citizen-soldier. From Bowdoin College professor to wounded and decorated major general, Chamberlain never abandoned the soul-stirring idealism that motivated his devotion to the Union. His bravery and skill at Little Round Top brought him the Congressional Medal of Honor, but he never forgot those young men who gave their lives in the desperate struggle. "There they lay," Chamberlain wrote, "side by side, with touch of elbow still; brave, bronzed faces where the last thought was written manly resolution, heroic self-giving, divine reconciliation." PHOTO COURTESY OF JAMES A. TRULOCK

Bayonet!

Little Round Top, Gettysburg, July 2

In Don Troiani's earlier version of the subject, depicted in "Lions of the Round Top," Colonel Joshua Lawrence Chamberlain leads the 20th Maine in a desperate counterattack that helped secure the vital crest of Little Round Top for the Union. Surviving portions of Chamberlain's uniform and accoutrements, preserved at the Pejepscot Historical Society in Brunswick, Maine, proved invaluable to a proper rendition of the gallant commander.

COLLECTION OF PEJEPSCOT HISTORICAL SOCIETY

53rd Georgia Infantry

TEARING OPEN A PAPER CARTRIDGE—an act that required all Civil War soldiers to have a good set of front teeth—a private of the 53rd Georgia Infantry prepares to load his .69 caliber smooth-bore Model 1842 musket during the second day of the battle of Gettysburg. As part of General Paul J. Semmes's brigade of Lafayette McLaws's division, the Georgians lost eighty-seven men in the fight for the Rose Farm, a storm center of combat during Longstreet's assault on the Federal left and center. General Semmes, brother of the famed commerce raider Raphael Semmes, was mortally wounded during the fight.

The uniform worn by the 53rd Georgia was issued by the Confederate government in Richmond and was typical of the garb of many Southern troops at Gettysburg. Due to increasing supply problems, the wool jean cloth jackets had wooden rather than brass buttons, and the shoulder sling (and sometimes waist belts) that bore the Richmond-manufactured cartridge box and other accoutrements was often made of painted canvas rather than leather. Moreover, archival records indicate that only 80 percent of Semmes's soldiers had canteens. Many necessary items of equipment could be obtained only from captured or slain Yankees.

Despite the challenges the South faced in supplying its soldiers in the field, a measure of uniformity was obtainable, and the typical Confederate fighting man was far from the "ragged Rebel" of legend.

COLLECTION OF L. JENSEN

Saving the Flag

The Wheatfield, Battle of Gettysburg, July 2

Like many of the men commanding regiments at Gettysburg, the attrition of two years of grim war had seen Harrison H. Jeffords of the 4th Michigan Infantry rise through the ranks from subaltern to colonel. A month shy of his twenty-ninth birthday, the slender, dark-haired officer was a graduate of the University of Michigan Law School who had forsaken a lucrative practice in Dexter, Michigan, to answer his country's call. Jeffords had survived the carnage of the Seven Days battles and Fredericksburg, and he shared his comrades' regimental pride. Not long after his promotion to the colonelcy of the 4th Michigan, the unit had received a new set of colors. In accepting the flag, Harrison Jeffords had "pledged himself in decisive terms to be its special defender and guardian." It was a pledge he would redeem at Gettysburg.

Like much of the 5th Corps, Colonel Jacob B. Sweitzer's brigade—which included the 4th Michigan—had been called upon to salvage a Federal line broken by Longstreet's massive assault. As the Confederate onslaught rolled on from south to north, two Southern brigades—General George T. Anderson's Georgians and General Joseph B. Kershaw's South Carolinians—had converged upon a twenty-acre wheatfield on the Rose Farm. Troops of the Federal 3rd Corps had been driven from the field, and the Rebels were forced to give way before the counterattack of Brigadier General John Caldwell's division of the 2nd Corps. As Caldwell's three brigades forged ahead, his right flank lay open, and the general asked for Colonel Sweitzer's support. Colonel Jeffords's 4th Michigan, four hundred strong, now advanced into the trampled wheatfield, into the "whirlpool of death."

With the Michiganders on the right flank, Sweitzer's brigade began pushing forward against Kershaw's South Carolinians but soon encountered ominous signs of a Confederate presence on the wooded crest to their right and rear. As firing from that sector increased, the Michigan men could hear the rattle of tin cups and canteens, and branches breaking before what was plainly a large number of men headed in their direction. "Colonel, I'll be damned," Sweitzer's orderly blurted, "we are faced the wrong way."

In fact an entire Rebel brigade—five Georgia units led by Brigadier General William T. Wofford—was swinging south to

Colonel Harrison H. Jeffords of the 4th Michigan was mortally wounded by a Confederate bayonet thrust while attempting to save his unit's colors in the wheatfield. Like so many Civil War commanders, Jeffords' fate was inextricably bound up with that of his regiment, his state, and his flag.

Photo courtesy Massachusetts Commandery, Military Order of the Loyal Legion, and the U.S. Army Military History Institute

link up with Kershaw and strike the Yankees. Quickly Sweitzer shifted the 62nd Pennsylvania and 4th Michigan to face the threat. But by then the enemy jaws were closing: Anderson resumed his assault on the left, while Kershaw and Wofford hurtled down on the right. "There goes the 2nd Brigade," a staff officer remarked. "We may as well bid it good-bye."

As Sweitzer's line gave way, the soldiers of the 4th Michigan were enveloped in a tide of gray-clad troops, flushed with victory and screaming the Rebel yell. His regimental formation broken into desperate knots of frenzied men, Colonel Jeffords was trying to extricate his unit from the trap when he saw the banner he had vowed to guard and defend, fallen in the wheat with its stricken bearer.

His sword clenched in his hand, Jeffords ran forward to save the colors, followed by a group of officers and soldiers who engaged the Confederates in hand-to-hand battle. Colonel Jeffords cut down the man who had seized the flag but was instantly thrust through the chest by a Rebel bayonet. He fell to his knees.

Lieutenant Michael Vreeland fired his revolver into his colonel's assailants until he was himself shot in the chest and arm and clubbed to the ground with a musket butt. In the few confused seconds of the bloody grapple the precious banner was saved, but Harrison Jeffords and thirty-nine other Michigan men lay dead or dying amidst the bloodied stalks of wheat.

The survivors of Sweitzer's brigade managed to rally behind a stone wall at the edge of the wheatfield, where Union batteries hurled salvos into the oncoming Rebel lines. The Michiganders dragged their dying colonel with them, borne alongside the colors he had given his life to save. But Jeffords' last words were not of the flag; they were "Mother, mother, mother!"

COLLECTION OF JOHN OSCHER

Barksdale's Charge

Battle of Gettysburg, July 2

By 6 p.m. of July 2, the steadily escalating roar of gunfire made it clear to the anxious soldiers of Brigadier General William Barksdale's brigade that they would soon be engaged in battle. From south to north, brigade after brigade, division after division, the units of General Longstreet's corps were punching toward the Yankee lines in a series of trip-hammer blows—a full-scale assault *en echelon* that Robert E. Lee hoped would crush and sweep aside the forces of the Army of the Potomac south of Gettysburg.

As Barksdale awaited the inevitable order to begin his attack, batteries of Federal artillery poured shells upon his waiting ranks. The Yankee guns and their infantry supports held a projecting angle of the Federal line near two peach orchards—one mature and one recently planted—that stood alongside the Emmittsburg Road. The Peach Orchard salient lay in the path of Barksdale's advance, and he was eager to take it.

At forty-one, William Barksdale was a former Mississippi congressman whose stocky build and booming voice had made him a force to be reckoned with in turbulent House debates over the sectional crisis and the South's right to secede from the Union. At a time when congressional discussion often gave way to fisticuffs, Barksdale had been a noted brawler, and he had put his combative nature to good use on the battlefield. His four Mississippi regiments had won renown for their stubborn defense of Fredericksburg in the battles of December 1862 and May 1863, and they would soon prove that they were equally determined in the attack.

Barksdale's units, fifteen hundred strong, were positioned with the 18th Mississippi on the left, the 21st on the right, and the 13th and 17th in the center of the brigade line. "All were well shod and efficiently clothed," noted Lieutenant Colonel Arthur Fremantle, the British observer who accompanied Lee's Army. "The knapsacks of the men still bear the names of the Massachusetts, Vermont, New Jersey, or other regiments to which they originally belonged." These packs, issued to Barksdale's men in June, had been confiscated from Yankee prisoners captured in the battles of Second Manassas and Chancellorsville.

The brigades of Joseph Kershaw and Paul Semmes were well under way in their advance on Barksdale's right, when one of division commander Lafayette McLaws's staff officers finally brought word for the Mississippian to commence his assault. From atop his restless steed, Barksdale exhorted his troops, "Attention, Mississippians! Battalions, Forward!" And with the high-pitched scream of the Rebel yell, the four regiments rose up, emerged from the cover of Pitzer's Woods, and headed for the enemy position on the Emmittsburg Road. Barksdale rode at their head, waving his hat, the white hair that fringed his bald crown blowing in the wind.

The guns of Lieutenant John K. Bucklyn's Battery B, 1st Rhode Island Light Artillery, continued to fire on Barksdale's men as they brushed aside a Union skirmish line. The Peach Orchard salient was defended by Brigadier General Charles Graham's brigade—part of the 3rd Corps that had been shifted forward to the exposed position by corps commander Daniel E. Sickles—and Graham's defenders were already hard-pressed when the new threat materialized. As Barksdale's formations neared the Sherfy farmhouse and barn that lay just west of the Emmittsburg Road, the 114th Pennsylvania was ordered across the road to meet Barksdale head-on. It was a des-

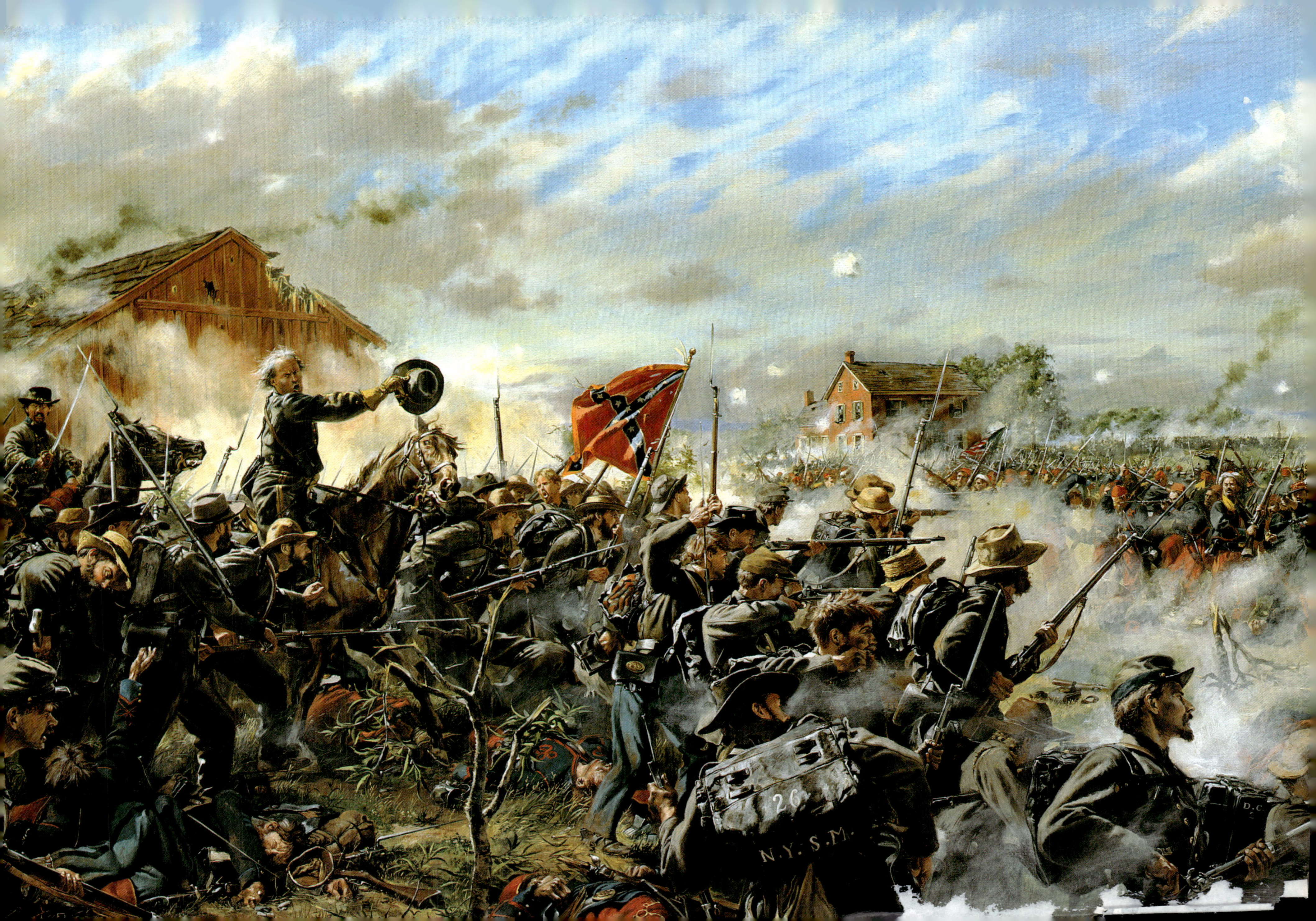
N.Y.S.M.

perate maneuver but one that had to be made if the battered Union artillery was to be saved from capture.

The 114th Pennsylvania was a Zouave outfit, one of several units in the Army of the Potomac that sported the red trousers, short jacket, and tasseled fez adapted from their French counterparts. Founded by an Irish-born Philadelphia lawyer named Charles Collis, at Gettysburg "Collis's Zouaves" were commanded by Lieutenant Colonel Frederick Cavada, the son of a Cuban father and American mother. Early in the battle Cavada collapsed with exhaustion and heat prostration, and it fell to senior regimental Captain Edward R. Bowen, all of twenty-three years old, to lead the three hundred Zouaves into the teeth of Barksdale's advance.

Scrambling over the fences that lined the road, Bowen's Zouaves sprinted through the yard of the Sherfy farm, formed line of battle, and opened a point-blank fire on the charging Mississippians. The 68th Pennsylvania, which had moved into support on Captain Bowen's left, was soon brushed aside, and when Barksdale personally led the 13th and 17th Mississippi against the Zouaves' front, the pressure was too great to withstand.

Spurred on by Barksdale's shouted command, "Forward, men, forward!" the flaming Rebel line shoved the 114th Pennsylvania back to the road, and Bucklyn's threatened guns were frantically limbered up and galloped away from their position. As the Zouaves crumbled, the 18th Mississippi on Barksdale's left plowed into the 57th and 105th Pennsylvania, which also gave way. Fired with victory, Barksdale's brigade split into two wings. The three left-hand regiments swung northward, herding the shattered Yankee formations up the Emmitsburg Road, while the 21st Mississippi forged ahead through the Peach Orchard, smashing a succession of Federal units.

The fight at the Sherfy house and Peach Orchard was only the beginning of Barksdale's epic assault. In the hours of combat that remained, hundreds of Mississippians and the stalwart general who led them would fall. But their legacy of valor remains one of the shining glories of the Army of Northern Virginia.

---

*C*lad *in typical Zouave fashion with loose pleated trousers, short jacket, and blue sash, this soldier of the 114th Pennsylvania, or "Collis's Zouaves" wears a turban wrapped about his tasseled fez. Originally organized as a company called the "Zouaves d'Afrique," the 114th was readily distinguished from other Northern Zouave units by the blue cuffs on their jackets.*

Possessed of a proud war record, in late 1863 the 114th Pennsylvania was honored with an assignment as Headquarters Guard of the Army of the Potomac. Their colorful garb and ready availability to visiting photographers made the 114th the Civil War's most photographed Zouave outfit. PHOTO COURTESY DAN MILLER

114th Pennsylvania Volunteer Infantry

"Collis's Zouaves"

Though largely attired in a uniform closely resembling that of their French counterparts, like many Civil War Zouave units the soldiers of the 114th Pennsylvania wore less baggy trousers than the French Zouaves. These brick red pants in fact more closely resembled those worn by the French Chasseurs, another branch of the light infantry arm of service.

Most Zouave regiments wore turbans—wrapped about the fez—and white gloves for formal occasions like guard mount and dress parade, although photographs and drawings reveal that some men also wore the turban into combat. The white canvas leggings were often covered with leather greaves, called *jambiéres.*

Retreat by Recoil

Battle of Gettysburg, July 2

As Longstreet's great assault rolled on, crushing through Sickles's 3rd Corps, all along the embattled Federal line units hastened to repel the attack. When General Barksdale's Mississippians pierced the Peach Orchard salient and thrust eastward toward the lower reaches of Cemetery Ridge, the gunners of Captain John Bigelow's 9th Massachusetts battery were called upon to check the ever-widening breach with the firepower of their six bronze smooth-bore Napoleons. The Baystaters—104 officers and men—had only recently joined the Army of the Potomac's Artillery Reserve from a year of garrison duty in the defenses of Washington, but on July 2, 1863, Bigelow's battery would write one of the most stirring chapters in the annals of Civil War artillery.

Shortly after 4 P.M. the 9th Massachusetts was dispatched in company with another battery from a position behind the Federal line toward the fighting that was intensifying along the Emmitsburg Road. After a brief halt near the Abraham Trostle farm, Captain Bigelow's drivers lashed their horses, and the six Napoleons dashed forward to the Wheatfield Road, just east of the Peach Orchard. Here the battery unlimbered and came into action alongside other Federal batteries that were hammering Longstreet's advancing lines.

When Barksdale's charge broke through the Federal infantry at the Peach Orchard, Bigelow's cannon continued to blaze until their brigade commander, Lieutenant Colonel Freeman McGilvery, ordered the captain to abandon the position lest his battery be overrun. But the movement could not be easily executed. A line of skirmishers from Kershaw's South Carolina brigade was closing in from the south, and the line of battle of Barksdale's 21st Mississippi from the west. In order to maintain his fire, Bigelow gave the order to "retire by prolonge." Ropes were uncoiled from each of the Napoleons and hooked to the limbers; as the horses pulled the guns rearward, the crews were able to load and fire, the recoil hurling the guns backward as the powder-streaked gunners went through the rapid, choreographed motions of loading and firing.

With the bullets of Kershaw's skirmishers tearing past their ears, the Massachusetts artillerymen managed to cover some four hundred yards, cannon firing all the while, until they gained a rocky corner of Trostle's pasture across from the farmhouse and barn. Having successfully held the Confederates at bay, Bigelow ordered his guns limbered up and withdrawn. But at that moment Lieutenant Colonel McGilvery again galloped on the scene and ordered the captain to stand his ground: "Hold your position at all hazards, and sacrifice your battery, if need be." With no infantry on hand, the 9th Massachusetts battery were the only Federals remaining between the Confederates and Cemetery Ridge.

As the Southern troops came nearer, Bigelow's guns were pressed back into an angle of the pasture that was enclosed by stone walls, with only one narrow opening into the Trostle lane. As the caissons started to the rear, the cannon were deployed in a semicircle, and

---

In addition to a wealth of primary accounts, Don Troiani was able to draw on the many detailed wartime sketches by bugler Charles Reed, whose bravery at Gettysburg won him the Medal of Honor.

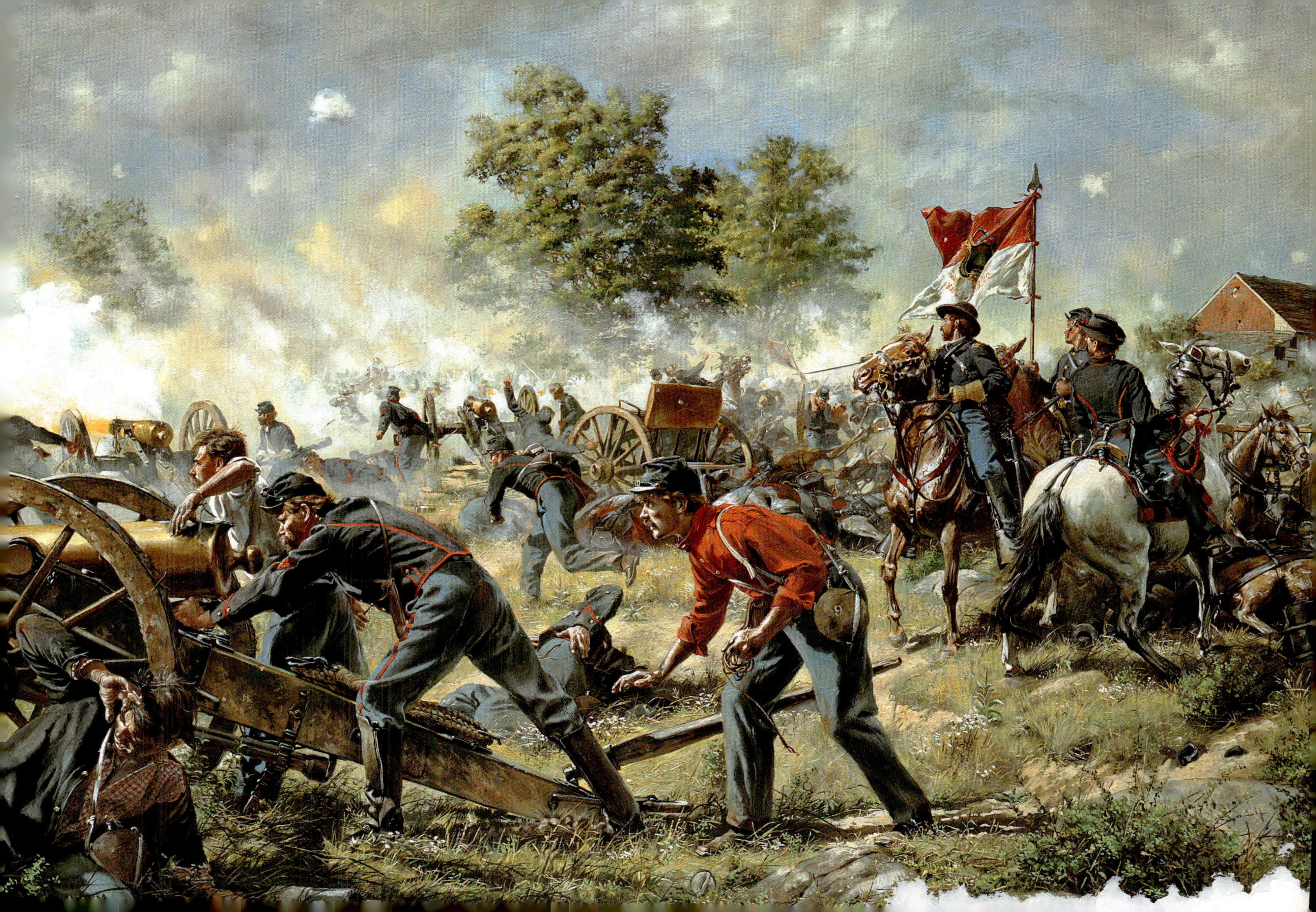

with ammunition piled alongside each gun, the desperate fight continued. Second Lieutenant Richard S. Milton's two-gun section began firing shotgunlike blasts of canister at Kershaw's skirmishers, while the sections of First Lieutenant Christopher Erickson and Second Lieutenant Alexander H. Whitaker prepared to meet a line of enemy troops that was advancing under the cover of a knoll only fifty yards to their front. These Confederates were Colonel Benjamin G. Humphreys's 21st Mississippi, and as the gray formation crested the rise, the four Napoleons facing them switched from solid shot to canister.

As the Mississippians broke into a charge, Erickson and Whitaker ordered their gunners to fire double-shotted canister. "The enemy crowded to the very muzzles," Bigelow recalled, "but were blown away." But the Confederates, "yelling like demons," were taking an ever-increasing toll of gunners, and most of the battery's eighty-eight horses were down. Bigelow shouted at Lieutenant Milton to pull his section out of the bullet-swept cul-de-sac, break a way through the wall, and make his escape. As the two guns started for the rear, the 21st Mississippi re-formed and surged down upon the four remaining cannon.

Lieutenant Erickson, a twenty-eight-year-old Norwegian, had so few men left to

This photograph, presented by Captain Bigelow to a fellow veteran of his battery, shows at center the monument erected to mark the first position of the 9th Massachusetts battery on Wheatfield Road.

At the Trostle Farm, visible in the background, the survivors of Bigelow's battery erected a second monument (lower right) at the scene of their last stand. PHOTO COURTESY DON TROIANI COLLECTION

work the guns that his section was virtually out of action. Wounded and bleeding from the mouth, Erickson spurred his horse over to Lieutenant Whitaker but was knocked from the saddle by six bullets and killed. Then the Mississippians stormed into the battery.

Captain Bigelow was also struck in the side and hand by the fire of Kershaw's South Carolinians, who had continued forward when Milton's section pulled out. The captain's faithful bugler, Charles Reed, had attempted to block the enemy fire by interposing his horse between the Rebels and his commander, but now all he could do was help the wounded Bigelow make his escape. Only four rounds of canister remained, and when the captain saw Confederate soldiers "standing on the limber chests and firing at the gunners," he gave the command, "Cease firing, and get back to your lines as best you can."

Abandoning their guns, the survivors of the 9th Massachusetts scattered toward Cemetery Ridge, where a hastily established line of cannon and infantry supports had managed to take position, thanks to the thirty minutes purchased in blood by Bigelow's gallant battery. At the Trostle farm a tangled wreck of smashed limbers, slain horses, and fallen gunners lay about the four abandoned cannon, grim testimony of the heroic stand.

This pendulum hausse and case was used by artillerymen to accurately sight their piece. Weighted on the bottom and mounted on a gimbals, it always hung true and thus could compensate for uneven ground that made it difficult to place the sight in an absolute vertical position. PHOTO COURTESY DON TROIANI COLLECTION

1st Minnesota Volunteer Infantry

Battle of Gettysburg, July 2

THE BATTLE OF GETTYSBURG WITNESSED countless acts of sacrificial gallantry. Soldiers of both armies mastered their fears and displayed almost superhuman bravery for the sake of ideals they cherished more than life itself. Gettysburg offered no more powerful example of this transcendent heroism than the charge of the 1st Minnesota Volunteer Infantry on the late afternoon and early evening of July 2, 1863.

Proud veterans of some of the war's bloodiest battles—at First Bull Run, the Seven Days, and Antietam—the tough westerners had earned a matchless reputation as one of the finest outfits in Hancock's 2nd Corps. Many men had fallen to bullets and disease since the 1st Minnesota departed Fort Snelling in the spring of 1861, and the unit numbered fewer than four hundred men as they commenced the grueling march to Gettysburg. Their colonel, thirty-three-year-old William Colvill, Jr., was a tall, barrel-chested former newspaper editor who had risen from a captaincy to regimental command. In the course of the march Colvill had suffered the ire of General Hancock's stern chief of staff, Colonel Charles Morgan, for allowing some of his soldiers to cross the Monocacy River on logs and planks rather than splash across as instructed. At Morgan's order, brigade commander William Harrow had temporarily placed Colvill under arrest.

By the summer of 1863 Colvill and his men were used to such arbitrary acts of military martinetism. It was part of what it meant to be a soldier, and there was no more soldierly corps in the Army of the Potomac than that commanded by "Hancock the Superb."

By 5 P.M. on the afternoon of July 2, the tide of battle was rolling relentlessly toward Cemetery Ridge, the 2nd Corps, and the 1st Minnesota. Initially in reserve, supporting batteries of artillery posted along the southern reaches of the low elevation, the advance and subsequent collapse of Sickles's 3rd Corps caused Hancock's troops to be fed piecemeal into the maelstrom, to check Longstreet's juggernaut. Colvill's 1st Minnesota found itself occupying a position that had earlier been held by General John Caldwell's entire division. To make matters worse, two of the Minnesota companies had been detached, leaving only 262 men in line to meet the threat.

Though the Napoleon guns of Lieutenant Evan Thomas's Battery C, 4th U.S. Artillery, were blazing, General R. H. Anderson's division was rolling steadily forward, shoving aside the remnants of the 3rd Corps. "The stragglers came rushing through the lines," Minnesotan Alfred Carpenter noted, "whom we in vain tried to stop and at last gave it up entirely, believing they were more injury than help to us." On the Rebels came, Brigadier General Cadmus M. Wilcox's Alabamians in the vanguard, pushing across the brushy swale of a dry streambed and heading for the strategic crest of Cemetery Ridge.

As he did so often that crisis-filled day, General Hancock took personal charge of the Federal defense. Accompanied by a single aide, the stalwart corps commander took in the situation at a glance. As he later confessed, "I saw that in some way five minutes must be gained or we were lost." Checking his horse alongside Colonel Colvill's line, Hancock exclaimed, "My God, are these all the men we have here? What regiment is this?"

"First Minnesota," Colvill responded.

Hancock pointed to the oncoming Confederate battle flags and snapped, "Advance, colonel, and take those colors!"

Colvill called his men to attention and ordered them forward. Muskets carried at right shoulder shift, with bayonets fixed, the slender line guided on the colors and started down the gentle slope at the double-quick. Alfred Carpenter remembered, "Comrade after comrade dropped from the ranks; but on the line went. No one took a second look at his fallen companion. We had no time to weep."

As the ever-thinning line neared the woody swale and the blazing Rebel ranks, Colvill—afoot and leading the advance in person—ordered his men to halt and fire. At a distance of thirty yards, the volley felled dozens of the enemy. Then Colvill shouted the command to charge. Down came the muskets of the front rank, flashing with steel, and the Minnesotans plowed into Wilcox's first line, hurling it back on those that followed. "I never saw cooler work done on either side," Colvill claimed, "and the destruction was awful."

As the deadly, close-range fight swirled through the brush and across the ravine, Colvill was twice wounded, and his second in command was hit six times. Captain Nathan Messick was in command when the forty-seven survivors pulled back to their starting point, having bought Hancock and the Union those precious five minutes and then sometime paid for in the blood of more than two thirds of those who made the charge.

COLLECTION OF U.S. ARMY NATIONAL GUARD BUREAU

Band of Brothers

Culp's Hill, Battle of Gettysburg, July 3

When the Army of Northern Virginia crossed the Potomac River into Maryland in the summer of 1863, no troops were more jubilant or more hopeful of success than the four hundred men of the 1st Maryland Battalion. Their loyalty to the South had made them exiles; their loved ones were behind enemy lines, their state under the heel of Yankee occupiers. But on June 18, with General Richard Ewell's corps wading the Potomac at Boteler's Ford, the sons of the Old Line State were once again on native soil.

The Marylanders were some of the finest soldiers in Lee's army—well drilled, well uniformed, and proud of their battle honors. Hard fighting at Manassas, in the Shenandoah Valley, and through the Seven Days had thinned their ranks and seen their unit nearly disbanded. Of necessity their regiment had been reorganized as a five-company battalion. But the sufferings of the past was forgotten in the joy of the moment.

Major William W. Goldsborough noted that the men of the battalion "could not restrain their feelings, and many were moved to tears, whilst others acted as though they had lost their reason." Quartermaster John E. Howard claimed their habitually reserved brigade commander, Brigadier General George H. "Maryland" Steuart, was so overjoyed he "turned seventeen double somersaults before he ceased, and then stood on his head for five minutes, all the while whistling 'Maryland, My Maryland.'"

With the rest of Ewell's corps the Marylanders pushed on into Pennsylvania, north to Carlisle, and threatened the state capital at Harrisburg before the escalating conflict at Gettysburg called them southward. Marching hard, they passed the carnage of battle and took position below Culp's Hill, on the left of the Confederate line. On the evening of July 2, Ewell's belated and futile assaults on the fortified Yankee lines at Culp's Hill claimed a number of Marylanders, among them the battalion commander, Lieutenant Colonel James R. Herbert. With Herbert wounded, Major Goldsborough took charge of the 1st Maryland and readied for battle.

On the morning of July 3 Major General Edward Johnson launched his division in another assault on Culp's Hill. Twice the attacks were hurled back with severe loss, but Johnson determined to try again, this time aiming his assault on the southern flank of the wooded slope. As General Steuart's brigade prepared to charge across a clearing known as Pardee's Field, with the Marylanders shifting into position on the right of the line, Major Goldsborough told a staff officer, "It is nothing less than murder to send men into that slaughter-pen." Placing senior Captain William H. Murray in charge of the right wing, Goldsborough took charge of the left. As the major walked along his line, he gazed into the grim, determined faces of his valiant battalion. "It was a dreadful moment," Goldsborough remembered, "the moment before the order was to be given that would usher so many souls into eternity."

Shortly after 10 A.M., Steuart's brigade started forward, with General Junius Daniel's North Carolinians in support. Crossing a stone wall, they had barely entered Pardee's Field when the Yankee line erupted in flame and men toppled from the ranks by the dozen. With arms at a right shoulder shift, and General Steuart leading in person, the Marylanders

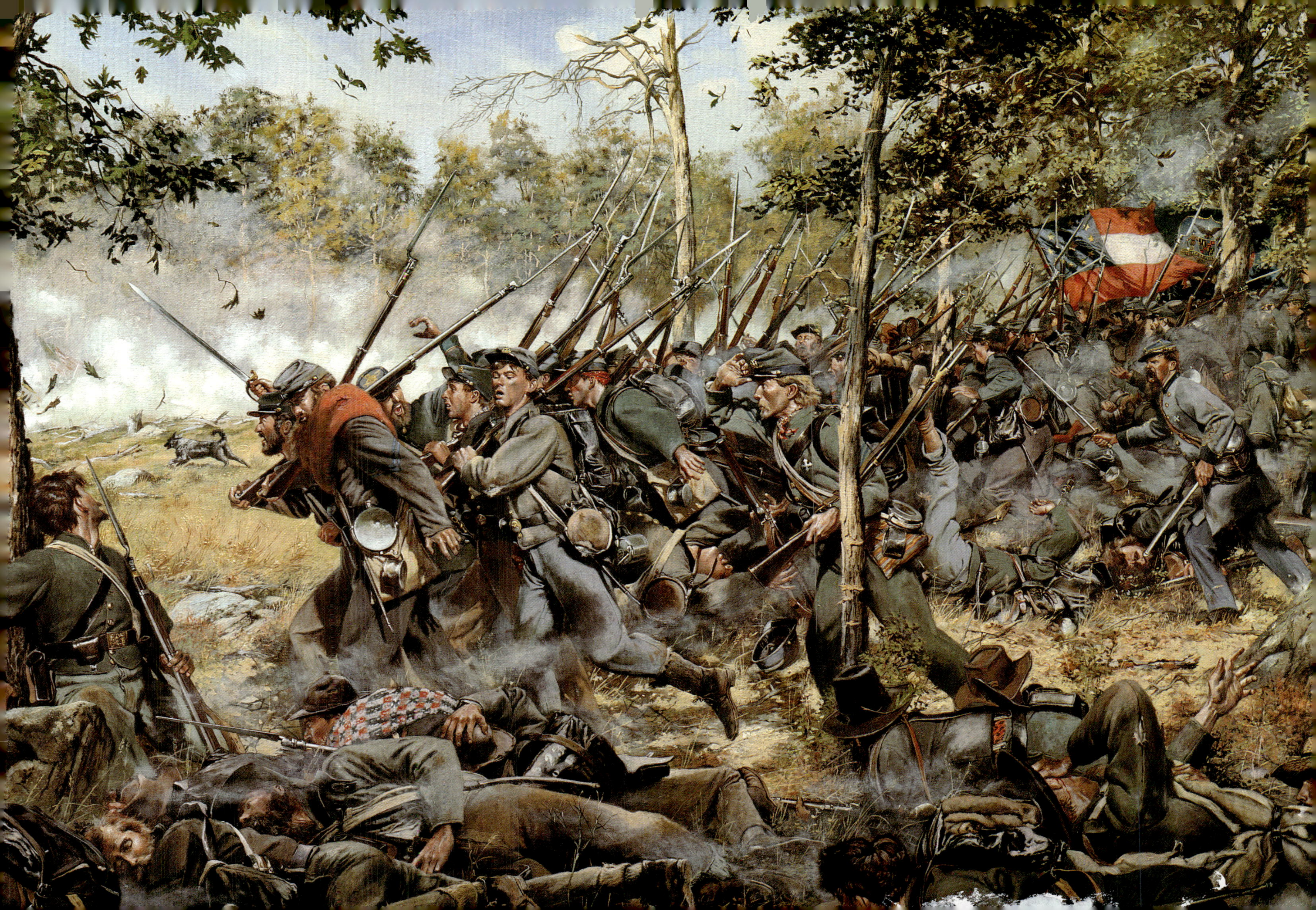

kept moving, passing over and hurling contempt upon the men of the 37th Virginia who had fallen prone and refused to advance further into the inferno.

On the little band of brothers pushed, closing the gaps, dressing the line, their pace breaking into a run as they neared the Union breastworks. Captain Murray was killed, Major Goldsborough wounded, and even the battalion mascot—a small mongrel dog—was shot down with his human comrades in the forefront of the charge. "He licked someone's hand," Federal General Thomas L. Kane recalled, "after he was perfectly riddled."

Private David R. Howard was still on his feet, sprinting for the Federal earthworks, when he glanced to his right and "saw a sight which was fearful to behold. It appeared to me as if the whole of my company was being swept away." Moments later, a Yankee bullet smashed one of his legs and brought him to the ground.

With Captain John W. Torsch in command, the survivors of the 1st Maryland Battalion fell back to the cover of the woods and assessed their losses. Tears streaming down his face, General Steuart exclaimed, "My poor boys! My poor boys!"

The killing did not end with the retreat. "It is a hard thing to say," stated the wounded Private David Howard, "but I am convinced the Federals deliberately shot at us while we lay there helpless on the field." Assailed by the groans of dying comrades and the thud of enemy bullets into the fallen soldiers, Howard straightened himself out, folded his arms over his chest, "and waited for my time to come." Another stricken Marylander reloaded his musket, placed the weapon to his head and snarled at the startled Yankees, "I will die before you make me a prisoner!" Then he depressed the trigger with his ramrod.

The casualties sustained by the 1st Maryland amounted to nearly 50 percent of their number: 56 killed, 118 wounded, and 15 missing. On a day of misfortune for the Confederacy, the sacrifice of the gallant Marylanders would stand as one of the greatest tragedies.

1st and 2nd Maryland Infantry, C.S.A.

Though their uniforms were often as dirty and worn as the other hard-marching and undersupplied troops of the Army of Northern Virginia, the men of the 1st Maryland and their successor battalion—later known as the 2nd Maryland Infantry—were noted for their attention to appearance and soldierly bearing. A New York Zouave who surveyed a batch of Confederate prisoners taken in the Antietam campaign commented that the Marylanders "were noticeable at that early stage of the war, as the only organization we saw that wore the Confederate gray, all other troops having assumed a sort of revised uniform of homespun butternut."

Perhaps one explanation for the Marylanders' reputation for uniformity was the fact that unlike most other Confederate soldiers, the men of the Old Line State generally favored the rakish cap or kepi over the more common slouch hat. "They had the remains of fancy clothes on," Union Colonel Theodore Lyman noted of a group of Maryland prisoners in August 1864, "including little kepis, half grey and half sky-blue." The Marylanders were also fortunate to have a cadre of civilian benefactors who exerted themselves to obtain replacement uniforms from North Carolina, or even smuggle clothing through Yankee lines.

The survivors of Gettysburg went on to serve through the bloody battles of 1864 as the 2nd Maryland Infantry, and by autumn their number was reduced to a mere one hundred effectives. Overrun on April 2, 1865, by the massive Federal assault on Petersburg, those who managed to cut their way out battled on, thin and exhausted but unwilling to give up the cause. Only sixty-three men, commanded by Captain John W. Torsch, were left to surrender with Lee.

PRIVATE COLLECTION

THE HIGH WATER MARK

Battle of Gettysburg, July 3

AFTER TWO DAYS OF TERRIBLE COMBAT THE battle of Gettysburg—and the fate of the divided Union—had yet to be resolved. Having determined to break the Federal line on Cemetery Ridge, Robert E. Lee placed that heavy responsibility in the hands of his "Old War Horse," General James Longstreet. Doubting the wisdom of a full-scale assault on the very center of the Union line, Longstreet nonetheless readied the divisions of James Pettigrew, Isaac Trimble, and George Pickett for the task. The infantry would step off in the wake of a massive artillery bombardment, which every Confederate hoped would damage the enemy ranks so that the Yankees would be unable to stave off the Southern juggernaut.

For nearly two hours the big guns thundered, and the earth trembled under the concentrated fire of the Confederate batteries. The Union batteries responded, splintering the trees that sheltered the waiting Rebel infantry and mangling scores of men who hugged the ground in anticipation of the still greater carnage to come.

Flamboyant Major General George E. Pickett, whose Virginia troops had been the last of Longstreet's corps to arrive on the field, formed his division in two lines. The brigades of Brigadier Generals Richard Garnett and James Kemper would lead the advance, with Brigadier General Lewis A. Armistead's five regiments going forward in the second wave. As the artillery fire began to slacken, Pickett ordered his men to their feet, and the disciplined ranks emerged from the cover of the woods and formed line of battle. With parade-like precision, the Virginians dressed their lines, guiding on the red battle flags that marked each unit's center.

At forty-six, Lewis Armistead was a grizzled veteran of the Regular Army who had lost two wives during his arduous prewar service on the western frontier. Born in North Carolina and reared in Virginia, he was heir to a proud military heritage: His uncle had commanded Fort McHenry and defended the "Star Spangled Banner" from a British naval assault in the War of 1812. Armistead walked along the line, exhorting his troops to fight for their families and their native state, then led his Virginians forward.

Soon the Yankee artillery began to tear bloody gaps in the Confederate formations, but the survivors closed ranks and pushed on across the mile-wide expanse that separated them from the low stone wall and copse of trees that marked the enemy position. As Garnett's and Kemper's men crossed the stout rail fences that lay astride the Emmitsburg Road and filed past the brick farmhouse and wooden barn of the Codori farm, they were met with a sheet of flame—the deadly volleys of the Union 2nd Corps, commanded by Armistead's old army friend, Major General Winfield Scott Hancock.

With the leading brigades torn and broken before him, Armistead led his men onward, jabbing his hat onto the tip of his sword and holding it aloft as a beacon on which to guide. "They caught his fire and enthusiasm," one officer noted, "and then and there they resolved to follow that heroic leader until the enemy's bullets stopped them." Armistead shoved his way through the jostling crowd of soldiers that staggered before the holocaust of flame that fringed a projecting angle of the stone wall. "Come on boys!" he shouted, "Give them the cold steel! Who will follow me?" and the screaming mob of gray-clad troops surged forward, to the wall.

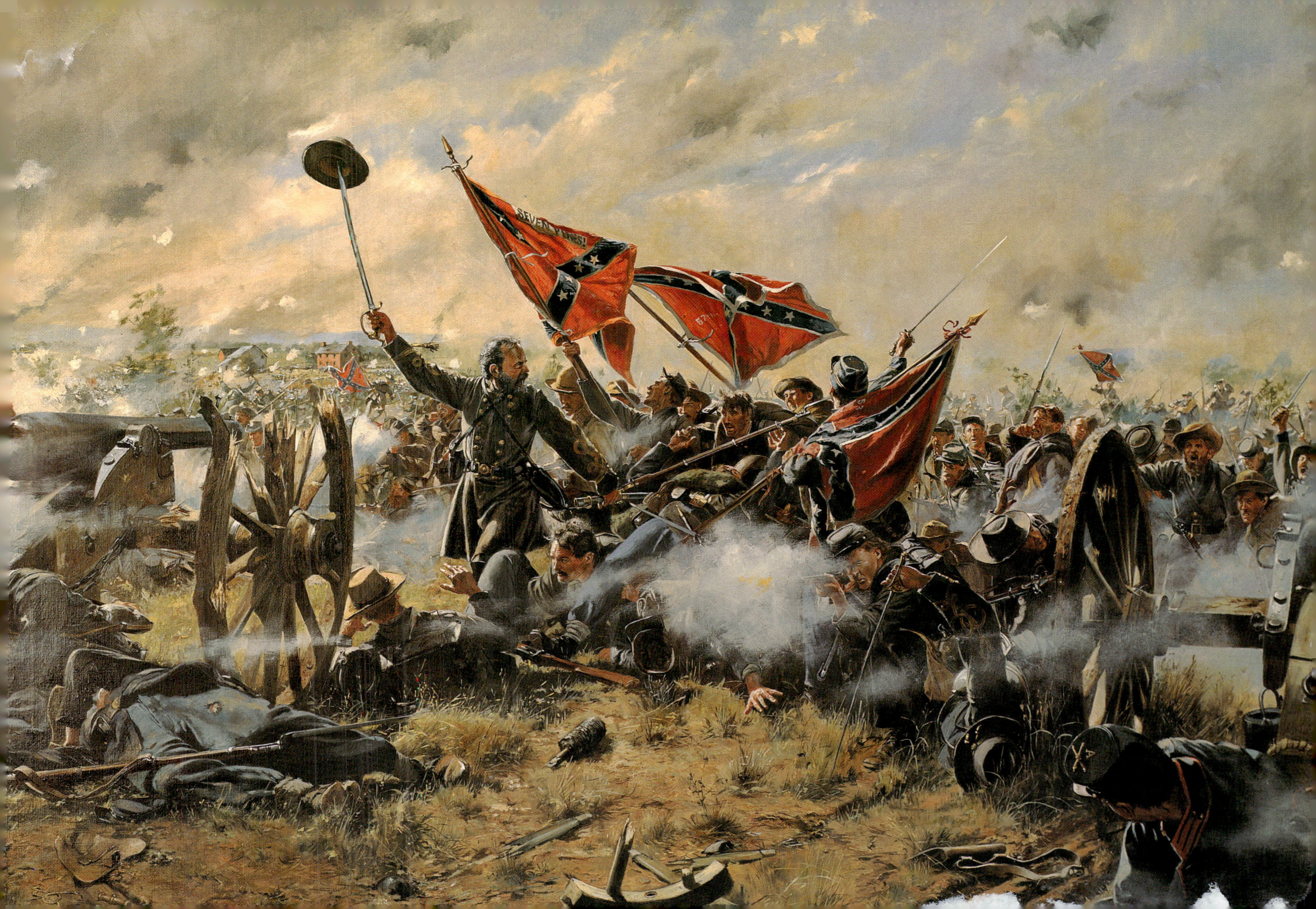
SEVEN

Armistead crossed the wall and leaped amongst the carnage-strewn wreckage of Battery A, 4th U.S. Artillery. The Federal officer in command of these guns, Lieutenant Alonzo Cushing, had been cut down with his third and fatal wound, and First Sergeant Frederick Fuger had loosed a last deadly salvo of canister before the surviving gunners bolted for the rear. A gap opened, and into it poured the gallant warriors of the Southern Confederacy, trampling over the bloodstained dead and flailing wounded. The flags of the 14th, 57th, and

---

Believed to be a rare portrait of Lewis Armistead in civilian garb, this carte-de-visite *photograph dates to the prewar years when he served as captain and brevet major in the 6th U.S. Infantry. Distinguished for gallantry in the Mexican War, Armistead had attended West Point but was forced to resign in 1836— allegedly for breaking a plate over the head of his classmate, future Confederate General Jubal A. Early.*

When the Civil War began, Armistead was on duty in California, where his close friend, Captain Winfield Scott Hancock, was also stationed. When the two comrades parted, Armistead presented Hancock with a major's uniform and presented Hancock's wife, Almira, with a prayer book, to be sent to his family in the event of his death.

As Armistead lay dying from the bullets of Hancock's 2nd Corps, he again remembered his friend, who was himself severely wounded while contesting Pickett's Charge. According to General Hancock's aide, Captain Henry Bingham, Armistead said, "Tell General Hancock that I have done him and you all an injury which I shall regret as long as I live." While some took this to be a recantation of the Confederacy, the words most likely stemmed from his concern for a friend he would never meet again. PHOTO COURTESY BILL TURNER AND LARRY JONES

53rd Virginia clustered about the intrepid Armistead, with the colors of the 28th and 56th Virginia close behind. At least one of the precious banners had fallen ten times, only to be raised again, and carried on.

Some 150 soldiers followed General Armistead and Lieutenant Colonel Rawley Martin of the 53rd Virginia into the angle, and the 71st Pennsylvania Regiment gave way before them. The right flank of the 69th Pennsylvania was submerged in a tide of gray, and the Confederates pushed on through a cross fire from the survivors of the 69th to their right and the 72nd Pennsylvania to their front.

While Union Brigadier General Alexander Webb struggled to hold his Philadelphia Brigade to their duty, Federal reinforcements came rushing from elsewhere along the line to bolster the embattled Pennsylvanians.

As Lewis Armistead placed his hand on one of Cushing's abandoned guns, he was cut down by Yankee bullets. Within minutes all who had followed the general into the angle were killed or captured. The high-water mark of the Confederacy had crested, and two thirds of Armistead's men had been left behind in its wake.

Exhausted and bleeding beside the cannon, Armistead gave the Masonic sign of distress and was recognized by fellow members of the order, who came to his aide. Captain Henry Bingham, one of General Hancock's aides, arrived and though bleeding from a wound to his head, did what he could to succor the stricken officer. As jubilant Federal soldiers gathered the fallen banners of Armistead's brigade, the general who had given his all for a doomed cause was carried to an improvised field hospital. There, two days later, Lewis Armistead succumbed to his wounds.

"Give Them Cold Steel, Boys"

Battle of Gettysburg, July 3

At the climax of Pickett's Charge, with hat jammed onto his sword and shouting, "Give them cold steel!" General Lewis Armistead led a determined band of Virginians across the stone wall and into immortality. With Lieutenant Colonel Rawley Martin of the 53rd Virginia at his elbow, Armistead pushed through the wreck of Cushing's battery, where he and virtually all of his followers were shot down or captured.

Don Troiani recalls this earlier version of "The High Water Mark" as "one of the most difficult paintings from a historical perspective I've ever undertaken. Recreating the fence lines, trees, fences and other features in the background was daunting, to say the least. I could have obscured everything with smoke, but that would have been the easy way out."

Research revealed that the original stone wall on Cemetery Ridge was three to five feet high, a good two feet taller than it is today.

COLLECTION OF JOHN OSCHER

Private, 72nd Pennsylvania Volunteer Infantry

Baxter's Fire Zouaves

Organized in the summer of 1861 by Colonel DeWitt Clinton Baxter, the 72nd Pennsylvania drew its volunteers from the ranks of the Philadelphia Fire Department. Clad in a modified version of the popular Zouave uniform, "Baxter's Fire Zouaves" served with credit on the Peninsula and at the battle of Antietam, where they suffered heavy losses in the fight for the West Woods.

In June 1863 the 72nd received new Zouave garb and a month later found themselves at the epicenter of the fight for Cemetery Ridge on the second and third days of the battle of Gettysburg. Attached to General Alexander Webb's Philadelphia Brigade of the 2nd Corps, the Fire Zouaves played an important, if somewhat controversial, role in the defense of the famed angle. Though they failed to immediately counterattack Armistead's breakthrough, their casualties—192 of 458 men engaged at Gettysburg—testified to their fighting ability.

PRIVATE COLLECTION

It is interesting to note that the ranks of Baxter's Fire Zouaves included both the father and uncle of comedian W. C. Fields. Fields's uncle was killed on July 2, 1863, and is buried in the Gettysburg National Cemetery.

First Sergeant, 13th Pennsylvania Reserves

The 13th Pennsylvania Reserves, also known as the 42nd Pennsylvania Infantry, was one of several wartime units whose members were selected for their skilled marksmanship. Emulating the European practice of raising detachments of jaegers, or riflemen, Philadelphia attorney Thomas L. Kane recruited a cadre of hardy outdoorsmen who pinned bucktails on their forage caps to symbolize their status as crack shots. Initially organized in two battalions, by September 1862 the seasoned veterans were reunited as a regiment and armed with the double-set trigger Sharps Model 1859 rifle—a weapon that suited their status as elite sharpshooters.

Attached with other regiments of the Pennsylvania Reserves to the Army of the Potomac's 5th Corps, the Bucktails entered the Gettysburg campaign 349 strong. Their commanding officer, twenty-three-year-old Colonel Charles Frederick Taylor, had been captured and exchanged earlier in the war, and was eager to display his unit's prowess in the defense of their native state.

Advancing with their brigade late on the afternoon of July 2, the Bucktails waged a deadly firefight in the woods bordering the famous wheatfield. Pushing forward to encourage his men, Colonel Taylor was cut down by Rebel fire, but as night fell the regiment still held their ground. The next day, the 13th Reserves launched an attack that netted two hundred prisoners and the flag of the 15th Georgia, a deed that won a Medal of Honor for Sergeant James Thompson and another accolade for the famed Pennsylvania Bucktails.

A Confederate Officer with His Men

When British military observer Colonel Garnet Wolseley noted the Confederate soldiers' "unmistakable look of conscious strength," he saw the fruition of their commanders' leadership. Even Federal officers like General Meade's aide, Lieutenant Colonel Theodore Lyman, commented on the inherent dignity and "superior bearing" of his Southern counterparts. "They have a slight reserve and an absence of all flippancy," Lyman wrote, "on the whole an earnestness of manner, which is very becoming to them."

With the Confederacy fighting for its very existence, it is perhaps not surprising that Southern officers would manifest "an earnestness of manner." But the fearless gallantry and intrepid deeds of the Confederate soldier owed much to the inspiration of the men who led them into battle.

10th New York Volunteer Infantry

"National Zouaves"

One of the best known Federal Zouave units was the 10th New York, which had its origins in a prewar organization called the National Zouaves. Mustered for two-year service in the first weeks of the war, the 10th New York was stationed at Fortress Monroe on the Virginia Peninsula before joining McClellan's Army of the Potomac. Temporarily deprived of their worn-out Zouave garb, the 10th was bloodied in the fight at Gaines's Mill and lost 133 men in the disastrous battle of Second Manassas, where the regimental colors were captured by the 18th Georgia.

Following the battle of Antietam the National Zouaves were transferred from the 5th to the 2nd Corps, with which they served in the hopeless assault on Marye's Heights at Fredericksburg. At the conclusion of their two-year term of service, the 10th New York was reorganized as a veteran battalion, and wearing their distinctive version of the Zouave uniform fought bravely to the end of the war.

The 10th New York was noted not only for their colorful garb but for the fact that the unit contained an active branch of the Masonic fraternity, the National Zouave Lodge. "Here the beautiful tenets of our institution tempered the rough and rugged life of the soldier," Zouave Charles Ludwig wrote, "and nerved his heart for the dangers and trials in the path before him." Captain Salmon Winchester, master of the Zouave Lodge, was killed in action at the battle of Fredericksburg.

COLLECTION OF WILLIAM RODEN

Union Drummer

U.S. Army regulations specified that each company of infantry be allotted two musicians—a drummer and a fifer—to be "instructed by the drum-major or principal musician." When on the march, or at drills and dress parades, "All the musicians are united in a body." During the Civil War the Old Army habit of enlisting boys under eighteen to serve as musicians continued, though it was required that the underage recruits obtain the permission of a parent or guardian.

Just as the soldiers in the ranks had to master an often bewildering litany of commands and maneuvers, so the musicians had to learn the dozens of calls that punctuated the daily military schedule. One Regular Army veteran recalled, "I watched the boys practicing and noted how difficult it seemed to be for some to hold the drum-sticks properly and beat the first exercise, called 'Mammy-Daddy,' without hitting the rim of the drum as often as the drum-head, which would bring down upon them a reprimand from the instructor, or in some cases a rap across the knuckles for some persistently awkward boy."

By late 1863 the drummers, like their infantry comrades, were veterans, and knew their business. As the regiment formed for battle, the musicians who had led the march prepared for another and far grimmer duty. They would serve as stretcher bearers and hospital orderlies, assisting the regimental surgeons in the desperate task of saving the torn and mangled wounded.

Rebel Yell

One Southern veteran called it "that do-or-die expression, that maniacal maelstrom of sound; that penetrating, rasping, shrieking, blood-curdling noise that could be heard for miles on earth and whose volumes reached the heavens. . . ." It was the famous "Rebel Yell," that high-pitched Southern battle cry that could send shivers down the spine of even the most hardened veteran in Federal blue.

Invariably let loose amidst the crash and roar of battle, as the gray-clad soldiers broke from the jogging double-quick to the charge, another Confederate remembered, "It drove all sanity and order from among us." It was a primal bond of sorts, a reminder that through the smoke and chaos there were thousands of others—kindred spirits—willing to hurl themselves upon their foes despite the flaming cannon blasts and spitting minié balls. "Most of us, engrossed in the musketwork, had forgotten the fact," this soldier wrote, "but the wave after wave of human voices, louder than all other battlesounds together, penetrated to every sense and stimulated our energies to the utmost."

Charging upon a Federal battery at Second Manassas amidst an intermingled mob of frenzied troops, Alexander Hunter of the 17th Virginia saw men foaming at the mouth: "They had run mad for the time," he recalled. Over the mangled dead and dying they surged, submerging the Yankee artillerymen and their guns, all the while howling that eerie, inhuman war cry that once heard was never forgotten.

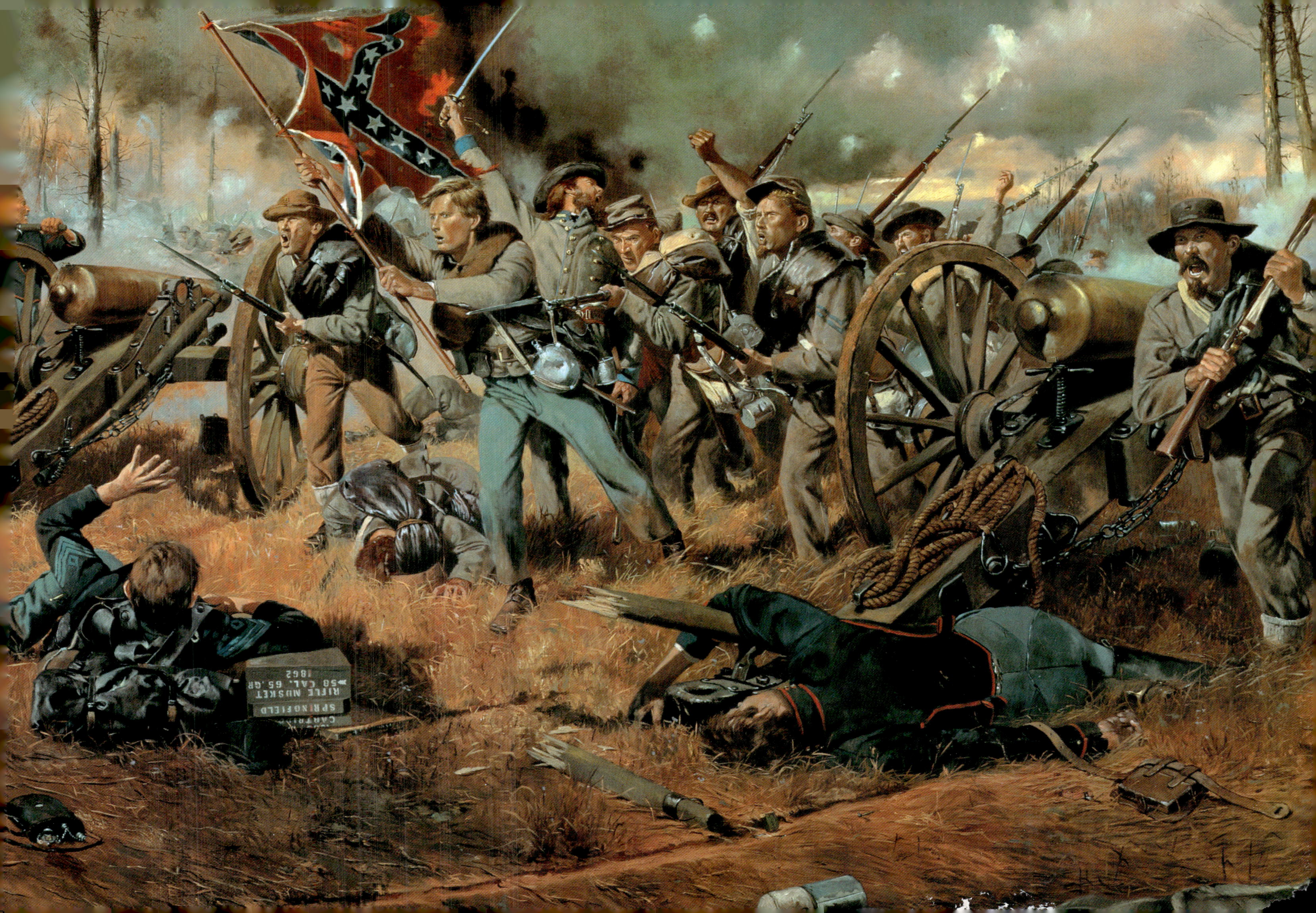
1862
RIFLE MUSKET
.58 CAL. 65.GR
SPRINGFIELD

Trooper, 7th Virginia Cavalry

Armed with a Confederate-manufactured Robinson Sharps carbine, toting a Jennifer saddle, and wearing an English overcoat of dark gray cloth, a trooper of the 7th Virginia Cavalry prepares for yet another foray against his Yankee foes. By the autumn of 1863 the Southern horsemen knew their enemy was at last coming on par with Jeb Stuart's riders, but their self-confidence remained as strong as their hope for Confederate victory.

The 7th Virginia had fought with distinction in countless cavalry fights. Their commanding officer, Lieutenant Colonel Charles Marshall, was a direct descendant of John Marshall, famous chief justice of the U.S. Supreme Court, and their natural familiarity with horseflesh had been well honed in two years of combat.

In September and October of 1863, the 7th and other units of their brigade served under Colonel Lunsford Lomax in a series of clashes with General Alfred Pleasonton's Union cavalry. Several of these fights occurred near Brandy Station, where the 7th Virginia had participated in the Civil War's largest cavalry engagement the previous June.

COLLECTION OF MICHAEL FLANAGAN

Union Standard Bearer

3rd U.S. Infantry

By November 1863, the Army of the Potomac's Regular Army troops were but a shadow of the stalwart band who had followed McClellan to the gates of Richmond a year and a half earlier. Little over three hundred remained of the 3rd U.S. Infantry, and the six regiments in their brigade fielded only some two thousand combined.

The tough veterans comprising the color guard of the 3rd U.S. had "seen the elephant" in the terrible combat of the Seven Days; had been pinned down in the deadly no-man's-land at Fredericksburg, skirmished through the tangled wilderness at Chancellorsville, and seen their comrades cut down in the slaughter of Gettysburg. When draft riots set New York aflame, the government called on the Regulars to put down the insurrection. And now, as General George Meade vainly sought to stop Robert E. Lee's Army of Northern Virginia in the frigid woodland along Mine Run, the Regulars still stuck by their color sergeant and the banner whose stars and stripes were the tangible symbol and embodiment of their sacrifice.

In September 1863 the 3rd U.S. had been able to field only 166 officers and men. The arrival of recruits and draftees increased their number in time for Meade's fruitless campaign in late November, but it was clear to all that the glory days of the Regulars lay, with their comrades, in the past—buried on the Peninsula and at Gettysburg. But those who proudly wore the white Maltese cross of the 2nd Division, 5th Corps would fight on, in the coming summer of bloodshed.

PRIVATE COLLECTION

1864

Confederate Standard Bearer

"Soldiers! You tread, with no unequal steps, the road by which your fathers marched through suffering, privation, and blood to independence!" So General Robert E. Lee addressed his Army of Northern Virginia as the proud Southern warriors girded for the great battles of 1864. Dauntless and devoted in their resolve to fight on, every soldier in that army knew that their greatest trial lay ahead.

The color sergeant who proudly bore his regiment's blood-red battle flag was entrusted with a piece of bunting that was more than mere symbol or a point on which to guide amidst the smoke-enshrouded battle line. The banner was the very incarnation of the dream of Southern independence so powerfully evoked by Lee. The battle honors that had been painted on this third-pattern issue flag at the Richmond Depot evoked the legacy of past glories and the memory of fallen comrades.

Knowing well that in the hell of combat his precious charge would make him the target of a hundred rifles, the Confederate standard bearer also realized his own tenacity could fuel a common valor. He knew also that if he fell others would not flinch to raise the banner anew, that other hands would fearlessly bear, with heartfelt pride, the symbol of their cause to victory.

PRIVATE COLLECTION

Excelsior

The 140th New York Volunteer Infantry in Saunders's Field

BATTLE OF THE WILDERNESS, MAY 5

During the long winter of 1863–64 the opposing armies hunkered down in their snug quarters along Virginia's Rapidan River. It was a time for rest and refitting, a time to fill the vacant ranks, to drill, to prepare for the inevitable bloodletting that would come with the spring. And in the first days of May 1864 General U. S. Grant set in motion the great campaign designed to tackle and destroy Robert E. Lee's vaunted Army of Northern Virginia. The war had entered its final and bloodiest stage; and the first great clash would come in the tangled thickets of the Wilderness.

The two-day slaughter commenced on May 5, when Federal troops of Major General G. K. Warren's 5th Corps lashed out at General Richard Ewell's Confederates in one of the few open spaces amidst the scrub oak and pine—a clearing known as Saunders's Field. The Yankee soldiers chosen to initiate the assault there were the most conspicuous in the Army of the Potomac: Brigadier General Romeyn Ayres's Zouave Brigade.

Ayres's units included several detachments of Regular Army men, as well as the 91st Pennsylvania Volunteers. But three of his regiments—the 140th and 146th New York and the 155th Pennsylvania—were clad in gaudy Zouave regalia, uniforms issued to them as reward for their proficiency at drill. Each unit was proud of its distinctive version of the Zouave uniform. "I assure you the brigade presents a very gay and dashing appearance," Major Henry H. Curran of the 146th New York had written his mother. "Our prominence will serve to spread abroad only a good reputation." Private Joseph Moon of the 140th New York thought his red-trimmed, dark blue outfit "the prettiest and best uniform in the army."

Largely recruited in the Rochester area, the 140th New York had arrived at the front in the autumn of 1862, just before the battle of Fredericksburg. Initially clad in standard Federal blue, in their first months of service the "Rochester Regiment" had lost more men to disease than to bullets. But on the second day of the battle of Gettysburg they had shown their bravery in the terrible contest for Little Round Top. Among the fallen that day was their commanding officer, the charismatic young West Pointer Patrick H. O'Rorke. His successor as colonel of the 140th was another graduate of the military academy, George Ryan, whose strict adherence to drill and decorum had brought the unit to a high state of military proficiency. It was as recognition of their prowess that early in 1864 the 140th New York had received their colorful Zouave uniforms.

Shortly after noon on May 5, General Ayres's Zouave brigade commenced their advance, forming in two lines under cover of the woods and deploying in Saunders's Field. The 140th New York was in the first wave of the assault, their left resting on the rutted track of the Orange Turnpike. The Regular Army units were largely out of sight in the woods to their right—supported by the 155th Pennsylvania Zouaves and the 91st Pennsylvania—while the 146th New York Zouaves were in the second wave, several hundred yards behind the Rochester men.

The first volley unleashed by their hidden Rebel foe felled a dozen men and wounded colonel Ryan's horse, forcing the colonel to dismount and lead his men on foot. Briefly the Zouaves halted, dropped prone beneath the zipping bullets, and fixed bayonets. Then Ryan shouted, "Stand up; right shoulder shift, forward, double-quick, charge!" With a roaring cheer the New Yorkers rushed toward the flame-fringed wood line to the front, men falling dead and wounded at every step. Ryan jogged alongside the regimental colors, waving his hat, his sword having been inadvertently left behind with his disabled horse. Youthful Adjutant Porter Farley pressed on beside his commander, yelling to the frenzied Zouaves to close up the gaps, dress the line, and maintain their alignment.

Downslope, across a little hollow, then up against the concealed enemy they pressed, angling to the left as they went, so that by the time they gained the woods the center of their line lay upon the Orange Turnpike. It was not until the Zouaves entered the woods that they began to return fire, and briefly Ewell's Southern troops began to pull back from their defenses. But the 140th had outdistanced their Federal supports on the right and rear and were exposed to a galling cross fire. "After getting into the woods the line of our regiment seemed to melt away," Lieutenant Farley recalled. "Off Ryan rushed," he recounted, "wild with the effort to hold the position."

Although the 146th New York swept into the woods and joined the desperate attempt to seize the Rebel stronghold, they too had lost heavily, and a Confederate counterattack hurled the broken Union formations out of the woods and back into the open field. Salvos of canister from two Federal artillery pieces that had unlimbered on the pike proved as deadly to friend as to foe, and by the time the remnants of the Zouave brigade rallied at their starting point, Saunders's Field was carpeted with bodies. To add to the horror, the bramble-choked field caught fire, consuming dead and wounded alike in the rolling smoke and flames.

"My God," Colonel Ryan gasped to his adjutant, "I'm the first colonel I ever heard of who came out of such a fight as that and couldn't tell where his regiment was." Of the 140th New York's 529 men who started the charge across Saunders's Field, only 274 emerged unscathed.

PRIVATE COLLECTION

146th New York Volunteer Infantry

The first unit in the Zouave Brigade to replace their Federal blue uniforms with Zouave garb was the 146th New York, who received their yellow-trimmed, light blue uniforms in June 1863. A month earlier some two hundred veterans of the 5th New York (Duryée's Zouaves) had been amalgamated with the 146th, and the decision was likely made for that reason.

Manufactured by the Schuykill Arsenal, the uniforms were closely modeled on those worn by the French Tirailleurs Algeriens, or "Turcos," units that were distinguished from the Zouaves by being recruited among native North Africans. Clad in their unique version of the Zouave uniform, the men of the 146th New York fought at Gettysburg, where they helped to defend Little Round Top. In the carnage of the Wilderness the regiment lost 312 men their colonel and lieutenant colonel were among the 65 who were killed or died of wounds.

PRIVATE COLLECTION

155th Pennsylvania Volunteer Infantry

Like the 140th New York, the troops of the 155th Pennsylvania were issued Zouave uniforms early in 1864 as a tribute to their precision on the drill field. While most Civil War Zouave uniforms were of American manufacture, those given to the 155th were a notable exception. Earlier in the war the Federal government had imported some ten thousand French *Chasseur à Pied* uniforms, many of which were too small for use by brawnier American troops.

But enough large-sized blue-gray Chasseur trousers were on hand to outfit a regiment, and the capes, or "talmas" of the same color—also part of the imported Chasseur uniforms—were converted to Zouave jackets. With bright yellow trim and false vest fronts stitched to their jackets, the men of the 155th Pennsylvania were a curious hybrid of French and American Zouave fashion.

The Pennsylvanians served with General Ayres's Zouave Brigade in the battle of the Wilderness. While the 140th and 146th New York were being cut to pieces in Saunders's Field, the 155th Pennsylvania waged an equally grim though less costly battle in the woods to their north. "Everywhere a gentle steady rain of twigs and leaves was falling to the earth," one survivor noted, "pruned by the same hail that penetrated the flesh and splintered the bones of the devoted men."

Transferred to the 2nd Division of the 5th Corps later in the campaign, the regiment would serve proudly through to the final victory at Appomattox. The last Federal soldier killed before Lee's surrender was a Zouave of the 155th Pennsylvania.

PRIVATE COLLECTION

Lee's Texans

Battle of the Wilderness, May 6

THE EIGHT HUNDRED SOLDIERS OF THE FAMED Texas Brigade, commanded by Brigadier General John Gregg, were issued three day's rations and late on the afternoon of May 4, 1864, marched with the other troops of Major General Charles W. Field's division from their camp near Gordonsville. Over the next two days they covered nearly thirty miles, leading Longstreet's 1st Corps toward the battle that raged through the tangled undergrowth of the Wilderness.

Robert E. Lee, knowing that Grant would call on his vastly superior numbers for the second day's fight, dispatched orders for Longstreet to make a night march that would bring his corps to the field in time to meet the expected Federal assault by dawn of May 6. Shortly after midnight the tired soldiers got under way, marching by moonlight toward the battlefield ten miles away.

Longstreet's men were slowed by difficult terrain, and the Yankee attack was well under way before the Southern troops neared the scene of combat. Still in the lead, Gregg's Texas Brigade moved down the Orange Plank Road, passing crowds of walking wounded and dazed stragglers. Up ahead Winfield Scott Hancock's 2nd Corps was in the process of smashing the better part of A. P. Hill's corps. The Federals were pressing close to the clearing at Widow Tapp's farm, where Lee and his staff had taken position alongside the blazing cannon of Lieutenant Colonel William T. Poague's artillery battalion. The men of Heth's and Wilcox's brigades came stumbling back, past the legendary commander of the Army of Northern Virginia, whose face bore an expression of grim resolve as he watched the disintegration of Hill's corps.

Lee's staff officer, Colonel Charles Venable, galloped back to Longstreet and informed his chief's "Old War Horse" of the emergency. The pace increased to a double-quick, and the Texans came panting and sweating the last mile and a half. With ranks packed together eight abreast, Longstreet's vanguard shoved its way through the broken ranks of Heth and Wilcox. "Here's Longstreet," some of Hill's beaten troops yelled, "The Old War Horse is up at last. It's all right now."

With General Gregg urging them on, the Texas Brigade entered the Widow Tapp's field, and at Field's order they made a right wheel into line behind Poague's embattled gunners. Colonel Venable observed that the Texas Brigade deployed in line of battle "with a steadiness unexampled even among veterans, and with an élan that presaged restoration of our position and certain victory." With General Benjamin Humphreys's Mississippi Brigade forming on their right, Gregg's soldiers prepared to meet the enemy onslaught north of the Orange Plank Road. Sensing they had to seize the initiative from the enemy, Longstreet told General Field, "charge with any front you can make."

Caught up in the drama, the habitually stolid Lee rode up to General Gregg, asking "General, what brigade is this?"

"The Texas Brigade," Gregg replied.

"When you go in there," Lee said, "I wish you to give them the cold steel—they will stand and fight all day, and never move unless you charge them." Invoking the proud history of the brigade, Lee told Gregg, "I want every man of them to know I am here with them."

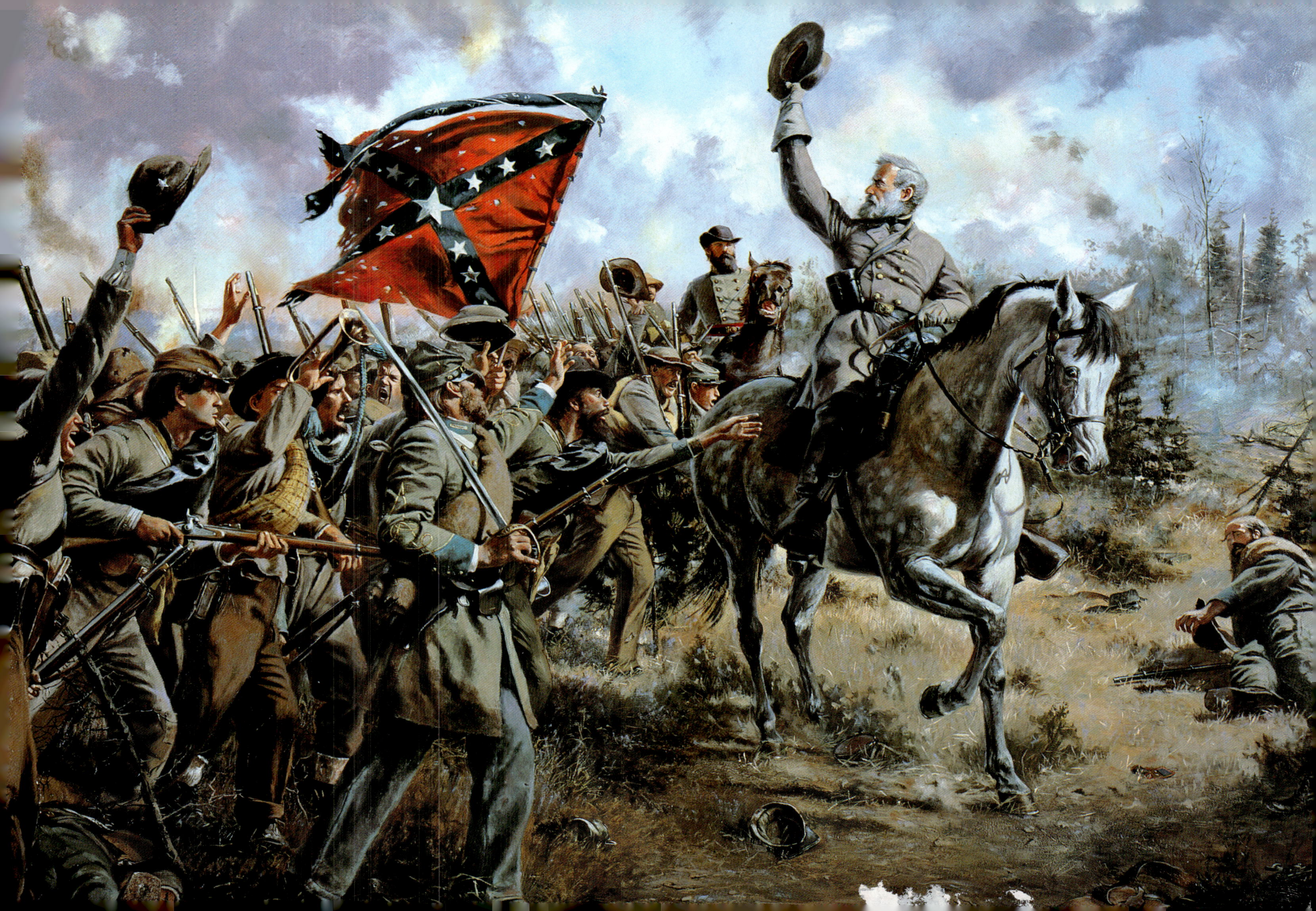

Wheeling his horse, Gregg admonished his eight hundred soldiers, "Attention, Texas Brigade! The eyes of General Lee are upon you! Forward, march!"

Lee rose in his stirrups, raised his hat, and shouted, "Texans always move them!" The men responded with a yell that one soldier thought "must have been heard for miles around." Fired by the passion of the moment, Lee spurred Traveller through the advancing ranks of the 5th Texas and prepared to lead the charge in person. Concerned for their beloved commander's safety, several soldiers grasped at Traveller's bridle, imploring Lee not to risk his life and shouting, "General Lee to the rear!" Colonel Venable later noted that with the advance rolling forward, "There came from the entire line as it rushed on the cry, 'Go back, General Lee! Go back!'" Some soldiers refused to continue the assault until Lee's safety was assured.

With Private Leonard Groce Gee of the 5th Texas clinging to Traveller's bridle, Venable and General Gregg finally convinced Lee to withdraw to his post by Poague's artillery, and the charge surged across Tapp's field. Though men fell from the ranks at every step, the Texas Brigade crashed into the underbrush on the far side and began driving Hancock's Federals back to the shelter of log breastworks at the intersection with the Brock Road. By day's end 565 of 811 men in the brigade had fallen, but Lee's Texans had played a pivotal role in staving off defeat in the Wilderness.

The Bonnie Blue Flag

The Mule Shoe, Spotsylvania, May 12

ON THE EARLY MORNING OF MAY 12, 1864, as darkness began to give way to the half light that precedes the dawn, the Army of the Potomac unleashed one of the largest and most spectacular assaults of the Civil War. Massed in tight columns, rank on rank, nearly twenty thousand men of Major General Winfield Scott Hancock's 2nd Corps advanced on a salient of Confederate earthworks near Spotsylvania Court House, Virginia, that soldiers called the "Mule Shoe."

The western flank of the Mule Shoe salient had witnessed heavy fighting two days earlier, when a Federal strike force led by Colonel Emory Upton had temporarily broken the Southern line. Many officers in Robert E. Lee's Army of Northern Virginia felt this projecting arm of the entrenched Confederate positions at Spotsylvania was too exposed. But at dawn on May 12, when Hancock struck, General Richard Ewell's corps was still in place within the Mule Shoe.

Hancock's men had been instructed to advance in silence—not to fire, not to cheer until they were within the Rebel lines. But as they overran the advanced Confederate pickets and picked up their pace to a jogging double-quick, there was no restraining the Yankees' enthusiasm. A mighty cheer roared out, and the wave of men in blue washed over the startled defenders of the Confederate front line.

The troops of Brigadier General Stephen Dodson Ramseur's North Carolina brigade were awake and under arms that damp, misty morning when the Yankee juggernaut struck, overwhelming the units at the apex of the Mule Shoe salient. As the crashing tumult escalated to his front and right, Ramseur positioned his 2nd North Carolina as a reserve, facing north, while his other three regiments hunkered down behind their breastworks, fronting west to meet any enemy threat from that direction. Here the Tarheels waited, their stalwart young general eager and alert for the summons to combat.

A little less than a month shy of his twenty-seventh birthday, Dodson Ramseur was an outgoing and popular graduate of the West Point Class of 1860 whose career as a Confederate general officer, while not without its controversies, had always been marked by bravery and devotion. Slight in stature, Ramseur's full dark beard and receding hairline made him appear older than his years. His wife, Nellie, was pregnant with their first child, and like so many soldiers in this terrible war, all his future hopes and dreams were deferred as he confronted the stern demands of duty.

As the Federal assault pressed on, taking thousands of prisoners and thrusting deep into the Confederate salient, Lee and his generals struggled to shore up the widening breach. Orders came from Ramseur's division commander, the intrepid Major General Robert E. Rodes, instructing his subordinate to "check the enemy's advance and drive him back." Ramseur's units filed into an open field not far from the McCoull House and fronted facing northwest, where Brigadier General Junius Daniel's brigade was in serious difficulty. Ramseur's men were being cut down even before they finished their deployment, and the general quickly gave the command to advance at the double-quick and charge.

The 14th, 4th, 2nd, and 30th North Carolina, as they formed Ramseur's line from left to right, rushed toward the Yankee-occupied earthworks, wheeling to their left as they charged to hit the enemy head-on. Dead and wounded strewn in their wake, the North Carolinians and their gallant general—who seemed to one admiring officer "an angel of war"—slammed into the Union troops and began to fire at point-blank range. Ramseur's horse was struck from under him, and a moment later a bullet ripped through his right arm below the elbow.

With Ramseur down, Colonel Bryan Grimes of the 4th North Carolina took charge and urged the men on, shoving the Yankees back toward the original line of the Mule Shoe. Though faint with loss of blood, Ramseur ignored his wound and pushed forward with his men. The Confederate formations were fragmented and companies and regiments intermingled, the battle flags of the 4th and 14th North Carolina side by side. As officers struggled to sort out the alignment, Private Tisdale Stepp of the 14th began to sing "The Bonnie Blue Flag," and soon scores of men were belting out the stirring Southern anthem even as they poured musketry into their determined foe.

With the skies unleashing a torrential downpour, Ramseur's brigade pressed their counterattack and soon regained the first line. There both sides fought the most sustained and horrific close-range fight of the war. Dead and wounded sank into the muddy trenches, trampled underfoot and suffocating in the mire. For ten hours the battle raged and casualties mounted until at last the fighting sputtered out in stalemate.

That Lee's army was able to recover from such a blow and counter the Federal onslaught with their own unquenchable devotion owed much to Dodson Ramseur. The wounded Carolinian received the thanks of Lee himself, and the whole army sang the praises of the gallant Tarheels.

COLLECTION OF WILLIAM RODEN

The Forlorn Hope

1st Maine Heavy Artillery, Battle of Petersburg, June 18

On the morning of May 15, 1864, the 1st Maine Heavy Artillery, some sixteen hundred strong, marched down Pennsylvania Avenue through the center of the nation's capital and boarded a transport on the Seventh Street dock. Their destination was Belle Plain Landing and a new assignment with the 2nd Corps of the Army of the Potomac—a force bled white as Grant battled Lee through day after day of unprecedented carnage.

The 1st Maine, along with other heavy artillery units, were bound for the front as replacements. For nearly two years, since their muster in at Bangor, the Maine "Heavies" had been garrison troops, comfortably barracked in the seventy-odd earthen forts that guarded the approaches to Washington. As Private Robert Libby recalled, "Drilling, building forts, felling trees, and guard duty was our daily life." But soon the unblooded downeasters would become hardened veterans.

Organized and drilled to function either as gunners or foot soldiers, heavy artillery units were by their nature considerably larger than infantry regiments. Rather than ten companies of one hundred men each, heavy artillery regiments comprised twelve companies of two hundred men each. While losses to illness and detached service reduced the total strength, the typical heavy artillery unit of 1864 was larger than many veteran brigades.

Led by their commanding officer, Colonel Daniel Chaplin, the 1st Maine Heavy Artillery marched rapidly from Belle Plain, through Fredericksburg, and on to the front lines near Spotsylvania. With their red-trimmed frock coats, polished brass, and stainless colors, the "Heavies" were quickly made the butt of jokes by the cynical, dirty veterans who regaled the new arrivals with shouts of "Fresh fish!" "Abe's pets!" and "Paper collar soldiers!"

On May 19 the 1st Maine and the other untried units of their brigade were committed to the meat grinder at the battle of Harris Farm. Battling in the rain and mud with General Richard Ewell's Confederates, the regiment lost 476 men, 147 of whom were killed or mortally wounded. This horrific baptism by fire began a grim month of constant marching and fighting that brought the regiment and the

---

This McDowell-style forage cap from the artist's collection was worn by William Hosford of Company A, 1st Connecticut Heavy Artillery. One of the first heavy artillery outfits to reach the front, the Connecticut unit saw extensive service in General McClellan's Peninsula Campaign. Regiments like the 1st Maine, which joined Grant's forces in 1864 and fought as infantry in the bloody battles of the overland campaign and the siege of Petersburg, suffered some of the war's greatest losses. Of the ten Federal regiments sustaining the most fatalities, four were heavy artillery units. Photo courtesy Don Troiani Collection

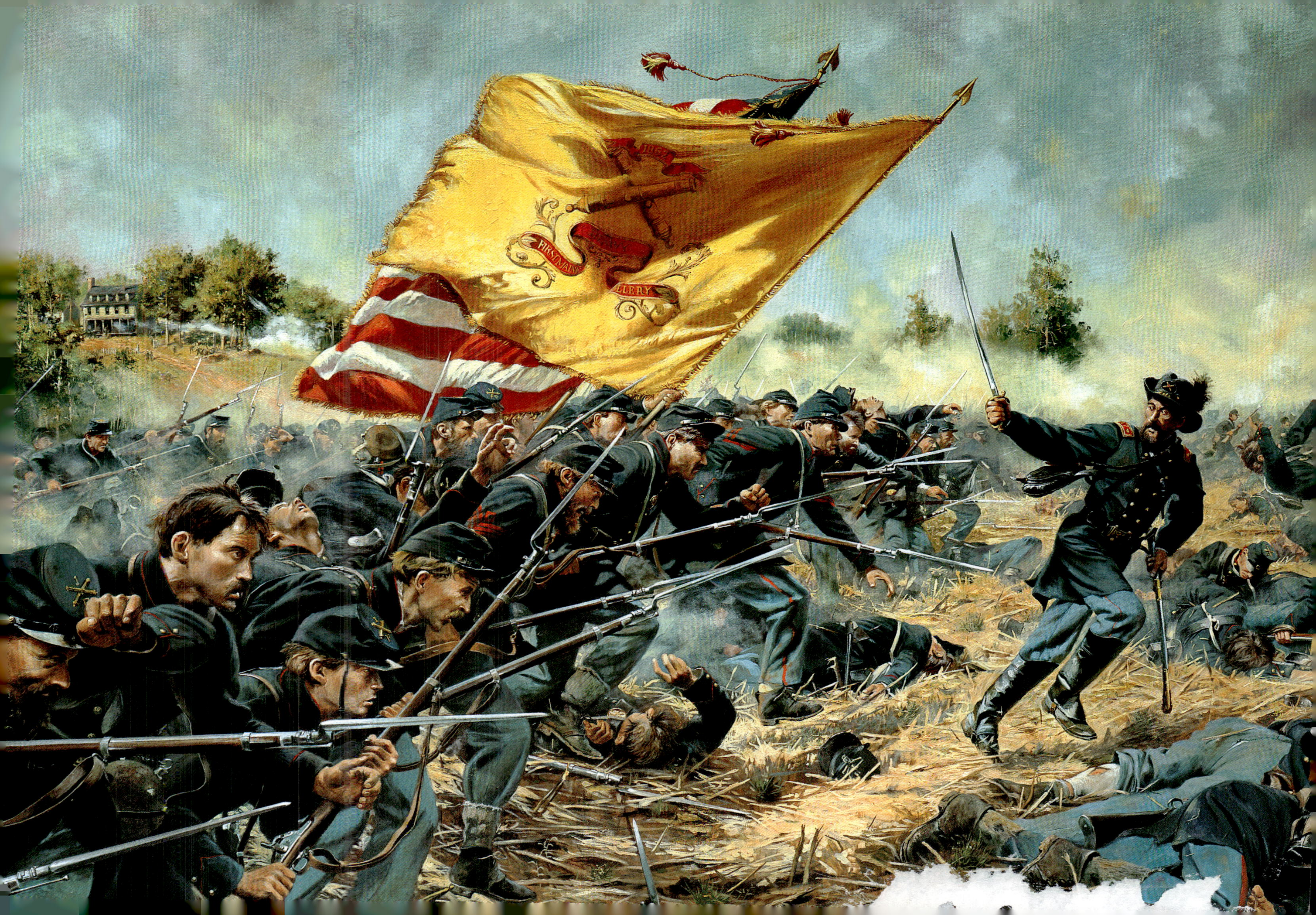

Army of the Potomac to the heavily fortified defenses of Petersburg. There, on June 18, the 1st Maine Heavy Artillery would earn what Lieutenant Horace Shaw called "a record it did not seek"—the greatest number of unit casualties sustained in a single engagement by any regiment in the entire war.

At 4:30 P.M. as Grant and Meade initiated a series of head-on assaults on the Rebel entrenchments, an aide rode up with orders for Brigadier General Gershom Mott to commit his division to an attack on a salient defended by General Colquitt's Georgia brigade. Mott protested the order, but he was overruled. The 1st Maine, aligned in three battalions of four companies each was designated to spearhead the charge. Colonel Robert McAllister, whose own brigade had been brought to a bloody stalemate, realized the assault was doomed. "As they moved, I held my breath," McAllister wrote, "knowing their destruction was sure."

General Mott watched as the 1st Maine started forward from a fringe of pines, their well-dressed lines surging on "like a blue wave crested with a glistening foam of steel." While the soldiers swept down a slope toward a sluggish brook that lay midway to the Southern earthworks, their formations were lashed with musketry and artillery fire. As Lieutenant Shaw remembered, "The field became a burning, seething, crashing, hissing hell."

With Colonel Chaplin acting as brigade commander, the charge of the 1st Maine Heavies was led by Major Russell B. Shepherd, who went forward with the first wave, urging the men on at a double-quick. According to plan, once Shepherd's battalion cleared the barrier of fallen trees and abatis and gained a footing on the Rebel works, the following battalions under Major Christopher V. Crossman and Captain Whitney S. Clark would exploit the breakthrough.

But human valor could not stand against the wall of flame and lead, and the onrushing lines were torn to pieces and brought to a halt before the Southern line. Private Joel Brown could hear the Rebels shouting, "Come on Yanks!" as they blazed away at the crumbling formations. "The wave of heroes was shattered against the rampart of earth," General Mott reported, "and was blown to pieces by the whirlwind of death."

Only after night fell were the dazed survivors able to withdraw from no-man's-land and make their way back. "The men came in through the darkness singly or by twos," Corporal Charles J. House recalled. "We had been in service twenty-one months and had learned to trust and love each other as brothers, and is it any wonder that tears came unbidden, tears of sorrow that so many had fallen and of joy that so many had escaped?"

It was impossible to aid the wounded. "After the Maine Heavies retired, the ground was strewn with wounded and dying crying 'Water! Water!'" Colonel McAllister wrote. "No help or relief could be sent them. . . . Hundreds of wounded thus died in our sight." Of the 900 men who commenced the charge, 241 were dead or dying and another 371 wounded. Weeping and enraged, Colonel Chaplin berated the veteran units who had failed to support his regiment. "There are the men you have been making fun of" he shouted. "You did not dare follow them."

Largely because of their sacrifice at Petersburg, the 1st Maine would eventually stand above all other Civil War regiments in total battle casualties: 23 officers and 418 enlisted men killed or fatally injured, and 922 wounded, in less than a year of frontline service.

ONE OF FORREST'S MEN

A GRITTY, HARD-BITTEN FIRST SERGEANT reflects the tough reliability and defiant will of those who followed the general called "The Wizard of the Saddle." Many Rebel troopers of the war's western theater abandoned the saber in favor of one or more pistols and often carried a rifle rather than the shorter carbine. Few wore the yellow trim of the cavalry branch on their jackets, preferring to leave flashy affectations and military trappings to their despised Yankee enemy. These were men with a purpose, and the star on their hats reminded them that their homes in Tennessee, Mississippi, and Texas were threatened with occupation by a numerically superior foe.

PRIVATE COLLECTION

SOUTHERN STEEL

Major General N. B. Forrest at the Battle of Okolona, February 22

GEORGE WASHINGTON'S BIRTHDAY WOULD never be a cause for celebration for Major General William Sooy Smith and the seven thousand Federal horseman of his independent command. For on February 22, 1864, the Yankee riders ran afoul of the Confederacy's most brutally effective cavalry leader—the dauntless Major General Nathan Bedford Forrest.

At thirty-three, General Smith was a West Point–educated engineer who had been transferred from an infantry command to take charge of most of the Union cavalry in the war's western theater. In early February 1864, while William T. Sherman's army pushed east from Vicksburg to Meridian, Mississippi, Smith was instructed to strike deep into the state on a large-scale raid intended to spread confusion through Southern forces still off balance following the surrender of Vicksburg the preceding summer. Sooy Smith was late getting his corps under way from their base at Memphis, Tennessee, and by the time the Federal horsemen launched their foray, Sherman had already started back to Vicksburg.

Slowed by steady rain that turned roads to quagmires, it was February 18 before Smith's cavalry had crossed the Tallahatchee River and reached the Mobile and Ohio Railroad at Okolona. Two days later, the Union troopers attacked and shoved aside a brigade of Confederate riders near the town of West Point. There, having learned of Sherman's withdrawal, Smith halted and decided to retrace his route back toward Okolona and ultimately the safety of Memphis.

Facing this faltering Yankee incursion were the twenty-five hundred men of General Forrest's "critter" cavalry—perhaps the best fighting troopers, man for man, in all the Confederacy. Though outnumbered nearly three to one, Forrest was never a man to be intimidated by odds, and with Smith's Yankees on the backtrail, on February 22 Forrest took the offensive. He expressed the hope, in his peculiar vernacular, to put the "skeer on Sooy Smith and his corps."

With Forrest and his escort in the vanguard, the Southern horsemen attempted to pinch off the Yankee rear guard with converging brigades. For a time the enemy was able to frustrate these efforts, continuing their retreat through Okolona northwestward on the Pontotoc Road. At Ivey's Hill, six miles beyond the town, Smith's troopers made a stand. Dismounting and opening fire with their repeating carbines from the cover of hastily erected barricades of logs and rails, the Federals repelled a succession of fierce Rebel assaults.

Leading his men in the charge, General Forrest's younger brother, Lieutenant Colonel Jeffrey Forrest, was shot through the neck and killed. Learning of his brother's fall, the general hastened to his side, cradling the slain officer in his arms and kissing his cold forehead. "Jeffrey, Jeffrey," the general moaned. He ordered his brother's body taken to a secure place, and then, in a voice choked with grief and rage, Bedford Forrest turned to bugler Jacob Gaus and ordered him to sound the charge.

With some of his men fighting on foot on either flank, Forrest led the mounted attack, hitting the center of the Federal line, which broke and scattered in confusion. One Yankee was felled by Forrest's revolver, and the charge pressed on. Hampered by the muddy roads, a bulky supply train, and scores of fugitive slaves, General Smith was forced to make another stand to cover the continuing retreat.

As he neared this new roadblock, Forrest

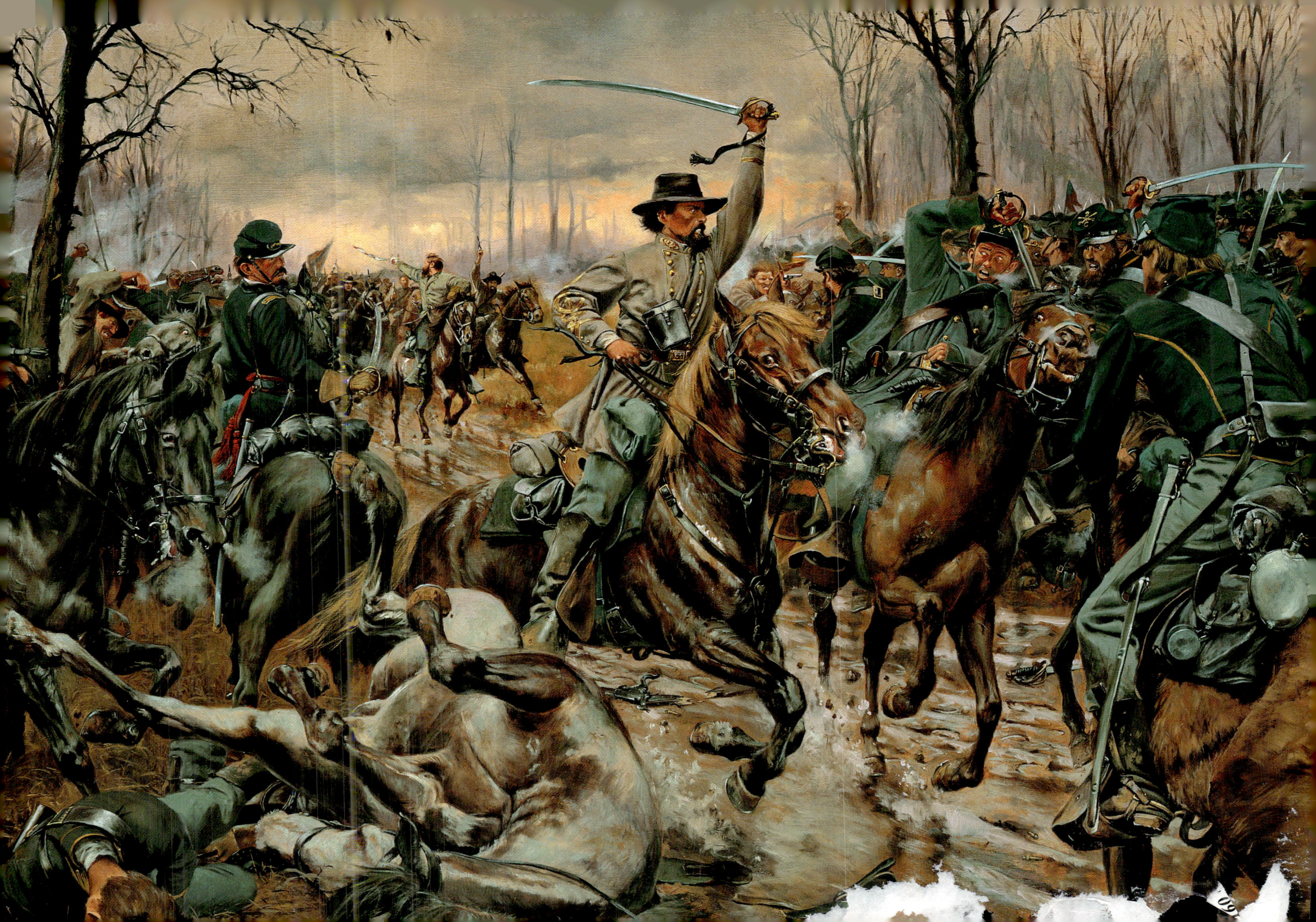

unhesitatingly spurred into the very midst of the Yankee defenders. Standing tall in the saddle, the general reminded one soldier of "a Scandinavian Berserk," while another thought him "so rash as to savor madness." Surrounded by enemy troopers, the powerful warrior exerted all his strength, as well as his ability to use saber or pistol in either hand. Three Federals died by the enraged general's hand.

Seeing his commander surrounded by blue uniforms, Colonel Robert McCulloch—whose right hand was swathed in bloody bandages from an earlier wound—shouted, "My God men, will you see them kill your general? I'll go to the rescue if not a man follows!" With his bandages unraveling and streaming behind, "Black Bob" McCulloch led his troopers into the fray.

Again the Yankees gave way, and a mile farther on they again made a stand, forming in three lines on a ridge halfway between Okolona and Pontotoc. Undaunted, Forrest led his tired riders on. His horse was shot under him with five bullets in the body and three others in the saddle. Forrest remounted a trooper's horse, which was then also killed. By the time the last Federal position was broken, Forrest was on his third horse of the day, which was wounded but still able to keep on its feet.

Although Forrest was forced to call a halt to his exhausting pursuit, Sooy Smith's corps had been shattered. Federal brigade commander Colonel George Waring recalled Smith's retreat to Memphis as "a weary, disheartening, and almost panic-stricken flight." The Federals had lost nearly three hundred men, twice as many as their relentless opponents, and Nathan Bedford Forrest had added to his laurels as "The Wizard of the Saddle."

Federal Infantry Officer

By the third year of the conflict, company commanders like this Union infantry captain had few illusions of glory. They were veterans now, and warfare was a grim business. Most of the officers who had marched off to war with dreams of patriotic glory had fallen in battle or been sent home because of wounds or disease. The men who wore the shoulder straps in 1864 were likely to have risen from the ranks, and merit counted more toward promotion than political connections.

The officers' uniforms had changed as well. Gone were the tasseled sashes—except for occasional dress functions—and many officers abandoned the regulation frock coat in favor of a loose-fitting sack coat, like the one shown here, manufactured by the firm of Niehaus and Hock of Belleville, Illinois.

But even though their garb had become more serviceable, officers were still expected to exude a bearing—and display a bravery—that would inspire their men to deeds of daring.

Thunder on Little Kennesaw

Lumsden's Alabama Battery, June 25

IN EARLY MAY 1864, AS FEDERAL FORCES under U. S. Grant were marching against Lee's army in Virginia, the other arm of the mighty Union offensive got under way in the war's western theater. Major General William T. Sherman launched one hundred thousand Yankee troops against General Joseph E. Johnston's Army of Tennessee. Sherman's goal was Atlanta, a city of immense strategic value to the Confederacy and a symbolic bastion of Southern hopes.

For nearly a month and a half Sherman battled his way southward into Georgia. Johnston's troops used the rugged terrain to their advantage, digging in atop ridges, entrenching beside rivers, and contesting every mountain pass. Johnston waged a skillful fighting retreat, not unlike that of Revolutionary War hero Nathaniel Greene's campaign against the British in the Carolinas. But as Johnston gave ground and Sherman's columns moved closer and closer to Atlanta, Confederate President Jefferson Davis—no friend of Johnston's to begin with—grew increasingly frustrated with his commander's performance.

By June 19 the Army of Tennessee was again preparing to make a stand, this time a mere twenty-five miles from Atlanta. The twin peaks of Kennesaw Mountain—the last significant high ground north of the city—were, in Sherman's opinion, "the key to the whole country." If the Kennesaw line could be breached, the next battle would be for Atlanta itself.

Confederate soldiers and engineers felled trees and threw up earthen entrenchments along Kennesaw's slopes, and Johnston's artillery rolled into positions from which to rake Yankee attackers with a deadly fire. One battery deployed on the crest of Big Kennesaw comprised four twelve-pound Napoleon guns under the command of Captain Charles Linnius Lumsden. A talented graduate of the Virginia Military Institute Class of 1860, the outbreak of war had found Lumsden employed as assistant instructor of tactics for the University of Alabama's corps of cadets. Recruited and organized at Tuscaloosa, Lumsden's battery reported for duty at Mobile and commenced a distinguished career with the Army of Tennessee.

By June 1864, Captain Lumsden's Alabamians were a tough, professional outfit, veterans of the battles of Corinth, Murfreesboro,

> IN PREPARATION FOR HIS PAINTING OF Lumsden's Battery, Don Troiani garnered useful first-hand accounts from David Evans, a respected authority on the campaign for Atlanta. Guided to the surviving earthworks by local historian Bill Erquitt, Troiani photographed the location but had to visually reconstruct the terrain, which is now largely overgrown with timber. The discovery of a period view by photographer George Barnard proved crucial to an accurate depiction of the scene.

and Chickamauga. Attached to Major Joseph Palmer's battalion in the artillery reserve, they had so far seen little combat in the Atlanta campaign. But their courage would be put to the test in dramatic fashion at Kennesaw Mountain.

After darkness had fallen on the evening of June 24, Captain Lumsden was ordered to pull his guns out of their position on Big Kennesaw and relieve another battery in the line on Pigeon Hill, a southern spur of Little Kennesaw. When Lumsden found that the narrow trail chopped through the woods by Confederate pioneers was too steep for his exhausted battery horses to scale, the gunners began the backbreaking ordeal of hauling guns, limbers,

PRIVATE COLLECTION

caissons, and ammunition up the slope by hand. With the help of infantrymen from Major General Samuel G. French's division, the tired Alabamians managed to come into battery atop the ridge, where they dug in behind a stout breastwork of logs and earth.

With the muzzles of his Napoleons projecting through the embrasures and ammunition close at hand, Captain Lumsden awaited the next Yankee move on the muggy dawn of June 25. General French, whose position encompassed Lumsden's guns, observed the Federals moving toward the Confederate left, and at 10 A.M. he ordered several of his batteries to open fire. "The enemy replied furiously," French recalled, "and for an hour the firing was incessant."

Lumsden's battery did not participate in this initial episode, but early in the afternoon the captain decided to probe the enemy lines with a few shells. One of General French's staff officers approved the move and saw to it that a battery further up Little Kennesaw added its fire to Lumsden's cannon. The echo of the Alabamians' salvos had barely faded when the Federals responded with counterbattery fire from twenty-four guns.

An artillery duel ensued all along the Kennesaw line, though as General French discovered, most of the Yankee shells overshot the crest, posing more of a danger to the camps in the rear than to the men on the front line.

But Lumsden's battery was a tragic exception. A Yankee shell came shrieking through one of the embrasures, narrowly missing the soldier who was swabbing out the bore of Lumsden's number three gun, cutting down gunner Jacob Gurley, and plowing into a caisson. The ammunition chests exploded, and the falling flames and debris set off fuses, friction primers, and nearby musket rounds that whizzed through the dazed artillerymen. Lieutenant A. C. Hargrove seized a sponge bucket and tossed water over the flames, averting an even greater disaster.

Lumsden ordered his gunners to cease fire. As Sergeant James Maxwell noted, "We found out what the enemy had over there, and we did not stir up that hornet's nest again." Two days later, Sherman's effort to take Kennesaw Mountain by storm ended in bloody reverse. But Johnston would again pull back, as Atlanta itself become the target of Yankee shells.

29th Alabama Infantry

The hard-bitten soldiers of the 29th Alabama, part of Major General Edward C. Walthall's division of the Army of Tennessee, were in the thick of combat during the Atlanta campaign. On July 20, 1864, in obedience to General Walthall's orders to "kill or capture everything" in their front, the Alabamians participated in a furious onslaught at Peach Tree Creek that overran nearly a mile of Yankee-occupied territory. Four months later, in the terrible slaughter at Franklin, the gallant men of the 29th managed to plant their battleflag on the enemy works. Though the banner and its staff were literally shot to pieces, an officer succeeded in bearing the precious fragments to safety.

This private carries an Enfield rifle and wears accoutrements of English manufacture—documented through research in the National Archives. The short jacket with round blue cuffs is typical of uniforms issued to the Army of Tennessee.

PRIVATE COLLECTION

33RD NEW JERSEY VOLUNTEER INFANTRY

"2nd Zouaves"

THE ATLANTA CAMPAIGN

WITH THE WAR WELL INTO ITS THIRD YEAR, recruiting officers who sought patriotic volunteers rather than draftees or bounty men for their new regiments would sometimes use the promise of a distinctive uniform as an incentive for enlistment. Such was the case with the 33rd New Jersey Volunteer Infantry, which left Newark on September 8, 1863.

The 33rd was outfitted in a variant of the Zouave style, with a uniform similar to that of the 9th New York, "Hawkins's Zouaves," and a kepi like the ones worn by the 95th Pennsylvania, "Gosline's Zouaves." The choice of uniform was in large part the brainchild of the 33rd New Jersey's commanding officer, young German-born colonel George W. Mindil.

Mindil had hoped to fill his ranks with veteran soldiers, but in fact the 33rd received many draftees, and desertion rates were high. Nonetheless, the regiment fought bravely in Sherman's Atlanta campaign as part of the 11th—and later the 20th Army Corps. At the battle of Peach Tree Creek on July 20, 1864, the 33rd lost its state color while conducting a fighting retreat.

On September 14, the regiment chose to abandon its worn Zouave garb in favor of the more easily obtainable regulation Federal uniform. The only portion of the original uniform that persisted was the cap, which continued to be issued by the U.S. Quartermaster Department.

PRIVATE COLLECTION

Waiting for Dispatches

Harpers Ferry, the scene of abolitionist firebrand John Brown's 1859 raid, was a supply and staging area for several Federal campaigns aimed at winning control of Virginia's Shenandoah Valley. The Union cavalry played an important role in these efforts, but it was not until the advent of Major General Philip Sheridan, in the late summer of 1864, that the mounted arm would be consolidated for use as an offensive strike force.

For much of the war Federal cavalrymen were used principally as scouts and messengers. Like the dispatch rider shown here, troopers would frequently be detached from their regiment for duty as staff orderlies and couriers, serving brigade, division, and corps commanders. But Sheridan recognized that the cavalry's innate maneuverability, coupled with the firepower of their carbines, made the troopers a force to be reckoned with. Much of the credit for ultimate Union victory in the Shenandoah Valley was due to "Little Phil's" cavalry.

PRIVATE COLLECTION

12th Virginia Cavalry

In July 1864, Jubal Early had carried the tide of war to the very doorstep of Washington, D.C. But while the irascible general could take comfort in the thought that he had "scared Abe Lincoln like hell," the great Rebel raid had actually done little to alter the Confederacy's deteriorating strategic situation. By late summer Early's force was back in Virginia, and a new Federal army, led by combative Major General Philip H. Sheridan, was preparing to wrest control of the fertile Shenandoah Valley from Early's defenders.

The troopers of the 12th Virginia Cavalry, along with their comrades in the famed "Laurel Brigade," would have their hands full contesting the revitalized, well-led and numerically stronger Yankee cavalry. Organized in June 1862 from the veterans of Turner Ashby's sprawling command, the men of the 12th were natives of the Shenandoah Valley and would thus be defending their homes as well as their cause. Unfortunately it would prove to be an impossible task, and the coming campaign shone little glory on the Laurel Brigade.

Like much of the Southern cavalry arm, the arms and uniforms of the 12th Virginia were far from standardized. Ordnance returns indicate that as many as eight different types of carbine and musket were carried within a given company, along with a variety of pistols, including the English-manufactured Kerr percussion revolver. Uniforms were mixed as well, including gray or black jackets and trousers of gray or varying shades of blue. Both caps and slouch hats were in evidence, many adorned with the distinctive badge of the Laurel Brigade. Curiously, despite the unit's mounted duties, far more shoes than boots were issued, and spurs were in short supply.

Gone were the glory days of the Southern Cavalry. Ahead lay humiliating defeat and surrender.

PRIVATE COLLECTION

3RD NEW JERSEY VOLUNTEER CAVALRY

"The Butterflies"

PERHAPS THE MOST UNUSUAL UNIFORM WORN by any Federal mounted unit was the braided hussar jacket, visorless cap, and hooded cloak, or "talma," issued to the 3rd New Jersey Cavalry. Given this curious hybrid of European military fashions, it is perhaps no wonder that the New Jerseyans were given the nickname "Butterflies" when they joined the Army of the Potomac's Cavalry Corps in 1864.

But the Butterflies soon proved their fighting prowess. Armed with the rapid-firing Spencer carbine, these New Jersey hussars took part in the grueling Shenandoah Valley campaign and were in the thick of the action in the war's final battles at Five Forks, Sayler's Creek, and Appomattox.

IN MODELING HIS DEPICTION OF THE 3rd New Jersey cavalryman, artist Troiani drew upon his significant collection of militaria, which includes one of the few surviving hussar jackets and the only known example of the orange-lined talma.

PRIVATE COLLECTION

Ranger Mosby

"Mosby is an old rat, and has a great many holes." Thus Union Colonel Charles Russell Lowell sought to explain his cavalry's futile efforts to capture the man known as "The Gray Ghost." Coupling daring hit-and-run tactics with a phantomlike elusiveness, Colonel John Singleton Mosby was the most effective guerilla leader of the Civil War. His very name struck fear into the hearts of the blue-clad soldiers, and his Partisan Rangers were an ever-present thorn in the side of the Union war effort.

This forage cap, from the artist's collection, belonged to a trooper of Company F, 15th New York Cavalry. The regiment was one of many that learned to respect—and fear—the Gray Ghost of the Confederacy. PHOTO COURTESY DON TROIANI COLLECTION

Though Mosby never led more than 350 troopers on a raid—and often commanded less than a third of that number—the unpredictable forays of his Rangers intimidated and held back thousands of Federal troops who might otherwise have been deployed against Confederate armies in the field. "Hurrah for Mosby!" Robert E. Lee once exclaimed. "I wish I had a hundred like him."

Short and slight of build but possessed of an iron constitution and an indomitable will, the steely blue eyes of the former Virginia lawyer were often enough to enforce discipline amongst his swashbuckling followers. "I often watched him," Ranger James Williamson remembered, "intently gazing at a man—staring as though he were reading him through with those eyes, like a book." This dapper little man with the plumed hat was not to be trifled with. While a student at the University of Virginia, Mosby had seriously wounded a local youth who had bullied him, and he spent seven months in jail as a consequence. One Ranger advised a friend, "If you want to get along with Mosby, never disagree with him in anything. If he says black is white, you say 'Yes Sir' or keep quiet."

Age twenty-seven when the war began, Mosby left his wife and two children and enlisted as a private in the 1st Virginia Cavalry. Promoted to the rank of first lieutenant in April 1862, he soon left the 1st Virginia and joined the staff of General Jeb Stuart, whom Mosby came to value as "the best friend I ever had." It was Stuart who in January 1863 gave Mosby his first opportunity to lead an independent force behind enemy lines. The twenty-nine-year-old captain was so successful—capturing pickets, eluding pursuers, destroying railroad lines, and abducting befuddled Brigadier General Edwin Stoughton from his Fairfax, Virginia, headquarters—that Mosby was permitted to form a new partisan detachment: the 43rd Virginia Cavalry Battalion.

Enticed by the exciting, freewheeling nature of partisan service, adventuresome

COLLECTION OF MICHAEL FLANAGAN

young men from throughout the Army of Northern Virginia flocked to Major Mosby's outfit. He was also able to draw support from the residents of Loudoun and Fauquier Counties—areas that had long experienced the ravages of Yankee occupation.

Over the next two years nearly two thousand men would at one time or another serve under the Gray Ghost. Some stalwarts stuck with him to the end, while others came and went as their fancy struck them. While lacking the structure and bureaucracy of the typical Civil War unit, by the very fact of its ephemeral nature the 43rd Virginia Battalion was ideally suited to guerilla operations.

Mosby always attempted to strike his opponents hard and fast. Deftly exploiting the terrain or moving under cover of darkness, the Rangers would gallop down upon startled Yankee pickets and waylay pursuing horsemen. A crack shot, Mosby eschewed the saber in combat, and most of his men followed their leader's example of carrying a brace of pistols for close-order fighting. Before embarking on a raid, the routes in and out were always scouted in advance, as were potential hiding places, be they the homes and barns of sympathetic locals or secluded valleys of the rolling Piedmont. It was not long before the Rangers' zone of operations came to be known as "Mosby's Confederacy."

As the war progressed the North made repeated efforts to bring Mosby and his command to bay. Several times the Rangers were forced into pitched battle, and numbers of their finest riders fell. Mosby himself sustained two severe wounds that nearly cost him his life.

But even the most ruthless and determined efforts of U. S. Grant and Phil Sheridan could not eradicate this most intangible and resilient of opponents. Still undefeated when Lee's surrender sounded the death knell of Confederate hopes, Mosby chose to disband his unit rather than surrender.

Recalling that last farewell to his Rangers at Salem, Virginia, thirty years after the war John S. Mosby told his aging veterans, "Life cannot afford a more bitter cup than the one I drained at Salem, nor any higher reward of ambition than that I received as commander of the Forty-third Virginia Battalion of Cavalry."

Forward the Colors

Bearing aloft the severed staff and bullet-torn bunting of his regiment's second-pattern national color, a Confederate officer leads his grimly determined troops to almost certain death. Such hopeless gallantry was commonplace in General Hood's suicidal assault at Franklin, when the veterans of the Army of Tennessee advanced across the field in a formation one Federal called "a living wall of men and glistening steel." Another Yankee remarked on the Southerners' magnificent discipline amid the hurricane of fire as they "continued to advance in a solid body, with their hats down over their eyes, just as if advancing against a hailstorm."

"The battle of Franklin will live in history," wrote Colonel Virgil S. Murphy of the 17th Alabama. "It is a monument, as enduring as time to Southern valor."

PRIVATE COLLECTION

Opdycke's Tigers

Battle of Franklin, November 30

UNION MAJOR GENERAL JOHN MCALLISTER Schofield and Confederate General John Bell Hood had been friends at West Point, graduating together in the Class of 1853. In the winter of 1864, the two men would meet again, this time in one of the Civil War's most bitter and bloody campaigns.

The big-boned, dour-faced Hood, crippled and ailing from wounds received at Gettysburg and Chickamauga, was leading the veteran fighters of the Army of the Tennessee in a desperate offensive against the Union defenders of Nashville. Through a combination of incredible luck and a lack of direction on Hood's part, Schofield was able to escape entrapment at Spring Hill, Tennessee, and take up a formidable position behind the earthen defenses of Franklin. On November 30, 1864, while the Union supply wagons crossed the Harpeth River and continued on to Nashville, Schofield's two corps braced for Hood's onslaught—a head-on assault by which Hood hoped to destroy Schofield's army and redeem his faltering offensive.

That afternoon Hood's battle lines deployed from the slopes of Winstead Hill and began the most grand and awe-inspiring Confederate charge of the Civil War. Two corps under Generals Frank Cheatham and A. P. Stewart marched relentlessly forward astride the Franklin and Columbia Turnpike, guiding their two-mile advance toward an angle of the Federal earthworks marked by the red brick Carter House and nearby cotton gin. As the superbly disciplined Southern formations swept forward in parade ground order, they came up against the outlying Yankee brigades of Brigadier General George D. Wagner. Wagner had inexplicably failed to withdraw from his exposed position to the main Federal line, and he paid dearly for this error in judgement. Within minutes Wagner's troops were routed from their shallow rifle pits and fled in confusion, the screaming Rebels in hot pursuit.

Caught in the maelstrom, three Ohio regiments abandoned a two-hundred-yard stretch at the center of the Union line, and gray-clad soldiers poured into the breach, surging toward the Carter House and its outbuildings. It seemed likely that Schofield's army would be cut in half and its remnants driven through the town of Franklin and into the river beyond. Federal disaster was averted,

Emerson Opdycke, colonel of the 125th Ohio and fearless brigade commander at Franklin, would finish the war as Brevet Major General of Volunteers. He died in 1884 from an accidental bullet wound he received while cleaning a pistol.

PHOTO COURTESY U.S. ARMY MILITARY HISTORY INSTITUTE AND JOHN BRADSHAW COLLECTION

PRIVATE COLLECTION

however, and the victory was largely due to a thirty-four-year-old Union brigade commander, Colonel Emerson Opdycke.

Opdycke's six understrength regiments were exhausted by the stress and constant marching and skirmishing of the previous few days. Their duty as rear guard of Schofield's army had denied them sleep and even the opportunity to boil coffee, let alone eat a decent meal. When General Wagner ordered Opdycke to file alongside his outlying brigades, the irascible colonel had refused and instead marched his men on into the works at Franklin. Thanks to this fortuitous act of insubordination, Colonel Opdycke was now in a position to shore up the crumbling Federal line.

As Opdycke attempted to shift several of his units across the Columbia Pike to a better defensive position, Major Thomas W. Motherspaw of the 73rd Illinois mistook the order for a command to charge, and mounting his horse, he yelled out, "Go for them, Boys!" The veteran soldiers were taken aback, but urged on by their officers and sergeants, they rushed forward with leveled bayonets. "Stop that regiment! Stop that regiment!" Opdycke shouted, but nothing could halt the desperate counterattack.

Other units joined in the mad scramble, and as their roaring cheers rose above the crash of battle, Opdycke spurred his horse to his old regiment, the 125th Ohio, and drawing his revolver gave the command, "First brigade, forward to the works!" The 125th Ohio surged ahead, toward a fence and the bullet-spattered Carter House beyond.

The Rebel and Yankee masses crashed together with a force that caused a murderous rebound, and rippling aftershocks sent men tripping and sprawling in the tightly packed ranks that followed. All regimental order disintegrated in a wild, frenzied melee of point-blank shots, lunging bayonets, and clubbed muskets, and the wounded and dying were trampled underfoot. Unhorsed amidst the chaos, Emerson Opdycke sprinted to the front of battle, firing his revolver into the Rebels, and, when his ammunition was exhausted, swinging the butt down upon the heads of his assailants. When the revolver broke apart in his hands, Opdycke snatched up a dropped musket and continued to flail about him at the foe.

As the hand-to-hand fight swirled about the Carter House, Opdycke's men captured nearly four hundred prisoners, as well as nine Confederate battle flags. Within about twenty minutes, the Rebels had been pushed back over the second line of earthworks, though the battle raged on along the main line of defenses.

Hoarse with shouting, blackened with powder, and streaked with blood, Opdycke's troops fired round after round into the enemy at a range that could be measured in feet. When ammunition was exhausted they groped frantically in the cartridge boxes of the fallen. Only after nightfall did the terrible slaughter of Franklin subside. Hood had been repulsed, and Schofield was able to make his escape across the Harpeth and move on toward Nashville.

The battered survivors, having reconfirmed their reputation as "Opdycke's Tigers," had saved Schofield's army. Their valor was recognized by their commanders, and Emerson Opdycke soon boasted the well-deserved star of a brigadier general.

A postwar photograph of the battle-ravaged home of Fountain Carter provided useful documentation for Troiani's painting of Opdycke's charge. In the course of repairs, the side gables were altered from a stepped to a more traditional angle, evident in the different brickwork seen here. In one of the Civil War's most tragic ironies, Fountain Carter's son, Confederate Captain Theodoric "Tod" Carter, was fatally wounded in the charge at Franklin and died in the sitting room of his family home. PHOTO COURTESY MASSACHUSETTS COMMANDERY, MILITARY ORDER OF THE LOYAL LEGION, AND THE U.S. ARMY MILITARY HISTORY INSTITUTE

Pat Cleburne's Men

In the winter of 1864 the rugged veterans of the 33rd Alabama played their part in the tragic drama of General John Bell Hood's Tennessee campaign. With Sherman's army slashing through Georgia from Atlanta to the sea, the defiant Hood, ailing and nearly crippled by wounds, launched a desperate effort to destroy the Yankee forces of Major General George Thomas. Hood's gambit failed, and with it one of the last Confederate hopes.

In Hood's suicidal onslaught at Franklin, the 33rd, along with the other troops of Brigadier General Mark P. Lowrey's brigade, battled their way onto the Federal breastworks at great cost of life. None of the fallen was more regretted than Major General Patrick Cleburne, the Irish-born division commander whose unsurpassed heroism and battlefield skill had earned him the nickname "Stonewall Jackson of the West." Realizing that a head-on assault was bound to result in loss of life that the South could ill afford, Pat Cleburne nonetheless led the charge with the fiery passion that had made his name a byword for gallantry among his adoring soldiers.

The fighting spirit of his division died with Pat Cleburne at Franklin, and the disastrous defeat at Nashville that followed soon after made it necessary to merge the shattered remnants of the 33rd Alabama with the survivors of two other units. But the heroic litany of past triumphs, emblazoned on their blue Hardee-style battle flag, would ever remind these Southern warriors of the days of victory.

PRIVATE COLLECTION

1865

The Last Rounds

By the end of 1864 the once-unbeatable Confederate mounted arm had been largely eclipsed by the Yankee cavalry. Even in the war's western theater, where brilliant horsemen like Nathan Bedford Forrest were yet able to confound their Northern foe, the steady decline in numbers, armament, and horseflesh had weakened the strategic power of the Southern cavalry.

While many Union horsemen were now armed with rapid-firing Spencer carbines, the Rebel troopers were forced to rely upon muzzle-loading carbines and musketoons from firms like Cook and Brother of Athens, Georgia, J. P. Murray of Columbus, and government manufactories like the Richmond arsenal. Other cavalrymen preferred to carry infantry muskets, slung across their bodies or tied to their saddles.

Moreover, like their Yankee counterparts, the Southern troopers had learned to fight as mounted infantry—relying upon their animals for speed and maneuverability but dismounting to fight on foot once the battle was joined. As Union armies pressed relentlessly across the deep South, every ridge, tree line, and rock outcropping could become a defensive position, to hold as long as ammunition and determination remained.

PRIVATE COLLECTION

Confederate Pickets in the Snow

Winter was always a difficult time for troops called upon to stand duty on the picket line. Snuggled beside the smoky hearths of their log and canvas quarters, every soldier knew that guard and outpost duty was an unavoidable part of army life and that his turn would soon come. Two to four days on picket as advance guard made for an arduous spell of sleepless nights and ceaseless vigilance.

For Confederate soldiers the last winter of the war was a particularly somber time. Much of the South had fallen to the Federals, and communication with loved ones trapped behind enemy lines was virtually impossible. Clothing shortages meant that though some men might be fortunate enough to have a captured Yankee overcoat to wear, many others would have to ward off the frigid cold with merely a blanket thrown about their shoulders.

Ever watchful and alert for any sign of an enemy incursion, the shouted challenge of the picket could—and often did—lead to an exchange of fire, and another name on the long, long list of casualties.

PRIVATE COLLECTION

The Gray Wall

Hood's Pyrrhic victory at Franklin—the occupation of abandoned Federal breastworks before which so many of his men had perished in fruitless assaults—was followed by the calamitous advance on Nashville. With the Confederates outnumbered nearly five to one, there was little doubt what would happen once Union General George Thomas advanced to attack his understrength antagonists. Fortitude and determination on the part of subordinate officers and the individual soldier could not prevent a disaster that saw the once proud Army of Tennessee broken and swept from the field.

The remnants of the Army of Tennessee would fight on through the bitter winter of 1864–65, and some of those who survived Hood's tragic offensive would join General Joseph Johnston's patchwork command in a final effort to slow Sherman's juggernaut through the Carolinas. The clash at Bentonville in March 1865 showed that though they lacked the numbers to turn the tide, the rugged Rebels still had the ability to make the Yankees pay in blood for every foot of ground they gained.

On April 4, 1865, Lieutenant Bromfield Ridley of General A. P. Stewart's staff witnessed what he called "the saddest spectacle of my life, the review of the skeleton Army of Tennessee." The ranks, once full, were a shadow, marching past "with tattered garments, worn-out shoes, bare-footed, and ranks so depleted that each color was supported by only thirty or forty men." The review, Ridley said, "looked like a funeral procession." And, as he knew all too well, "the shades of sorrow" were closing in on the brave defenders of the Confederacy.

PRIVATE COLLECTION

Crutchfield's Virginia Heavy Artillery Battalion

VIRGINIA'S BATTALIONS OF HEAVY ARTILLERY were among the best-drilled soldiers available to Robert E. Lee in the last desperate weeks of the war. Trained to work the big guns of Richmond's earthen fortifications, and also able to maneuver and fight as infantry, the heavy artillerymen of Colonel Stapleton Crutchfield's brigade would pay a heavy price for their valor on the bloodstained road to Appomattox.

"They were splendid soldiers in external appearance and bearing," recalled Major Robert Stiles, who was transferred to the heavy artillery in late 1864. "Their dress-parades, inspections, reports, salutes, bearing in the presence of officers and on guard, were wonderfully regular, accurate, and according to the drill and regulations." Colonel Crutchfield, who had lost a leg while commanding Stonewall Jackson's artillery at Chancellorsville was an intrepid young man who was determined to do his utmost in the final battles, even though the Southern cause seemed hopeless.

With the collapse of the Petersburg and Richmond lines, Crutchfield's brigade abandoned their garrisons and joined in the march westward. On April 6, 1865, the heavy artillerymen were among General Richard Ewell's troops defeated at Sayler's Creek. After repulsing the initial Federal assault, Crutchfield's soldiers launched a ferocious countercharge that hurled the Yankees downslope to the banks of the stream. But success was only temporary; outnumbered and outgunned, and with Colonel Crutchfield dead, the gallant heavy artillery battalions were soon overwhelmed.

The Last Salute

With the war in its final hours, the battle-scarred intellectual warrior Joshua Lawrence Chamberlain rode at the head of two brigades bound for a final confrontation with the Army of Northern Virginia. General Chamberlain would never forget that grueling march to destiny: "They move—these men—sleepless, supperless, breakfastless, sore-footed, stiff-jointed, sense-benumbed, but with flushed faces, pressing for the front. It has come at last, the supreme hour." The end was in sight.

Eight days after the defeat of Five Forks, a week after the fall of Petersburg and evacuation of Richmond, three days after the disastrous fight at Sayler's Creek—Robert E. Lee and the surviving remnants of the Army of Northern Virginia conceded defeat at Appomattox Court House. On the afternoon of April 9, 1865, the great commander, supremely dignified in his most tragic hour, met U. S. Grant in the parlor of Wilmer McLean's home and signed the terms of surrender.

For all his bulldog tenacity and single-minded pursuit of victory, once victory was attained Grant displayed remarkable compassion to his defeated foe. The Confederate soldiers would be paroled and allowed to return to their homes. Officers were permitted to retain their swords and sidearms, and those who owned their horses could keep them as well. But the Federal commander did have one important stipulation—the Southern troops would be required to park their artillery and supply trains, stack their muskets and accoutrements, and surrender their battle flags to the officers appointed to receive them. This ceremonial abandonment of the tools of war would both disarm the Confederate troops and leave no doubt as to which side had ultimately triumphed.

The officer delegated to receive "the arms, artillery, and public property" was Joshua Chamberlain. No more fitting choice could have been made than the lean academic from Maine who had soldiered on, with unsurpassed gallantry, despite wounds that left him in almost constant pain. He cherished a profound respect for those who had risked all for ideals they valued above life itself. It mattered not whether they wore the blue or the gray, or whether they won or lost. "There is a way of losing that is finding," Chamberlain

Brevet Major General Joshua Lawrence Chamberlain. Photo courtesy James C. Frasca

once said. "It is only when a man supremely gives that he supremely finds."

On the chill, overcast morning of April 12, Chamberlain deployed the veterans of his old 3rd Brigade, 1st Division, 5th Corps along the Richmond-Lynchburg Stage Road. The general and his staff took position on the right of the line, alongside the 32nd Massachusetts and beneath the red Maltese cross of the division flag. Maintaining an awed silence, the Federal troops rested in place as their Southern counterparts began marching uphill toward the village of Appomattox to meet the men in blue for the last time. "It was," Chamberlain wrote his sister afterward, "a scene worthy of a pilgrimage."

At the head of the Confederate column rode thirty-three-year-old General John B. Gordon, like Chamberlain a man who had carried himself through four years of war with bravery and skill, and who bore the scars of near-fatal wounds. "As my command, in worn-out shoes and ragged uniforms, but with proud mien, moved to the designated point to stack their arms and surrender their cherished battle-flags, they challenged the admiration of the brave victors," Gordon remembered.

When the Confederates drew abreast of his command, Chamberlain called his troops to attention, then to shoulder arms, thus rendering a salute to Gordon's soldiers in their hour of heartbreak and grief. Recognizing the gesture as "a token of respect from Americans to Americans," Gordon saluted Chamberlain with his sword and ordered his own troops to return the honor.

From early morning to late afternoon, brigade after brigade of Southern soldiers filed up the road, stacked arms, unslung belts and cartridge boxes, and furled their flags. Choked with emotion, men of both sides wept unashamedly. "It was a proud, but sad scene," one Federal recalled, "and our men felt a soldier's sympathy for their brave antagonists." Many Yankees shared their scant rations of hardtack and salt pork with the famished and exhausted Rebels. Deeply appreciative of the Northerners' good will, a Confederate wrote, "We suffered no insult in any way from any of our enemies. No other army in the world would have been so considerate of a foe."

To the end of his long and honorable life, Joshua Lawrence Chamberlain would never fail to pay homage to the heroic legacy of the Confederate soldier. In a postwar address to the Society of the Army of the Potomac, Chamberlain echoed the message of that profound moment at Appomattox:

The Army of Northern Virginia! Who can help looking back upon them now with feelings half fraternal? Ragged and reckless, yet careful to keep their bayonets bright and lines of battle well dressed; reduced to dire extremity sometimes, yet always ready for a fight; rough and rude, yet knowing well how to make a field illustrious.

Who can forget them—the brave, bronzed faces that looked at us for four years across the flaming pit—men whom in a hundred fierce grapples we fought with remorseless desperation and all the terrible enginery of death, till on the one side and the other a quarter of a million fell—and yet we never hated....

Main force against main force—there was good reason why, when valor like that was exhausted, the sun should go down on thousands dead, but not one vanquished.

General John B. Gordon, C.S.A. PHOTO COURTESY MASSACHUSETTS COMMANDERY, MILITARY ORDER OF THE LOYAL LEGION, AND THE U.S. ARMY MILITARY HISTORY INSTITUTE

From American to American